Teaching Gifted Children
Special Educational Needs

Children with both giftedness and special educational needs are often found in mainstream classrooms. This essential resource provides an overview of existing knowledge about dual and multiple exceptionality (DME), examining the needs of gifted and talented children from both the class teacher's and SENCo's perspectives. Diane Montgomery explores both the specialist interventions that some children will need for at least part of their school life, as well as the general inclusive provision that every school can develop to meet the needs of all children. Focusing on evidence-based identification throughout, chapters in this accessible book cover:

- An analysis of the terms 'giftedness' and 'talent' and the different methods that can be used for identifying them and assessing their limitations.
- Identifying and supporting a range of difficulties, syndromes and disorders such as dyslexia, dyscalculia, DCD, ASD, ADHD and SEBD.
- How to manage classroom behaviour, improve school ethos and create a DME-friendly school through inclusive teaching and learning.

This invaluable resource will assist you in creating a DME-friendly school, helping to integrate learners with a range of difficulties and enabling them and others to learn.

Diane Montgomery is Professor Emerita at Middlesex University, UK, where she was Dean of Faculty and Head of the School of Education. She is a qualified and experienced teacher, teacher educator and chartered psychologist specialising in research on underachievement and dual and multiple exceptionality.

Teaching Gifted Children with Special Educational Needs

Supporting dual and multiple exceptionality

Diane Montgomery

Routledge
Taylor & Francis Group

LONDON AND NEW YORK

First published 2015
by Routledge
2 Park Square, Milton Park, Abingdon, Oxon OX14 4RN

and by Routledge
711 Third Avenue, New York, NY 10017

Routledge is an imprint of the Taylor & Francis Group, an informa business

British Library Cataloguing in Publication Data
A catalogue record for this book is available from the British Library

Library of Congress Cataloging-in-Publication Data
Montgomery, Diane.
Teaching gifted children with special educational needs : supporting dual and multiple exceptionality / Diane Montgomery.
pages cm
Includes bibliographical references and index.
1. Gifted children–Education–Great Britain. 2. Children with disabilities–Education–Great Britain. I. Title.
LC3997.G7M654 2015
371.950941–dc23
2014047178

ISBN: 978-1-138-89055-8 (hbk)
ISBN: 978-1-138-89057-2 (pbk)
ISBN: 978-1-315-71232-1 (ebk)

Typeset in Galliard
by Deer Park Productions

MIX
Paper from
responsible sources
FSC   FSC® C013056
www.fsc.org

Printed and bound in Great Britain by
TJ International Ltd, Padstow, Cornwall

Contents

Preface

This book is written for teachers, students of education and interested others. It is based upon principles derived from a career in teaching, teacher education and research. The main themes are:

The teacher is the key: The only effect size of any significance to emerge from meta analyses of research has been the quality of teaching.

Excellence for all children: No system of selection, pull-out programmes, acceleration and special provision finds and meets the needs of all our gifted and talented children or those with special needs. Only the selected few gain access to it and sometimes the provision is special only in name. Thus the regular teacher is the key to providing for all children's needs and drawing on resources and specialists to help. It is the right of every child to have the best there is.

Teaching is a complex profession: Teachers do not teach subjects; they teach children to learn subjects. This involves acquiring sets of higher order academic and professional skills, not just relating subject knowledge. Telling is not teaching.

Learning should be developmentally appropriate: Children's learning needs change as they develop and methods employed with adults are not appropriate for children. Concept development and acquisition stages require different methods of teaching and learning from the concept attainment phases of the later years.

Lifelong learning: Teachers' creativity needs to be released to enable them to develop pupils as self-organised and lifelong learners. They need to make learning interesting and fun.

The teacher-researcher: Because of the vast knowledge base that now exists about education, teachers have to become learners and researchers in their own classrooms to find what works best and to develop their personal theory and

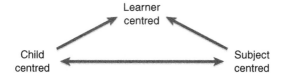

Figure 0.1 A focus on learner needs

practice of teaching. It made sense in an era when much less was known about teaching and it makes sense now when there is an overwhelming body of knowledge to select from.

Continuing professional development

Continuing professional development (CPD) is essential to build teacher knowledge and improve professional practice. 'Two things to do on Monday morning' has become a popular mantra at CPD courses but the effects soon disappear. Practice without theory is blind. The most effective methods for developing professional knowledge and skills are longer courses where shared ideas can be taken back to classrooms and verified or otherwise. Programmes of constructive self-organised learning can also be effective.

Terminology

In the UK and USA there is a tension between individual pathology models and ecological models in special educational needs (SEN). A major site for this conflict is in education. In Britain there is a resistance to medicalise conditions to avoid the negative consequences of placing emphasis on deficits rather than educational needs.

In the US the normalisation of medical labels to explain educational difficulties occurs because the legislation does not permit access to special services or resources without it. This makes the concept less threatening to their practitioners and the general population.

The hesitation to medicalise conditions is widespread in the UK. For example 'specific learning difficulties' is used in England for the US term 'learning disabilities' and 'difficulties' is preferred to 'disorders'. There is also a strong movement not to label conditions at all because of the stigma that might arise. This has tended to change the concept of SEN and in the specialist education SEN field in England and Scotland they are often referred to as 'Additional Needs'.

Students and pupils: 'pupils' is an English term referring to children and young people in schools. The term 'students' is used in international journals, books and research and can refer to children, pupils, youths and students in higher education.

Note:
The Ministry of Education: This title has changed many times over the years and as such references will be seen as DES, DfE, DfEE, DfES, DCFS and, again recently, DfE.

World Health Organisation (WHO) 1992 *The ICD-10 Classification of Mental and Behavioural Disorders: Clinical Description and Diagnostic Guidelines* Geneva: WHO. These guidelines are sometimes used by researchers and diagnosticians instead of those of the American Psychiatric Association (APA *DSM-IV* 1994 and *DSM-V* 2006).

Introduction

In the gifted education field double or dual and multiple exceptionality (2E and DME) are terms used to describe those who are intellectually very able (gifted) or who have a talent (a special gift in a performance or skill area) and in addition to this have a special educational need (SEN) such as dyslexia, or Asperger syndrome. They are 'twice exceptional'. If they are gifted with several special needs they are multiply exceptional and it is likely they will be more difficult to support. Having learning difficulties makes it likely that they will be underachieving in school.

There are thus two strands underlying the contents of this book, each underpinned by different bodies of theory and research: giftedness and special needs.

In the *gifted education field* high ability and exceptionally high ability and children's educational needs have been the focus of concern for over 100 years. But it was Goldberg (1956) reviewing 176 research studies who came to the conclusion that there were two major research needs: to find what would stimulate the love of learning among able students, and what kinds of assignments would most effectively develop independence of thinking and independence of effort. Some form of differentiation was needed but whether it was acceleration or in depth enrichment was not known.

Passow (1966) had similar concerns about the lack of creativity and the numbers of gifted children particularly from disadvantaged environments who were underachieving. Nearly 25 years later in an international review of research (1990: 8) he concluded that we still did not know what kinds of educational and social opportunity were needed to promote high ability and how we could nurture it in disadvantaged populations and develop creativity. These concerns remain to be answered although we have made some progress in the last two decades.

In the UK we have passed through an era in which the word 'gifted' could not be used. It was banned by some education authorities. Thus to address the children's needs we called the training 'study skills' programmes. Even UK publishers had adapted to this 'zeitgeist' and would not publish gifted titles. The publishing of *Educating the Able* (Montgomery, 1996) was a big step forward in this regard. Even so *Reversing Lower Attainment* (Montgomery, 1998) was not permitted to include a reference to the gifted especially in mixed ability settings for whom it was written.

In contrast to other countries during that era, little research funding in England found its way to teacher education but an underground movement developed to share research and practice. This was supported through the National Association for Able Children in Education (NACE). The quest today is still to find that interesting and challenging curriculum to motivate able learners and prevent underachievement (UAch). Leading the field are the European Council for High Ability (ECHA) and the World Council for Gifted and Talented Children (WCGTC). Nevertheless Persson (2012) showed ways in which gifted education is still dominated by American cultural assumptions.

Special educational needs provision can be traced back to the late nineteenth century when specialist schools were set up to meet the needs of deaf, blind and partially sighted children. Over the twentieth century provision was widened to cover ten categories of need including the 'maladjusted', 'speech and language disordered' and 'mentally retarded'. Today such stigmatising labels have been replaced with those that describe children's needs such as specific learning difficulties; speech, language and communication needs; social, emotional and behavioural difficulties and so on.

Twenty per cent of children were recognised as having some degree of special need and now these are referred to as 'additional needs' and specified in individual cases. Influences from the US do not seem to have permeated provision in the same way as in the gifted field.

Most countries that make provision for children with special needs (some are still unable to do this) have followed this pattern of developing provision. The same has not occurred in the education of the gifted. The most profoundly gifted and talented may have been selected and given a special curriculum more suited to their needs but 'bright' children in many countries are still enduring rote learning and repetition in uncreative environments. This can make them psychologically ill or drain their brains of innovation and creativity. Even in countries where special provision is made for some, the gifted and talented with special needs may be missed.

Learning and teaching: Regular Program for International Student Assessment (PISA) tests have established that South East Asian education systems produce the top scorers but this does not mean they give the best education. The curricula and time spent on it are extensive and the students' needs and experiences reflect a different ethos and culture.

These systems for example are highly didactic, focus on memorising and time spent can last up to 16 or more hours per day with extra tutoring and homework backed by 'tiger mums'. It has led to workers who believe that life is only about gaining 'tickets'. Even these systems are being reconsidered for this is not what countries need to survive in this new millennium. The creative talent pool needs widening and rote methods do not achieve this.

As the budgets of many countries tighten, specialist units, resources and teacher numbers are declining. Teachers in regular classrooms are expected to provide for a more diverse range of pupil needs. Of course the needs always existed but now we identify and know more about them. Exceptional children will have Individual Education Plans (IEPs). In some countries all children will be expected to have personalised programmes of learning or this is the aspiration. Can this fit with inclusion?

Differentiation and inclusion: These concepts developed especially in the area of special needs but have become key constructs in education as a whole. They do not sit comfortably within didactic systems and selective schooling; they can be contradictory.

DME: The incidence of DME in the research literature ranges from 2.5 per cent to 36 per cent of the gifted population (Baum and Owen, 1988; Silverman, 1989; Whitmore, 1982). However, in a more recent large-scale US survey Rogers (2010) found 14 per cent of the gifted had some form of 2E. Of the 14 per cent, 3 per cent had Specific Learning Difficulties (SpLD), 7 per cent had Attention Deficit Hyperactivity Disorder (ADHD), 3 per cent had Emotional and Behavioural Difficulties (EBD), and 1 per cent had Autistic Spectrum Disorders (ASD). In the UK the figures based on research by the different societies is made up as follows: 4 per cent SpLD; 1 per cent ADHD; 3 per cent EBD; 1 per cent ASD; 5 per cent Developmental Coordination Difficulties (DCD). Differences in definitions account for these figures. Research detailed later suggests that there are also a number of hidden difficulties not yet appearing in these figures corresponding to Whitmore's 36 per cent.

Dual exceptionality is well known in the SEN field where it is termed 'comorbidity'. Comorbidity often occurs in dyslexia when the dyslexic may also show symptoms of ADHD, Asperger syndrome (AS) or DCD (Developmental Coordination Difficulties – dyspraxia). The incidence of comorbidity in community studies is generally in the region of 30 per cent (Clements, 1966; Duke, 2002).

The four conditions – dyslexia, ADHD, AS and DCD – and in addition Social, Emotional and Behavioural Difficulties (SEBD) and the children's needs are the focus of this text. In these conditions there is also a high frequency of co-occurrence of handwriting difficulties, making a multiple exceptionality. It is this additional factor that is 'hidden in full sight'. It alone has a most powerful effect because so much time in schools is spent on writing yet insufficient attention is devoted to its acquisition and fluency development, especially in poor writers. This writing difficulty in many gifted underachievers results in an inability or an unwillingness to produce written work of a suitable quality to match the perceived potential. Silverman (2002) found it was the most common cause of underachievement in the gifted.

In addition, in the UK and no doubt many other countries family background is also a major determinant of success (DCFS, 2009). This means that very few children from 'working class' homes gain places at the top universities and access to high status jobs despite being gifted. Instead, 43 per cent of the high status jobs go to the 7 per cent from private schools.

Cultural disadvantage and low socio-economic status can also handicap understanding, expression and social communication and these too contribute to poor

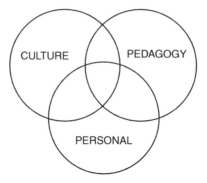

Figure 0.2 Triad of impairments in underachievement

writing and underachievement. This means that any success achieved by a child from these backgrounds indicates a very high ability and weightings should be given to allow them to gain access to higher status institutions.

Links between underachievement and multiple exceptionalities

The three factors in Figure 0.2 summarise the major underlying causes of under-achievement. In real life they interact with each other to create different patterns of underachievement and exceptionality. They consist of:

- The cultural and sub-cultural influences that mediate language, social communication and experience outside and inside school.
- The teaching methods and models across the years and the curriculum to which the learner is exposed.
- The personal factors such as ability, talent, personality, motivation and potential learning difficulties as in DME.

Case example – Alex

Alex, aged seven, a bright boy, was placed in a classroom where the teaching methods were mundane and there was no differentiation or intellectual challenge. He quickly became bored and sought other forms of entertainment. These included annoying other pupils and upsetting the teacher through misbehaviour and clowning. Over time Alex developed a reputation for having a behaviour problem and a career in disruption began, ending in exclusions.

This pattern is particularly likely to happen when children are from disadvantaged backgrounds and do not have the language and social skills to divert attention from their misdeeds, or when the teacher has poor classroom management skills. Here a dual exceptionality has been *created* in the form of SEBD. Gifted children in these circumstances will underachieve unless they have the good fortune to meet a mentor or are rescued from the situation.

Case example – Jess

Jess's personal qualities combined with being in a similar situation to Alex meant that she went to considerable lengths to fit in and conform. In the early years it involved helping other children by passing the time hearing them read and helping them write. She became teacher's aide and teaching assistant. As the classroom organisation became less flexible in secondary school she turned to inner mental resources and daydreamed the days away. Fortunately she had a home environment that promoted learning and helped compensate to some degree for the poor schooling. However, with lack of challenge and no failures to learn from she did not develop the advanced study skills needed to cope with university and dropped out after the first year.

Because of the lack of early intellectual challenge both these children had poor trajectories and did not achieve their potential.

The personal differences and learning difficulties that children bring to any learning environment can also create underachievement. One of the explicit signs that something is wrong may indeed be the emergence of SEBD. However, it may also be caused by inadequate pedagogy, poor classroom management skills and an irrelevant curriculum, and it may also be induced by poor quality rearing techniques and cultural disadvantage.

Case examples show that 'acting out' and 'acting in' patterns so often seen in SEBD depend very much on the personality of the children such as Alex and Jess. Gender is also an influence as boys are more prone to act out than girls. What we do know is that both patterns can be turned round by changes to the

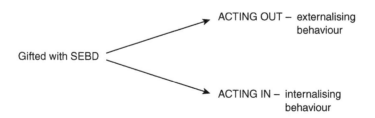

Figure 0.3 Different reactions in SEBD

teaching methods (Rayner, 1998) and the behaviour management strategies employed by the teacher (Montgomery, 2002). In DME poor quality teaching and curriculum need to be ruled out or dealt with at the same time as clues or indicants of dual and multiple exceptionality are pursued.

Identification of gifted children with SEN

It is not always easy to identify the gifted especially if they have special needs; however, three main patterns emerge from the data. These are:

Discrepancies

When an IQ test is given discrepancies can be used to identify gifted children with DME. Discrepancies may be found between and within IQ scores and school attainments or SATs. Educational psychologists may for example find a score of 120 on the verbal scale of the WISC – IV (2008, Wechsler Intelligence Scale for Children) and 105 on the performance scale instead of just a few points disparity. This large difference indicates some form of potential learning difficulty. A high IQ score of 120 for a 10-year-old and school attainments at the level of 10-year-old peers indicates significant underachievement and possibly a learning difficulty such as a writing problem. As the child functions at the level of peers too often no special measures are taken.

If comprehension scores are higher than accuracy scores on reading tests this indicates higher ability or mental age.

However, in over 50 per cent of cases no discrepancies are found within IQ tests scores but there is still a learning difficulty.

Deficits

Deficits in performance on tests and tasks can result in gifted children with SEN going unidentified. For example learning difficulties in verbal (phonological) processing in dyslexia can mask high abilities. It can result in deficits on the subtests – Arithmetic, Coding, Information and Digit span (ACID profile) – so that the global IQ may be some ten points or more lower than would otherwise be the case. It is for this reason that Silverman (2002) advised that ten points should be added to the IQ scores of children with learning disabilities if selection for special provision is to be made.

Deceptive

In this category gifted children are frequently unidentified because the social, behavioural and emotional difficulties obscure and distract the attention and become the focus of the analysis and intervention. They also spend more time off task and fall behind in school subjects.

General characteristics of special needs

Special needs are on a continuum from mild through moderate to severe and profound, rather like giftedness and talent. They all need the earliest intervention in the preschool years and the early years of schooling. This will help develop the talents and ameliorate the difficulties. Special needs also have a particular nature in that they may result from a disorder, delay or a deficit.

- *Disorder.* The development does not follow a normal pattern or clear up later. There will always be residual effects, as in Specific Language Impairment (SLI) and ASD, but can be improved by specific training.
- *Delay.* This is usually characterised by a developmental slowness, but it follows a normal pattern. These children may need a slower but normal programme to attain the developmental milestones, e.g. in walking and talking and the developmental tasks of the school-aged child – reading, writing and number – learning the basic skills.
- *Deficit.* This usually prevents the normal onset of the development, but may clear up later to some degree. It is argued that dyslexia, for example, may be due to a deficit rather than a disorder. When the deficit clears up it allows normal development to begin but at a late stage. It is usual to try to compensate for the deficit or remediate it by specific training programmes.

1. PSM – Physical, Sensory and Medical difficulties

These pupils are in the smallest numbers compared to the other groups. They include gifted pupils with the following difficulties:

a) *Physical difficulties* such as cerebral palsy and *medical difficulties* such as spina bifida, multiple sclerosis and epilepsies. They need not only access to the buildings but also to an intellectually challenging curriculum suited to their individual level of ability. This should be the least of the barriers they have to overcome.

b) *Sensory difficulties* which are the visual and hearing impairments. Although the measures generally used to aid identification also tend to recognise attainments they do not identify potential (Starr, 2003).

Further barriers arise if teachers are reluctant to include children with sensory and physical difficulties in their gifted projects because they lack experience of working with them and rarely meet them. For those with hearing impairment, using visual scales of tests and Raven's Progressive Matrices (Raven, 2008) as the marks of the potential can help identify giftedness.

Visually impaired gifted pupils often said they had to be better than gifted pupils without disabilities in order to be recognised (Corn, 1986). They share this in common with gifted girls and disadvantaged and minority ethnic groups.

In brief, when gifted pupils with PSM have their specific needs catered for then their educational needs are much the same as other gifted children and there is now an array of assistive technologies that can aid them. Even so a number will need as much pedagogical support as the other groups to be discussed because of the degree of underachievement.

2. SEBD – Social, Emotional and Behavioural Difficulties

These range widely from attention seeking to disruptive and aggressive behaviours and from minor anxiety reactions to school phobia and bullying. In more extreme cases, Conduct Problems and Oppositional Defiance (ODD) are considered to be disorders in the American Psychiatric Association, *DSM-V* (APA, 2006).

3. Learning disorders

a) *Asperger Syndrome* (AS) or *High Functioning Autism and Pragmatic Language Disorder:* These are Autism Spectrum Disorders (ASD). Those with ASD can have a triad of impairments (Wing, 1996) that involve social communication, imagination and fantasy, and language and thinking – or just one or two of the impairments depending on the condition. A very literal-minded way of thinking and understanding, and very immature social skills are characteristic. These are often accompanied by ritualistic and annoying behaviours.

b) *Specific Language Impairment* (SLI): This was originally termed Developmental Dysphasia, in which the ability to understand (reception) or use language (expression) or both is impaired and disordered. Language in some cases may not develop at all, as in cases of severe autism. However, nonverbal skills may be unaffected or even in the gifted zone. This can be a very frustrating condition and sign language is an essential tool at the earliest stage.

   These children need very special and individualised help from the early months and a sign language such as MAKATON can help parents communicate with them (https://www.makaton.org/).

   At school they prosper best in a small nurture group where individual language work can be undertaken.

c) *Attention Deficit Hyperactivity Disorder* (ADHD): The main problems are in attention, hyperactivity and inconsequence. The result is that the children have difficulties in learning. Their attempts have a trial and error approach. They also have difficulties in sitting down and listening or sharing and working with others. They roar about, constantly on the move fiddling with and breaking things. They shout out answers and comments and interfere with other pupils and thus they are seen as behaviour problems. Some have attention deficits without the hyperactivity.

4. SpLDs – Specific Learning Difficulties/Learning Disabilities

Specific Learning Difficulties is the term used in the UK. Learning Disabilities (LD) is used in the US and most other countries. These include:

a)   *Dyslexia* – a reading *and* spelling difficulty
b)   *Dysorthographia* – a spelling difficulty without reading problems
c)   *Dysgraphia* – a handwriting difficulty
d)   *Dyscalculia* – an arithmetical difficulty

In much of the research and UK government literature dyslexia is referred to as a specific reading disability and a reading disorder – these definitions will be challenged later.

5. DCD – Developmental Coordination Disorders/Difficulties

At the mildest and even moderate areas of difficulty the problems are developmental and can clear up with appropriate support, training or remediation. At the severe and profound end of the distribution the difficulties merge into disorder that cause significant motor deficits.

   Pupils may have:

*   gross motor locomotion difficulties that impair running, walking, cycling and swimming;
*   difficulties in fine motor skills that affect handwriting, bead threading and buttoning;
*   visuo-motor difficulties that affect ball skills and hand–eye coordination.

In some cases all these difficulties will be found in the one individual.

6. GLD – General or Global Learning Difficulties and talent

These are the slower learners. Their main difficulties are in the intellectual area, specifically with limitations in memory, language and thinking abilities. Intellectual giftedness can occur in all the categories of SEN except in those with GLD. Even so pupils with GLD may also be identified with specific talents so they must not be forgotten.

   They may have a talent in singing or playing a musical instrument or, for example, working with animals or plants. One young woman with an IQ of 57 was looking after her household and maintaining a job. This is very unusual but an exceptional talent.

Verbal or non-verbal learning difficulties and disabilities?

This is another way of classifying difficulties and there is a point to it. It is the verbal learning difficulties that are overt and appear to have the major impact on school attainment.

However, non-verbal learning difficulties such as dysgraphia, general motor coordination difficulties, attentional and behavioural problems can prove equally deleterious. They also have a powerful impact in lowering self-esteem. It is cruel never to be chosen to join the team; children feel such rejection very strongly. Remediation or intervention is seldom if ever considered necessary but it could make all the difference.

Art and PE come under the 'non-academic' part of the curriculum. It tells children that they are of less worth than so called 'academic' subjects. Sadly children skilled in these subjects or in designing and making can feel second class. If a child is an expert or gifted in a 'non-academic' area the talent needs to be extreme to be noticed and applauded. But it is so important for schools to identify talent whatever form it takes and to encourage and support it.

Small numbers of children have difficulties in drawing and singing or appreciating music (amusica, dysmusica). They may be 'tone deaf'. Because these are 'non-academic' subjects, school can be survived.

Missed gifts and talents

The gifts that are always missed are the leadership skills of those who do not always follow the crowd or the school rules and the humourists and clowns. Particularly problematic is identifying giftedness in pupils with English as an Additional Language (EAL) and dyslexia, and SEBD will always trump giftedness unless there is a sensitive mentor to support them.

Comorbidity – co-occurrence issues

If a child has both ADHD and dyslexia or DCD and dyslexia, the symptoms and 'disorders' are comorbid – they co-occur but are not related. When comorbidity is not identified the symptoms of the two dysfunctions are mixed and then the interventions are not appropriately targeted.

Kaplan (2000) argued that Atypical Brain Development describes variations of the brain's development and framework and can accommodate unusual disabilities and strengths. This means that labels may be irrelevant and the pattern of symptoms identified in an individual are the only relevant factor. This is becoming a popular view in education. However, as any clinician will confirm, despite the individual nature of a learning disability it will conform to a 'species' pattern. Identifying this requires training and experience and enables the intervention to be better targeted.

The first major community survey on the subject, of over 10,000 cases, by Clements (1966) found that substantial comorbidity did exist in the learning disability field and the proportion of overlap was 30 per cent.

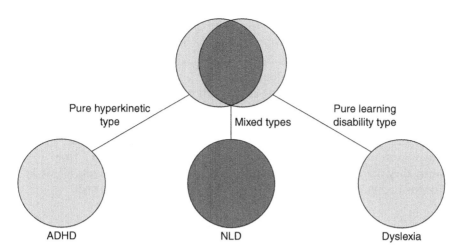

NLD Non verbal Learning Difficulties

Figure 0.4 Overlaps in comorbidities

Some problems arising from DME

1. Giftedness with SEN brings about special problems. Students given provision for their dyslexia such as remedial teaching and supportive strategies may be placed in the lowest classes or sets because of their low attainments. When they do not have the intellectual stimulation needed to match their high ability they can become very frustrated.
2. The result is they can develop behavioural and emotional problems as well and then become a multiple exceptionality case. At each point the SEN can be the focus for intervention and the high ability is overlooked. The special needs teachers may also not have been trained in the needs of the more able.
3. If the high ability is identified and special provision is made for that then the pupil may not perform well because there may be a lack of teaching skill in relation to the SEN.
4. There may also be the problem of needing dual funding to compensate for the dual needs but the system may not be set up to do this. Funding for one need cannot always be allocated to another.
5. The naming of a specific difficulty can stigmatise a learner. Some labels are unfortunately used in this way – 'SENs', 'Boffs', 'Disabled', 'Handicapped'. However, labels like 'dyslexia' can help explain a problem, remove fault and target provision and resources.

The inclusion paradox

Inclusion has been much advocated in the SEN field and many schools aspire to it. It means that children with a range of special needs are fully included in mainstream education and that the curriculum, pedagogy and school environment *are adapted to meet their needs.*

In the gifted education field there is a history of segregating pupils, a pressure to select for ability and offer segregated enrichment classes or acceleration through the grades and curriculum contents.

Inclusion thus raises questions about methods used in gifted education. In addressing the needs of twice and multiply exceptional children ideas will be offered to show how this conflict between disparate goals can be resolved.

Another issue raised by inclusion is that the principle can be over-applied. Children who need remedial 'catch up' sessions cannot benefit from them when they are in classrooms where another curriculum is running in parallel. Supporting pupils with DME can help clarify and resolve these issues.

1 Identification of giftedness and talent

Introduction

The use of the term 'gifted' is in itself somewhat controversial. It suggests that any form of talent is a gift from God and not subject to change or improvement. We either have it or we do not. It suggests only the highest level of talent is involved and that it is rare. In other words we are in the realms of prodigies such as Mozart and Picasso or Galton and Darwin.

Immediately we can see that few women come to mind yet we know they must exist, as a century of mental testing has demonstrated. In the seventeenth century Angelica Kauffman was more famous and earned more for her paintings than Holbein. She helped found the Royal Academy yet it is the statue of Sir Joshua Reynolds that we see. Ada Lovelace, gifted mathematician (and daughter of Lord Byron), helped develop the first computer program but is only now being rediscovered. The lesson is we must expect equal numbers of girls and boys in any gifted cohort.

Teachers were well aware that there might be a vast range of abilities and talents amongst the children in their classes and yet when the work of NACE and others began many teachers would insist they had never met a gifted child, and some still do!

There is of course a major difference between gifted achievement and gifted potential. Potential is far more difficult to identify and is often hidden or latent, especially in the school years. It has also become clear that there is not only a general range of ability in the population as a whole but there is also a range in the top echelons.

Gagne (1998) found that the wider the range of attributes included as 'gifts' or 'talents' then the larger the number of children who were likely to be included. He found over several large studies that there were some consistent features: 2 per cent of his subjects appeared as multitalented and nearly 50 per cent were in the top 3 of their groups for at least one attribute. In other words about 50 per cent of children can be regarded as gifted or talented in some respect. Yet in English schools the Department for Education and Employment (DfEE, 1999) instructed that only 5–10 per cent of pupils should receive some form of gifted education provision and be placed on the 'G and T' (Gifted and Talented) register.

According to Tannenbaum's (1993) meta-analysis of research, in order to identify most of the highly able, it is necessary to select the top 15–20 per cent by both ability and attainment and even then some of the most able or gifted will be missed. In the Welsh proposals (Raffan, 2003) the selection of a top 20 per cent is based upon comparisons with the size of the Warnock (1978) special needs group among other considerations.

Giftedness is usually defined as high general intellectual ability such as might be identified using intelligence tests. Talent is used to refer to a high level of ability in a specific performance area such as music, dance or art. It can be used to encompass leadership, communication, design and special mathematical abilities so that some call all high abilities 'talents' rather than 'gifts'.

Creative talent may or may not be associated with a high level of intelligence. Torrance *et al.* (1963) found that a threshold IQ of only 120 was needed for high creative productive achievement and Cropley (1994) concluded there was no true giftedness without creativity.

Gagne's (2004) definition in his Developmental Model of Giftedness and Talent (DMGT) is as follows:

> *Giftedness:* designates the possession and use of untrained and spontaneously expressed natural abilities (called outstanding aptitudes or gifts), in at least one ability domain, to a degree that places an individual at least among the top 10 per cent.
>   *Talent:* designates the outstanding mastery of systematically developed abilities (or skills) and knowledge in at least one field of human activity to a degree that places an individual at least among the top 10 per cent of age peers who are or have been active in that field or fields.
>
> (p. 120)

The notion of 'gift' also raised the fundamental question about whether prodigies were born or made, the nature versus nurture issue. Howe *et al.* (1998) and Radford (1990) argued that the early histories of prodigies demonstrated significant amounts of practice and nurture. It has led us to believe that with encouragement and education an aptitude can be translated into some form of productive activity or expertise. What this talent might become may also be subject to chance factors (Gagne, 2004).

Identification of giftedness by intelligence tests

Intelligence in the population as defined by IQ tests follows what is called a normal distribution under an upside down U-shaped curve. All this means is that most people are of average ability and there are fewer who are less able and more able at the two ends of the distribution. The individual's score on the test is called an intelligence quotient or IQ. Figure 1.1 shows the normal distribution of ability in the population.

The gifted end of the distribution represents about 3 per cent of the population and at the other end of the distribution there is a slight increase over and above 3 per cent thought to be due to birth difficulties and genetic mutations.

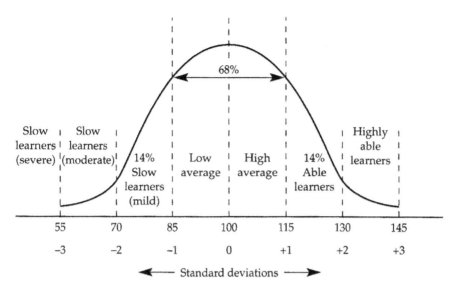

Figure 1.1 Normal distribution of ability in the population

IQ tests today are built upon the assumption that the range goes from 0 to 200 with a score of 100 being the mean with standard intervals of 15 points in between.

Scores of 0–55 define those with *severe learning difficulties* (SLD); 55–70 define those with *moderate learning difficulties* (MLD); 70–85 define those with *mild learning difficulties*. The score of 70/72 has been the cut off point for access to ordinary schools depending on the level of basic and social skills acquired. These slower learning children generally have poorer language, thinking and memory skills, hence their poorer scores on IQ tests. They take longer to learn from experience and more of them have coordination and language difficulties than is usual.

Scores of 85–100 are termed '*low average*', and 100–115 are '*high average*'.

Children with scores 115–130 are often called 'bright' or in test terms '*superior in ability*'. Many group IQ tests do not rise above scores of about 135; they have a low 'ceiling'. In one grammar school visited for work on 'study skills' all the 'A class' of 32 boys thus had scores between 130 and 134! These may also be called the 'more able'.

Scores of 130–145 represent the '*highly superior*' popularly termed 'gifted'. Only 3 per cent of the school population is predicted to fall into this category but this means we could have at least one in every classroom. They are also called the 'highly able' in many English texts on giftedness.

When local authorities were encouraged to make special provision for the gifted in the 1980s they very often established a threshold criterion of 145+ IQ points for referrals. This ensured that very few would meet the criterion and provision would cost as little as possible.

The IQs of the gifted in the top 3 per cent can range from 145–200 but only a few IQ tests give an accurate idea of where in this upper range an individual's real score falls. Individual tests such as WISC-IV and Binet Form L-M revised extend much further than 145 but WISC for example becomes less reliable at the extremes and can give very different results from Binet that can extend beyond 180. So there is no telling how able the gifted child might be even using these standard test measures.

WISC is now the most widely used IQ test world-wide by psychologists to identify patterns of ability. The Binet test form L-M used to be the most popular but its language bias created limitations in diagnosis especially in relation to socio-educational difficulties. However, IQ tests are tests of what has been learned, not of potential to learn or real world problem solving and creativity. It means that deprived linguistic and cultural environments can depress scores on these tests.

Intellectual or cognitive skills?

Many secondary schools prefer to give 'cognitive abilities' tests to their new intakes. It is for them a quicker and easier method for selection and diagnosis than reading the primary school reports. Despite the more mellow title 'cognitive abilities' the tests are group tests, or paper and pencil tests based upon intelligence test items.

Intellectual skills are about knowing 'that' and knowing 'how'. They include converting printed words into meaning, fractions into decimals, knowing about classes, groups and categories, laws of mechanics and genetics, forming sentences and pictures. They enable us to deal with the world 'out there'. Mostly these are taught in schools within subjects and also make up items on intelligence tests (Gagne, 1973).

Cognitive skills are internally organised capabilities that we make use of in guiding our attention, learning, thinking and remembering. They are executive control processes that activate and direct other learning processes. We use them when we think about our learning, plan a course of action and evaluate learning outcomes. These are seldom taught in schools or given value there. They form the basis of wisdom and are seldom tested except in real life situations.

The reasons for making these distinctions is to indicate that intelligence is not only about capacity but also the extent to which skills and knowledge have been taught or absorbed from contact with the environment; they are products of memory. Cognitive skills are different – they are higher order self-regulatory processes – and calling intelligence tests 'cognitive' could be a misinterpretation.

Gagne (1998) explained that the figures shown in Table 1.1 were based upon the top 10 per cent in each of four aptitude domains – intellectual, creative, socio-affective, sensorimotor – and possibly emotional intelligence. This means that the total percentage of gifted and talented individuals far exceeds 10 per cent and using peer nomination of multiple abilities he found 50 per cent in a sample of 2,500 of elementary school children.

An IQ score may sound accurate but it is based on a number of subtests made up of various test items all thought to be related in some way to our intelligence.

Table 1.1 Gagne's (2004: 131) metric-based system of levels within the gifted education population

Level	Label	Ratio in general popn.	IQ equivalents	SD
5	Extremely	1:100,000	165	+ 4.43
4	Exceptionally	1:10,000	155	+ 3.7
3	Highly	1:1,000	145	+ 3.00
2	Moderately	1:100	135	+ 2.3
1	Mildly	1:10	120	+ 1.3

SD Standard Deviation

But the inverted U-shaped curve simply demonstrates the random distribution of the errors of measurement. For example as soon as lots of sub-scores in school exams are added together the majority of pupils' results cluster around the mean with just a few doing well in all subjects. In fact it is misleading to add actual scores to obtain form or class positions; all the scores should first be standardised or brought to the same basis.

Even though a lot of work goes into an IQ test to standardise it and to make it valid (test what it sets out to) and reliable (consistently give the same score on each occasion), a simple score or set of scores can hardly define us especially if they result from only a paper and pencil test. There are, however, other ways in which giftedness or high ability might be defined to add to test information, such as the following.

Identification of giftedness by characteristics

In a meta-analysis Shore (1991) identified a number of characteristics by which highly able students were identified in researches. However, what are characteristics of groups can seldom be applied in total to an individual, although they can give indicators. Using them does overcome the problem of arbitrary cut-off points for referral to special provision.

Capabilities

- *Memory and knowledge* – They knew more, they knew what they knew better and could use it better.
- *Self-regulation* – They expertly guided and monitored their own thinking on task.
- *Speed of thought processes* – They spent longer on planning but arrived at answers more quickly.
- *Problem presentation and categorisation* – They extended representations beyond the information given, excluded irrelevancies, identified missing data and grasped the essentials of the task more quickly.
- *Procedural knowledge* – They used organised, systematic and flexible approaches to problem solving.

- *Flexibility* – They had the ability to see alternative configurations and adopt alternative strategies.
- *Preference for complexity* – They increased the complexity of tasks in play situations to increase interest.

It can be seen that in many respects these gifted learners were behaving as experts do. Nickerson *et al.* (1985) first researched this topic and it has become an aspect contributing to understanding in gifted education. Eriksson *et al.* (1993) found that it needed 10,000 hours of practice to become an expert in a performance field. Mozart, for example, undoubtedly had a talent or gift but he also put in a prodigious amount of playing and composing time from a very early age and this seems typical of experts and prodigies. He was also born into a musical family.

Traits and trait rating among the gifted

Traits are characteristic patterns of behaviour dependent on experience and the individual's personality. Underachievers or the twice exceptional may show a range of traits that give a clue to higher potential. Some of the positive ones are:

- inventive and original when motivated;
- quick to learn new concepts;
- very good at posing and solving problems ingeniously;
- asks awkward and penetrating questions about everything;
- persevering but only when motivated;
- streetwise and full of commonsense wisdom;
- perceptive about people and motives.

Many traits are thought to be on a continuum. When scale points are assigned, they can be linked as in a graph and a profile of the traits can be seen. As with IQ scores the numbers are not real scores that have equal appearing intervals so they cannot be added together.

Typologies

Typologies are less frequently encountered in gifted education procedures. They appear mainly in the literature on personality. Some think of the gifted or underachievers falling into broad categories such as:

- coasters – the 'invisible underachievers';
- overactive inattentives;
- class clown, humourist;
- dreamers;
- anxious conformist;
- disruptive, has behaviour problems;

- Absentee, truant;
- Doubly exceptional – masked gifted.

NACE research in 12 schools that were successful in making provision for the gifted (Wallace *et al.*, 2009) showed that effective schools intervened before these behaviour types evolved into problems. The schools were still, however, concerned that some pupils were coasting.

Niehart (2011) put forward a number of types of gifted patterns that she had observed in her research:

- *Type 1: The successful identified gifted.*
- *Type 2: The gifted with a creative style.*
- *Type 3: The underground gifted* – These were the underachievers, a group that included many disadvantaged individuals. They had to be taught social skills and needed a cultural broker. They also had to be taught to code switch – speak in the appropriate register when talking to other people. They also needed exposure to successful models and regular discussions about gender, class and race issues.
- *Type 4: The gifted 'drop outs'* – Niehart identified two groups of these:
  a) The 'pro-social drop outs' who were disaffected, emotionally troubled and at risk of becoming delinquents or addicts.
  b) The 'antisocial dropouts' who were a much smaller group who later became criminals – 'They don't just show up, they grow up'. If they are lucky enough to develop a caring relationship with an adult they can be rescued.
- *Type 5: The twice exceptional gifted* – These were children with disabilities and they showed a heterogeneous profile. Not surprisingly anxiety and depression were common in this group at adolescence. She found that about half the 2E group acted out social and emotional difficulties. They needed to be helped to develop self-advocacy skills, and persistence. Peer support was essential.

Niehart found that on average gifted children were two to four years more mature socially and emotionally than their peers, whereas those with 2E were two or more years less mature.

Identifying characteristics, traits and typologies are viewed as informal methods. However, they do have an objective base in clinical observation.

Checklists

Checklists are probably the most popular of informal assessments used in identification of gifted pupils. In primary schools they are essential as there may be no test data to back up or triangulate with success in the school curriculum.

Teachers in England will have been trained as part of CPD by their G and T coordinators to develop and use checklists to identify high ability and underachievement. Each secondary school department is expected to have its own agreed subject abilities checklist based on the school's general one.

Checklists focus teacher attention on factors wider than IQ, SATs and attainment test scores. They offer a more rounded view of the learner's task behaviour than success in school subjects.

Checklist to identify gifted learners

The following is an example checklist devised with teachers (Montgomery, 1996: 49–50):

- a wide range of interests and hobbies
- curiosity and investigative in approach
- an interest in and knowledge of questions about the origin of the universe, God, prehistoric monsters, the planets and solar and stellar systems at an early age
- keen powers of observation noting mismatches, patterns and analogies
- a facility in hypothesising and dealing with abstract ideas
- originality and initiative in intellectual and practical work
- unusual imagination and plenty of ideas
- pursues subjects or a subject in great depth
- a very powerful attention and attention span, concentrating and persevering for extraordinarily long periods
- frequently having learned to read self-taught, well before going to school, sometimes at about the age of two and a half
- superior reasoning powers and also powers of induction
- superior development of verbal skills and vocabulary, using complex and advanced sentences at a very early age
- works effectively independently, using the library with ease and frequency
- follows complex directions easily
- has a very good memory span for age
- may have high superiority in a particular area such as mathematical ability
- has a good sense of humour, unusually so for age
- may have a very rapid speed of thinking and working.

Items above with an asterisk indicate areas of learning disability that may mask high ability and lower success in school attainments.

Learning to read well before formal schooling begins can be a useful indicator of ability. It certainly facilitates progress in school subjects especially if the ability to write well soon develops. It is generally regarded as a sign of high potential ability when the reading and writing are five years above chronological age.

Checklist to identify gifted underachievers

- large gap between oral and written work
- failure to complete schoolwork

- poor execution of work
- persistent dissatisfaction with achievements
- avoidance of trying new activities
- functions poorly in groups
- lacks concentration in class
- poor attitudes to school
- dislikes drill and memorisation tasks
- difficulties with peers
- low self-image
- sets unrealistic goals
- clowns to avoid work and distract attention
- completes work satisfactorily to level of peers.

(Montgomery, 2009: 6)

Completing work satisfactorily to the level of peers may be deliberate so as not to attract the derision of peers for being a 'Boff' (boffin). If not deliberate it can indicate a learning difficulty. In both cases an ability test is needed. This demonstrates the importance of using a range of assessment techniques in a process of triangulation.

Checklist to identify gifted underachievers with good verbal skills

Compare the list above with the following checklist, devised for gifted children with good verbal skills and literacy difficulties:

- highly able orally and seems very intelligent
- able to engage in a mature way in adult conversations
- very good at oral problem solving
- answers oral questions well and asks difficult often impossible questions
- may have very poor, slow or illegible handwriting
- reads at a level that is possibly average for their age but well below their mental ability
- spells very poorly
- refuses to write anything down whenever possible
- as soon as they are asked to write they clown about, do very little and make excuses
- as more emphasis is placed on writing in late primary and secondary school they become difficult and exhibit behaviour problems; they may develop emotional problems as a consequence of their stress
- may prove highly able in mastering the computer to support written work.

(Montgomery, 1996: 51)

Checklist to identify gifted learners with poor verbal skills

The children who are so often still missed in a consideration of who is gifted are those who do not have good verbal skills. They may come from disadvantaging socio-cultural backgrounds where communication is limited or there may be a specific difficulty. The next checklist illustrates some of their problems and frustrations:

- good at design problem solving
- very advanced drawing and painting abilities, or cartoon drawing
- spends a lot of time on constructional activities, may later rebuild motor-bikes or old cars, clocks or computers from parts
- has surprising insights and gifts in certain kinds of creative problem solving
- does not contribute much in oral work
- may have been late talking and have mild difficulties in expressing ideas and forming words
- poor at reading and spelling
- exhibits behaviour problems as curriculum becomes more didactic and written work increases
- may develop special interests or gifts in sports, musical and artistic or dramatic activities, often outside school
- may become exceptionally able in a technical field such as computing.

(Montgomery, 1996: 52)

When gifts are not identified and supported and too great an emphasis is placed upon having good literacy skills as avenues to success in life, children who are different from this stereotype may become distressed and even emotionally disturbed if they are more vulnerable. Resilience building is very important for these children and for many gifted individuals in an era of doctrinaire educational processing and mass schooling.

Identification of giftedness by achievements

Prodigies

Peggy Somerville is characteristic of an infant prodigy. She was born into a family of artists and at three years old was painting vigorous lifelike expressionist water-colours. She held her first London exhibition at the age of eight and it was a sell out. She worked as an artist all her life but never achieved the status of a Picasso or Sickert. The musical talent of Jacqueline du Pré was equally identifiable at the age of five like many other gifted musicians. Characteristic of both girls was that they were born into cultured and relatively well-off families with plenty of opportunities to pursue their chosen field.

Most children only encounter such opportunities at school and not always then if musical instruments cannot be afforded and there is no art specialist to promote latent talent. Adult experts are often very skilled at identifying potential talent in the young such as for singing, ballet, diving, drama, football, etc. but children do not always encounter them.

Identification of potential Nobel prizewinners is far less easy. Even those with the highest intellectual gifts as measured by IQ do not necessarily achieve greatness. Terman (1954) concluded that out of the top 300 gifted in his research perhaps six might achieve national status and only one might become eminent.

In the histories of many who become recognised as gifted there is frequently the element of chance (Gagne, 2004): the chance that they will meet the one person or experience that will change the course of their lives; the chance that they will pick up and play the very instrument that will become their specialty.

Thus we have to conclude that many talented people will never discover their special 'gifts' and it is thus the role of the school to open the child's vista and experience to as wide a range of experiences as possible. In disadvantaged environments it is immensely important.

A talent portfolio

If a pupil does not have the opportunity to learn to play the flute, sing, paint in oils, act, or sail, etc., then the chances are that 50 per cent of them with a particular talent will never have that talent revealed and enjoy success in developing it.

Chance played an important role in talent development of many of the 'greats'. So schools especially need to extend the talent opportunities of their disadvantaged pupils beyond the curriculum subjects usually on offer and this can be done with the local community and the wider field. The pupils themselves say how much they appreciate this. If we encourage them to keep a talent portfolio or record of achievement they can record the opportunities they have had and enjoyed and plan what they might like to do in the future.

Using SATs and subject attainments to identify giftedness

English Standard Attainment Tests (SATS) are nationally devised and marked. Originally they were going to measure progress in both core and foundation subjects but this proved to be so time consuming and expensive that only core subjects – English, mathematics and science – were tested.

Initially pupils were tested in the core subjects when they were 7, 11 and 14-years-old. Pupils would go on to be assessed at 16 in GCSE examinations and at 18 in A levels or the Baccalaureate if they chose to stay in education. They often also had other tests in between. They were seriously over-assessed and SATs at 7 and 14 were subsequently discontinued, but a Foundation Year assessment was introduced in the Reception year (5 years in England). This does not identify the potentially gifted.

The collection of data from SATs at a national level enabled comparisons to be made between schools and year-on-year progress. Despite claims that the national curriculum and initiatives such as the national literacy strategy (DfEE, 1998) had improved literacy standards from 56 per cent achieving the set standard (level 4, in Year 6) in the 1950s to 84 per cent by 2014, the comparisons were false. Tymms (2004) found that there had been little improvement over that period to just over 60 per cent.

In order to do well in the league tables some teachers began to teach to the tests and this of course narrowed the curriculum. The repetitive nature of what is thus on offer can bore the more able and alienate them from school. It was found that at GCSE levels schools would focus on pupils who were likely to gain a D standard and give them additional support so that they might achieve a C and raise the status of the school in the league tables. All this had been predicted.

Research and appeals against grades show that markers are not entirely consistent and reliable in marking, especially of essay-type answers. They can downgrade scripts for slips of the pen and those that are difficult to read. Tolerance of these ambiguities is very variable.

Many of the test questions in the subject areas require knowledge of factual information and although gifted children retain information well they are not always interested in it or listening to it in class. Less able children may work very hard at revision and have extra tuition so they may score well in the tests. Thus SATs and subject examinations are less than reliable and valid as measures of high ability and yet schools still use them to determine pupils' abilities and potential. It is therefore essential that SATs are not the only identification strategy used. Triangulation is an important safeguard.

Identification of giftedness through provision

Many of the characteristics of giftedness are not included in any ability test but can be particularly useful as identifiers when observing pupils engaged in problem-solving types of curriculum activities – this is frequently referred to as authentic assessment.

Identification through Provision (IP), also known as *Curriculum-based Identification* (CBI), is useful. However, not all curriculum provision is fit for this purpose (see Chapter 7). If IP is linked with opportunities for children to self-refer many of the issues raised in identification can be resolved. The problem then could become one of resourcing; however, there are resolutions that can be found there also.

The schools observed in the NACE research project (Wallace *et al.*, 2009) were able to engage in a significant degree of identification through provision or *authentic assessment* because of the range and nature of the curriculum and peda-gogical approaches that they used. Many of the techniques involved pupils lead-ing and problem solving individually and in groups. This gave the teachers more time to stand back and observe what was going on. They could see how effective the learning was as well as how well the resources were working.

Grids

English schools now have registers for the gifted and talented and for pupils with special educational needs. Compiling a grid integrating this information is thus not a difficult task. The grid should be extensive, capturing as much information as possible and contributed to by the pupils, e.g. on out-of-school achievements and interests.

Table 1.2 Example grid/spreadsheet

YEAR	Class	S1	S2	S3	S4	S5	S6	S7	S8	S9	S10	etc.
VQ												
PQ												
RA												
SA												
HW speed												
SAT Eng												
SAT Ma												
SAT Sci												

A typical grid/spreadsheet has the pupils' names across the top and all the subject and test information available plus the outside school achievements and so on down the side, as shown in Table 1.2.

In the first set of six or so rows hard data should be recorded, along with test scores on VQ, PQ, Ma Q, RAge, SAge, R Comprehension and writing speed.

Stars: Teachers can put a star (*) in the subject column for those pupils they think are the best performers in their subject area. Alternatively they can rank all the pupils into A, B or C. These can be followed by a general assessment by each of the subject tutors. So as not to be burdensome the assessment should be a simple impression mark, e.g. 'A', 'B' or 'C', with 'A' representing more able/good, 'B' average and 'C' poor. An alternative is for staff just to give the coordinator a list of their 'stars' to insert in the grid.

This has proved a very powerful technique for highlighting performance patterns. A tick can be added for 'creatives' and a 'U' for underachievers to make it more sophisticated. After subject columns there should be columns for behaviour using an agreed code, then out-of-school columns and so on.

Just scanning these completed grids can reveal many different and interesting patterns. They can indicate need for interventions and support, praise and affirmation, or mentoring.

Shadowing

Pupils identified in the grids as being of concern can be followed for a day through all their lessons to see what is happening to them and their responses. Observing the daily diet of school to which pupils are subject can prove very revealing and enable plans to be developed for both teacher development and learner IEPs.

Mentoring

Many schools have adopted mentoring schemes for all pupils but it is difficult in a large school to find enough adult mentors to train and take on the role. There is thus room for schemes involving pupil mentoring, peer tutoring and 'buddies'; these can prove particularly beneficial for underachievers and gifted children with particular interests. However, it is beneficial for all pupils to have a mentor and the school benefits as well.

Conclusions

In statistical terms 16 per cent of the population have IQs of 115 and above, putting them in the 'more able' category, while talent and creativity may be distributed across the ability range. High IQ, however, is a less than accurate measure of potential or achievement in life or contribution to creative works. Personal factors such as persistence, interest and motivation play a considerable part, thus widening educational opportunities may prove more important than narrow selectivity. Schools therefore need to use multiple methods to capture and promote children's assets and achievements in and out of school.

One of the measures used for identifying disadvantage in the UK is pupils who qualify for free school meals. It is a crude way of allocating a 'pupil premium' to help schools overcome disadvantage. How the school uses the premium is a matter for debate but widening experience is an important consideration.

Not all disadvantaged children are in 'lower class' families; the reverse is also the case. Many rich families' lives are devoid of cultural, educational and linguistic opportunities for their children. This can be complicated by children being cared for by *au pairs* who may have a limited grasp of the English language. Language experience may thus be another need.

As officials have become aware of the depressing nature of social class and social disadvantage on achievement, 'value added' statistics have been introduced to moderate the league tables. But this is an outcome measure and we still need a system that qualifies pupils to enter into appropriate provision. An alternative is to make an enriched curriculum available to all.

Overcoming disadvantage, widening experience, increasing pupil talk and enriching the basic curriculum are the challenges. Chapters on identifying and including pupils with special needs follow, before overall pedagogical practices are detailed in the final chapter.

2 Identifying and supporting children with Developmental Coordination Difficulties

Introduction

In the early 1900s the term 'congenital maladroitness' was used to describe those who showed significant movement difficulties. Now the term *'movement difficulties'* itself has become widely used as it is compatible with other terms in the special needs area such as 'learning difficulties'.

In the interim the most popular term was 'clumsy' children (Gubbay, 1975). In 1992 the World Health Organisation used the term 'Specific Developmental Disorder of Motor Function'. But in 1994 *'Developmental Coordination Disorder'* (DCD) was adopted by the American Psychiatric Association (APA, 1994). The essential feature of Developmental Coordination Disorder (DCD) is a marked impairment in the development of motor coordination ... that significantly interferes with academic achievement or the activities of daily living. (APA, 2000: 56)

DCD is now the accepted term for what was once called 'clumsiness' and 'developmental dyspraxia'. 'Praxis' is the ability to motor plan, yet some children with coordination problems have no difficulties with it and so the medical term was dropped. In education 'DCD' stands for Developmental Coordination Difficulties.

Clumsiness is a relative term. The newborn is clumsy and also suffers relative temporary autism. The range of motor skill (IQ constant) is on a continuum. Appropriate common-use labels are difficult to find as Figure 2.1 suggests.

Children vary widely in gracefulness and dexterity. A locomotion problem may become apparent as the child walks across the room scattering belongings and other people's desks and work. He or she may not be able to climb a rope, do a forward roll (after the age of eight), catch a ball, and is the person no one wants in the team.

DCD had been regarded as a set of difficulties that did not affect academic learning but how wrong that perception was. They have been found to be a major cause of underachievement in the gifted (Montgomery, 2000; Silverman, 2002) and they are often comorbid with dyslexia, ADHD and ASD, creating not only dual but multiple exceptionalities.

| clumsy | awkward | average | skilled | graceful | (gifted) |

Figure 2.1 The DCD continuum

Bravar (2005) found that 70 per cent of Italian children referred for underachievement had writing difficulties. Of these, 47 per cent had poor handwriting and the writing of 23 per cent was illegible, but only 6 per cent had actually been referred for writing problems.

Between 5 and 10 per cent of the UK school population is estimated to have DCD (Barnett *et al.*, 2008). According to APA (1994) the incidence is between 5 and 6 per cent. The majority with gross motor difficulties will also have fine motor problems. Their exercise books are filled with scruffy, scrappy work loaded with crossings out and holes. Such pupils are not picked in team games and are frequently seriously bullied even by teachers and they become the butt of jokes and blame.

Despite the ungainly behaviour, and perhaps a lack of control of emotional responses, the individual may be highly intelligent trapped in a body that will not do as instructed unless specific training is given. If the writing is legible the DCD may be ignored, but the pupil is condemned to underachieve and is usually poor at spelling and maths (Chesson *et al.*, 1991).

DCD in school age pupils studied by Schoemaker and Calveboer (1994) showed that compared with controls those with DCD were more anxious, lacking in self-esteem, more introverted and judged themselves to be less able both physically and socially even in children as young as 6 years. The researchers put this down to the importance placed upon proficiency in physical activities by the child and the peer group. Some put success in sport especially football as a higher goal than success in the classroom. However, one of the major factors contributing to low self-esteem was the negative attitude of teachers to the work of children who could not write neatly (Montgomery, 1998; Roaf, 1998).

Schoemaker's long-term studies showed that those identified at 5 years with DCD still had problems at 15 years. Children do not generally grow out of DCD, contrary to popular belief.

Speech delay was a most frequently appearing concern in Chesson's study with over 50 per cent of their DCD sample having required speech therapy. They identified two distinct groups: those whose difficulties were identified before entry to school and those whose problems only became apparent after entering school. Half the group of 31 were doing well in maths at school but their problems in spelling and handwriting were hampering progress in other subjects. Twenty-three of the group were having learning support in mainstream and a further four required specialist provision within language units.

Characteristic difficulties in DCD

Children with DCD have difficulties in learning the skilled movements. However, once they have been learned, skills such as walking, riding a bicycle, writing, etc.

can be performed with relative ease. The child with DCD will continually fall off the bike and take a much longer time to learn to ride and a few may not be able to complete the task at all. Those with less determination may give up.

Even stopping a task is the product of learning. A child of 18 months told to put rings on a stick will continue to do so even when told to 'Stop!' Children have to learn to be directed by the human voice and some children may arrive at school from disadvantaged circumstances where confusion has reigned and they appear to ignore the teacher's instructions. In such cases a period of clear unambiguous training will overcome the problem. A child with DCD may take longer to learn these controls but can be helped by specific training.

Patterns of DCD

*   *Gross motor DCD* is easily identified when balance and coordination are required. The problems affect the coordination of the general movements of the body including fine motor coordination.
*   *Visuo-motor integration (VMI)* affects hand–eye coordination and spatial functions, e.g. jigsaw, knot tying, ball skills.
*   *Fine motor DCD* usually only affects the smaller more complex movements involving the hands, e.g. handwriting, bead-threading and buttoning.
*   *Isolated DCDs* in dressing, speech.

Gross motor DCD

The pupil with gross motor DCD may:

*   move too fast or too slow
*   show lack of control
*   be slow to react to signals
*   constantly fidget and fiddle with things
*   be easily distractible and inattentive
*   show organisational problems
*   have difficulties thinking through a plan of action and carrying it out
*   have difficulties in the recall of events and sequences as well as time
*   show inconsequential and impulsive behaviours
*   have difficulty with handwriting and copying from the board
*   slump and loll about in their seat
*   walk down the corridor veering to one wall
*   appear somewhat uncoordinated even when walking
*   show contralateral body movements
*   constantly fall off apparatus and bump into things
*   lose books and other belongings
*   leave a trail of devastation
*   spill food and knock over tables and chairs
*   have their clothes and hair awry

- have had problems in early years with buttoning, tying shoelaces and changing for PE
- find learning new skills challenging, e.g. constantly fall off when learning to skateboard.

Attentional difficulties, explosive outbursts, lack of inhibition and impulsive behaviours found in DCD can be confused with aspects of ADHD.

Visuo-motor integration (VMI)

Difficulties in this area may exist in the presence of adequate motor skills. The problem can be noticed when pupils follow a pencil with their eyes from right to left and their eyes jump as they attempt to cross the mid line. Pencils on the left will be picked up in the left hand and transferred to the right rather than using the right hand to cross the mid line. Jigsaws and figure drawing may show difficulties as well as spatial location and far point copying. Keeping the place in reading may also be difficult and the eyes will jump lines and segments of text.

Visuo-motor impairment is rare in cases of dyslexia (Vellutino, 1987) although it was once a common diagnosis and thought to be a cause. Ayres (1976) called them **sensory integration difficulties** – difficulties in integrating information from the senses with motor information.

Case examples – Marie and Sam

Two potentially bright pupils of the same age in Reception class are set to copy a pattern with counters. Both copy a pattern with counters such as a horizontal row of red yellow red yellow red yellow dots. When a similar pattern is shown as a diagonal Marie makes hers vertically. Sam makes his diagonally.

When they are asked to pick up a pencil with their preferred hand (right) and the pencil is placed in the left sector Sam can do it smoothly and easily and starts drawing. Marie starts the movement of the right hand then picks up the pencil with her left and passes it to her right at the mid line, then begins to draw.

It appears that Marie has perceptual difficulties but is this really so? She has already begun to read but Sam has made little progress. Marie's 'soft neurological' signs do not appear to be affecting reading but they will probably affect her writing and copying among other VMI skills. She would benefit from early systematic training in crossing the mid line through music and movement, e.g. 'The wheels on the bus go round and round'.

Visuo-spatial difficulties

Some individuals have a severe form of this difficulty and typically they say that even as adults they can get lost in any big store or supermarket. They may also have great difficulties reading a map, reversing a car, maintaining balance with eyes shut and walking in a straight line without wobbling and veering to the right and left. Walking along a balance bar in PE may be fraught with difficulties for them.

Verbal or oral dyspraxia – dysarthria

This affects just the speech apparatus that is controlled by 100 different muscles. The child will need speech therapy to become intelligible and may need help with breathing, timing and sequencing through daily exercises.

- Teachers need to ensure that others do not bully the child and no attempt should be made to correct the speech in front of others. Speech therapists advise that only the parents should correct it.
- Teachers are encouraged to help with particular sounds or remind the child of them.
- Reading is best taught to them using synthetic phonics methods.
- Cooperative learning methods are needed to promote social and communication skills.
- The Talking Curriculum (see Chapter 7) is essential to promote talk and develop speech.
- Work is needed on building self-esteem.

Developmental dysgraphia

Dysgraphia is an impairment in the fine motor coordination skills associated specifically with handwriting and drawing. It has a particularly deleterious effect on the learning capacity in schools because from an early age children are expected to learn to write and use it as a main means of learning and response. Gross motor locomotion and visuo-motor skills may be unaffected.

Handwriting difficulties are evidenced in lack of fluency and quality of composition (Berninger and Graham, 1998) with illegibility a major issue, leading to lower marks (Soloff, 1973; Sweedler-Brown, 1992). Rosenblum and Livneh-Zirinsky (2007) showed that children with dysgraphia took more 'on paper' and 'in air' time measured with a digitised pen recorder. They applied less pressure on the writing surface and had erased or overwritten significant numbers of letters. All this affects writing speed and legibility.

Pre-term children have also been found to be a population at risk from handwriting difficulties and Feder and Majnemer (2007) found that full-term controls in their study wrote at a higher speed and with greater legibility at 6/7 years.

Automaticity in handwriting relates strongly to success in composition. Medwell and Wray (2014) found that threshold speeds of 12 letters per minute using Christensen and Jones' (2005) alphabet test were needed by 6-year-olds (Year 1) and 22 letters per minute by 10/11-year-olds (Year 6).

As DCD is found across the ability range and up to 10 per cent of children will have some form of the difficulty we can predict that 10 per cent of any gifted group may also have the difficulties. However, in the research studies detailed below (Montgomery, 2008, 2014) 30 per cent of pupils across the age and ability ranges showed some difficulties with writing and it is the major cause of underachievement among the gifted.

It was observed that some gifted children attending National Association for Gifted Children workshops had almost illegible writing. Explanations were offered that their brains ran much too fast for their developing graphic skills. But on closer investigation it was found that DCD may have been involved in some of the cases alongside dyslexia and also as an entity on its own (Montgomery, 1997). It had been noticeable over a number of years that some gifted undergraduates gained lower second degrees instead of upper seconds and the only reason seemed to be their writing speed. Some had slower writing because it was very precise and neatly formed, others used italic, many used semi print forms and some just wrote slowly. Calligraphy, or 'beautiful writing' often dominated the need to use a rapid running hand in note taking and examinations. They were unable to write down enough ideas and arguments. This has been borne out by the research of Connelly *et al.* (2005) with their undergraduates.

Investigations by Berninger and Graham (1998) showed writing operates at two levels:

- lower order skills of spelling and handwriting; and
- higher order skills of composition.

Writing at first seems essentially to be a motor activity for it is possible to write a name and address with the eyes shut, but it is conceptually driven when a person is engaged in free writing and perceptually driven when copy-writing. Far point copying is memory loaded and more difficult than near point copying. In free writing correct spellings have to be assembled automatically to express the ideas; if spelling is poor this slows down writing speed whilst the writer pores over the spelling or selects a different word.

Difficulty with spelling distracts the attention from both the message and the motor act (Myklebust, 1973) and takes up much more brainpower than fluent spelling. Spelling problems slowed down the speed of writing by at least two words per minute in free writing in Year 7s (Montgomery, 2008). Berninger (2004) found that the ability to recall letter shapes in an alphabet test contributed more to handwriting than motor skills and performance on the letter test correlated highly with scores for good composition in SAT at Key Stage 1 (Medwell *et al.*, 2008).

Identification of DCD in the school years

Gubbay (1975) devised a questionnaire to aid in the identification of children with DCD as follows:

- Is the formation and neatness of handwriting much below average?
- Is the sporting ability and body agility much below average?
- Is the child unduly clumsy?
- Does the child fidget excessively in class?
- Is the conduct much below average?
- Is the overall academic performance much below average for the age and ability?

Screening examination questionnaire after Gubbay (1975)

1. Whistle through parted lips (pass or fail)
2. Make five successive skips (without a skipping rope) (pass or fail after three attempts, with two demonstrations by examiner if necessary)
3. Throw a tennis ball up, clap hands up to four times, then catch the ball with two hands or dominant hand (number of claps – fails if only claps twice or less)
4. Roll a tennis ball with dominant foot in a spiral fashion around six matchboxes at 30 cm intervals (18 seconds allowed)
5. Tie a single shoelace with a double bow (15 seconds allowed)
6. Thread ten beads (in 38 seconds) (beads 3 cm in diameter, bore of 0.8 cm, string with stiffened end)
7. Pierce 20 holes in graph paper (in 24 seconds) (use a hat pin, two rows in 3 x 3 mm squares)
8. Posting box: fit six different plastic shapes into appropriate slots (two seconds) (fails if takes longer than 18 seconds)

The clumsy children were selected by Gubbay on the following basis:

- 8-year-olds: 6 or more failures
- 9-year-olds: 5 or more failures
- 10-year-olds: 4 or more failures
- 11-year-olds: 3 or more failures
- 12-year-olds: 2 or more failures

Tom's spiky writing (see Figure 2.2) suggests a more severe DCD problem than Gary has. Gary's profile is a dyslexic one with milder DCD and handwriting difficulties.

Gary's (11 years) open-ended writing

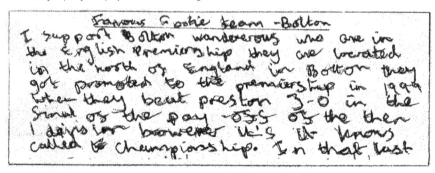

Tom's (11 years) open-ended writing

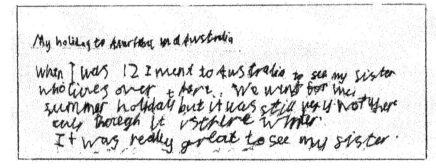

Figure 2.2 Gary and Tom's dysgraphic writing

Comparative case analysis – Gary and Tom

Gary and Tom are two 11-year-old boys who have just moved into secondary school Year 7. An educational psychologist has diagnosed both with dysgraphia (see Table 2.1). The learning support teacher has compiled a comparative table of indicants from Gubbay's checklist to determine the sort of learning support they may need and how their patterns of difficulties vary because this was not clear from the psychologist's reports.

Most attention in relation to underachievement has been directed to encouraging children to want to write and to stimulate their compositional ideas (Wray, 2005). However, if the sub-skills of spelling and handwriting are not automatic and fluent too much cerebral capacity is taken up with them rather than with the ideas and logical exposition. In disadvantaged populations the language of education can be beyond the experience of the learners (Warwick, 2009) and this too contributes to their underachievement.

Table 2.1 Differences between Gary and Tom

Gary	Tom
Was able to walk on tiptoes for a brief time	Made an inept attempt, flat-footed
Hopped on one leg three times, just	Made a stumbling inept attempt
Jumped on both feet without falling over	Unable to do it
Struggled to coordinate movements for crawling, persisted and was able to do it but had to concentrate intensely	Managed a semblance of crawling but poor in cross-lateral coordination
Was able to run fast and then speed up but was not a proper fast sprint	Was only able to jog slowly and was unable to increase his speed
In the laterality tasks he scored 1–2 points because in all of them he had to think carefully about each one. They were all completed correctly each time	Kept changing his mind about which was left or right and in the end guessed for each one and only sometimes was correct
Completed the balance task OK	The balance tasks were very difficult for Tom. He only managed to walk a few steps along a line before falling over
Was unable to feed five beads onto a thread in 30 seconds	Was unable to feed five beads onto a thread in 30 seconds
Able to tie a loose bow	Unable to tie a bow at all and became frustrated
Able to cut out shapes but not neatly	Able to cut out shapes but not neatly
Apparently normal gait	Has an awkward gait
Occasionally bumps into things	Always bumping into things and knocking things over
Always fiddling with objects on desk	Always fiddling with objects on desk and moving legs and tapping feet
Unable to hold more than one thing in mind at a time	Unable to hold more than one thing in mind at a time
Struggles with organisation and planning	Struggles with organisation and planning
Confusion with time, forgetful	Confusion with time, forgetful
The Ed Psych's report also showed	*The Ed Psych's report also showed*
Gary was slow to learn to talk and parents found it difficult to understand him	Tom talked at the usual time and no difficulties in being understood
12 points decrement in PQ (VQ 110 and PQ 98)	28 points decrement in PQ (VQ 117 and PQ 89)
Spelling age: 8 years	Spelling age: 12–13 years
Reading age: 8 years	Reading age: 11–12 years
Diagnosed as also dyslexic	
Some difficulties with social relationships. Highly emotional	Some difficulties with social relationships. Highly emotional

The examination of over 1,000 scripts for this chapter and previous data suggests that by the age of 7/8 years as in the Kingston Project (Low, 1990) most children could be fluent writers but poor pedagogy conspires to prevent them.

The Sutton Trust research (Jerrim, 2013) found that by the end of the Reception year children from poor homes were 11.5 months behind middle income and rich peers in reading. Writing research in Reception (Montgomery, 2014) showed that by the end of the Spring term poor children were already five months behind the rest. Figure 2.3 shows examples of handwriting difficulties across the age range. None had a diagnosis of DCD.

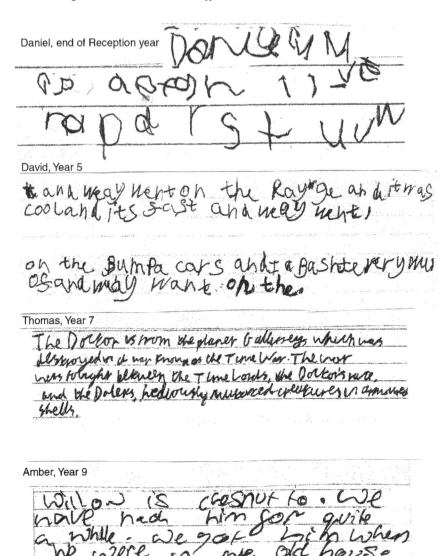

Figure 2.3 Dysgraphia across the age ranges

Issues in handwriting and dysgraphia

Writing speed

Adults can generally write at a speed of 40 words per minute but it takes time and practice to achieve this rate. Tests on several thousands of teachers in CPD training sessions showed that their speed varies in range from 25 to 56 words per minute when writing the Lord's Prayer or some other well known piece. Teachers clearly need to write speedily enough to obtain their degrees.

However, 80 per cent of teachers in primary schools did not direct attention to speed (Stainthorp *et al.*, 2001) but focused on legibility and neatness. Even the National Literacy Strategy (DfEE, 1998) did not address the subject. The National Curriculum framework (DfE, 2014) only directs teachers to encourage increased speed in Years 5 and 6, the end of junior/elementary school.

Print script

Children in England are still permitted to learn an unjoined print script (manuscript) in Reception (see Figure 2.4) transferring later to a running joined hand (cursive): 'Joined handwriting should be taught in Year 2' (DfE, 2014: 15).

Although most children can learn the new set of cursive motor programmes easily, Wedell (1973) and Montgomery (1997) found that children with DCD can not. They need to start off with a form of cursive so there are no transfer problems to set them back. Although many Reception teachers may think this is too difficult, during the early decades of the twentieth century all UK children were taught cursive from the outset as children still are in the French school system among others (Thomas, 1998). In the revised National Literacy Strategy (DfEE, 2001) the only concession was to advocate ligatures – flick up strokes.

Research by Morin *et al.* (2012) showed that those taught cursive from the outset made more progress in speedy writing of words, followed by semi-joined and slowest were those taught print. They advocated teaching cursive from the outset as switching was too hard for children.

Other researchers (Overvelde and Hulstijn, 2011) specifically recommend not allowing children to trace letters (using pencil and paper) because doing so delays memorisation of letter forms. Individual letters need to be made with

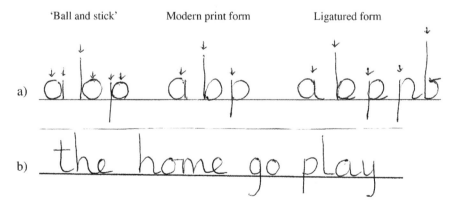

Figure 2.4 a) Print and ligatured scripts and *b)* Semi-joined script

one continuous line drawn in the air then practised on the paper; no tracing or copying as used with dyslexics. This is an essential step forward from 'ball and stick' print that was once widespread and even more problematic for dysgraphics.

Preliterate 5-year-old children printed, typed or traced letters and shapes, then were shown images of these stimuli while undergoing functional MRI scanning (James and Engelhardt, 2012). A previously documented 'reading circuit' was recruited during letter perception only after handwriting – not after typing or tracing experience. The researchers found that the initial duplication process mattered a great deal. When children had drawn a letter freehand, they exhibited increased activity in three areas of the brain that are activated in adults when they read and write: the left fusiform gyrus, the inferior frontal gyrus and the posterior parietal cortex. By contrast, children who typed or traced the letter or shape showed no such effects. They attributed the differences to the messiness inherent in free-form handwriting: not only must we first plan and execute the action in a way that is not required when we have a traceable outline, but we are also likely to produce a result that is highly variable. The variability may itself be a learning tool for different forms of the same letter. This shows that free-form handwriting is better for teaching writing and underpins reading and spelling.

Alice (see Figure 2.5) has been taught to form the letters with ligatures but has not been taught their purpose and how to join them. In early learning, lead-in strokes may not be recorded but they are essential in remedial writing for dysgraphics. In the early years as soon as one letter has been learned with its ligature it should be used to link to another to make simple words and syllables. This helps develop fluency and speed. To aid spelling, all syllables (beats in words) should be written as one writing unit as soon as feasible and especially whole common words such as 'and' and 'the'.

Penhold

The most efficient pen/pencil hold for fluent speedy writing is the standard 'dynamic tripod' grip illustrated in Figure 2.6.

In the standard tripod grip the pen is held between the thumb and second finger and the forefinger rests on top, making the tripod. The next most efficient is the 'rigid tripod' grip where the forefinger and second fingers rest on top of the pen

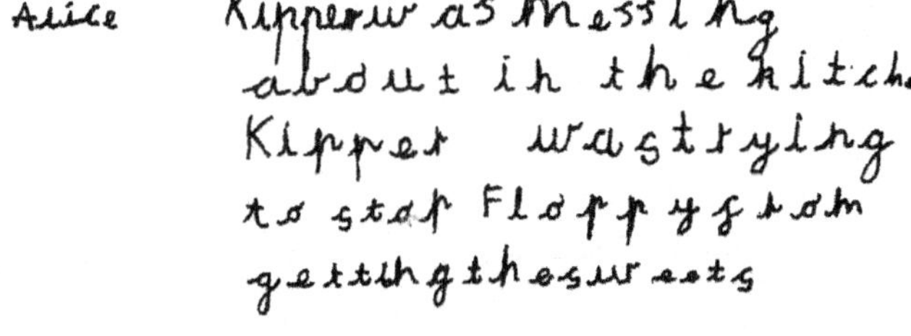

Figure 2.5 Poorly taught ligaturing (two-thirds of original size)

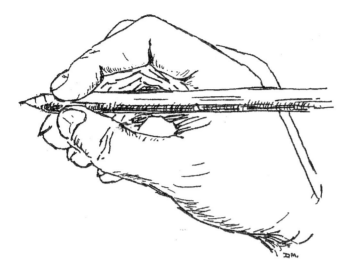

Figure 2.6 The flexible standard tripod grip

and the thumb and third finger hold the pen. This restricts movement somewhat and the action is a little stiff. It can more quickly lead to fatigue. The 'thumb over' grip is also popular. The most immature grip is the full fist (stab) grip that obscures the writing and is slow. In between there are all manner of grips that children use to gain control over the pen. Bendy joints in little fingers, pens that are too large and lack of strength all contribute to difficulties in developing a correct penhold.

Schwellnus *et al.* (2012) compared speed and legibility of children writing with 'dynamic tripod' versus a 'lateral quadruped' grip (thumb crosses over the pen against the side of the index finger and all four fingers initiate the pen movement). The children aged nine years copied five sentences in two minutes. It was found that grasp had no effect. Thus they questioned the practice of trying to change writing grips once they were well established. However, essay writing at lengths of 10 to 20 minutes might reveal pain and differences in speed.

If the fingers are weak and bendy then they can be supported by special or built-in pencil holds until strength and the correct grip can be developed. Strengthening exercises are essential such as play with sand and playdough, cooking, using eating tools and finger painting. Writing movements in the early years can be prefaced by painting, singing and music and movement games.

The results of poor penhold and DCD problems can mean that children write more slowly and develop fatigue and illegibility towards the end in the 20-minute test scripts (Montgomery, 2008). Alston (1993) found that 40 per cent of her sample found writing painful and 60 per cent avoided it whenever possible.

However, in the scripts from school C above (Figure 2.3) it was noticeable that some children with DCD could write very rapidly, e.g. Amber wrote 425 words. They were all correctly spelled but difficult to decipher at first.

Handwriting grips follow a developmental pattern from 'stab grip' in the early years to 'digital pronate' (as in a fork hold), static tripod and then dynamic tripod or lateral tripod (thumb over) (Schneck and Henderson, 1990).

Left-handedness

Left-handers should learn to develop the standard tripod grip but they need to hold the pen further from the point so that they can see their writing as they form it. They also need to be allowed to slope their writing paper 40 degrees to the left, far more than right-handers to the right. Left-handers should sit on the left of other children to allow free movement of the arm.

'Hookers' hold the pen with the palm upwards. This may not be a grip that is open to change. It is thought this grip is used by those who should be writing with the other hand but are not able to because of some neurological reason. They may need to write with the paper at 90 degrees to the horizontal.

Legibility

Research into eight Reception year classes (Montgomery, 2014) indicated that some teachers do not teach children how to make their letter forms at all but set them to trace or copy without oversight and feedback (see Figure 2.7). To improve legibility, letter formation and penhold need to be taught and observed and feedback given. Only Lana's and Amber's scripts show that there has been a direct and systematic attempt to teach correct letter formation and movement. The others are drawing their letters and letter-like shapes. This follows from tracing and copying methods of learning.

In the later years a test of writing form (Figure 2.8) shared with a child with writing difficulties can be used to help develop legibility. In the remediation period the child can be given sheets with double lines in which to write the bodies of the letters to get them all the same size and to clearly write the ascenders and descenders which must all slope in the same direction. Mark and the other children's attempts can be seen in Figure 2.9. The intervention should be short, for example five minutes daily practice for a fortnight, as in Mark's case.

Lines

In Reception, contrary to many teachers' custom and practice, lines should be given for little children to write on. It does not hamper creativity (Burnhill and Hartley *et al.*, 1975) and helps them find where to start and organise their marks on the paper both in free and copywriting (Figure 2.7).

Laterality

Studies of normal subjects show that large numbers have crossed laterality or mixed laterality. It is therefore not of use as a diagnostic indicator or 'soft neurological sign'. Assessments include dominant eye, hand and foot.

(a) Millie (Oct 2012)   *I go to nanny's*

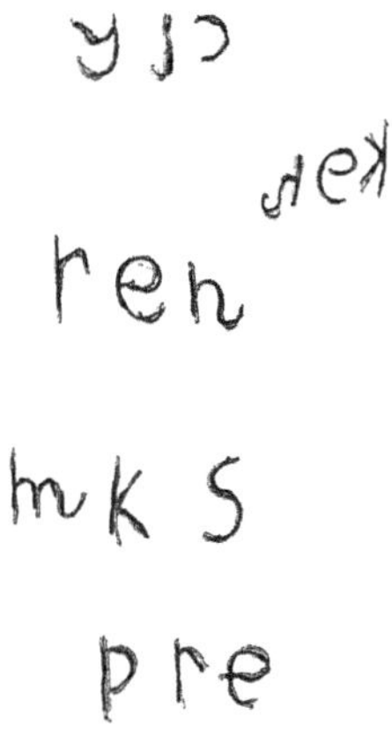

(b) Lana (Oct 2012)   *Little red hen makes the bread*

(c) Harrison (Oct 2012)   *About my holiday in Majorca*

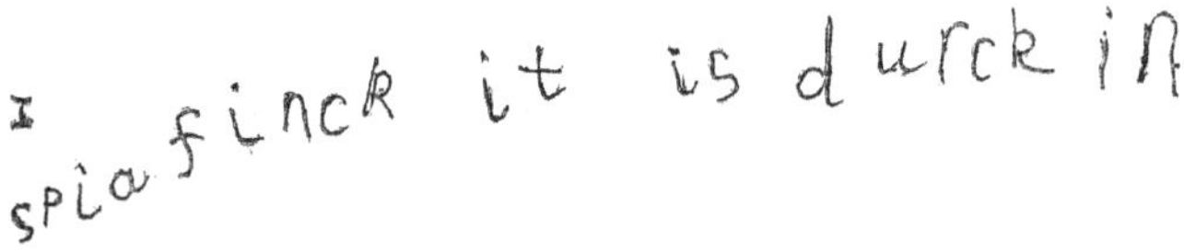

(d) Amber (March 2013)   *I think it is dark in space*

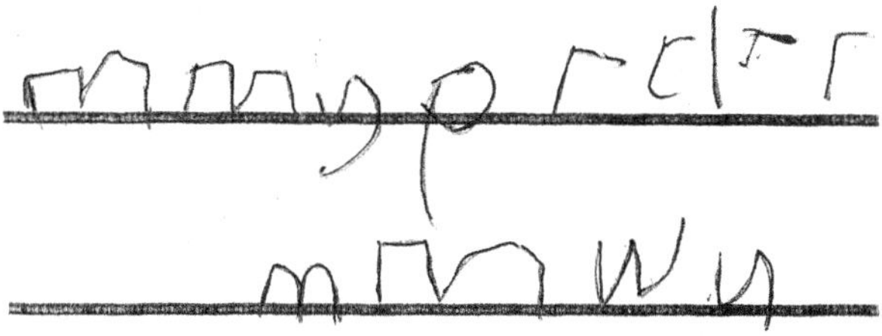

(e) Darcey (2012)   *I went swimming in my holiday house*

Figure 2.7 Writing with and without lines in Reception

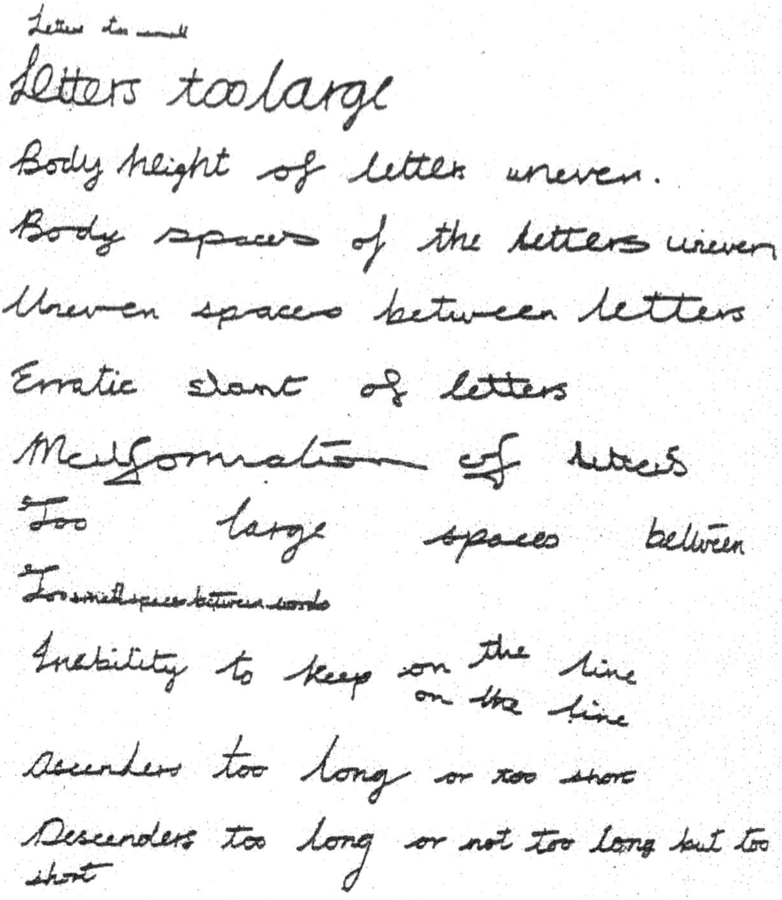

Letters too small

Letters too large

Body height of letter uneven.

Body space of the letters uneven

Uneven spaces between letters

Erratic slant of letters

Malformation of letters

Too   large   spaces   between

Too small space between words

Inability to keep on the line   on the line

Ascenders too long   or too short

Descenders too long   or not too long but too short

Intervention Procedure

Whatever the errors identified give the pupil some double lined paper and ask him or her to write name and address between the lines. The target is to get the body size of letters all the same. Note any malformed letters.

Figure 2.8 Handwriting form and legibility test (T-HFL), Montgomery (1990)

Figure 2.9 shows the results of remediation following the use of the Test of Handwriting Form and Legibility (T-HFL).

Lateralisation does not become evident until a baby is over 10 months old when a preference will begin to emerge. What is of concern is when lateralisation is very evident at this stage. It suggests that the child may have a problem with the non-preferred side. The right-hand side of the brain controls the left-hand side movements of the body and vice versa. The left hemisphere is also usually 'dominant' for language.

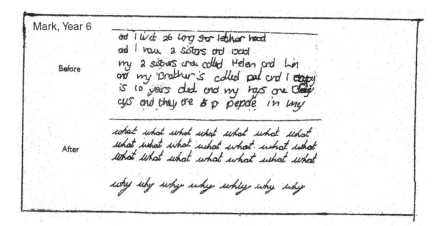

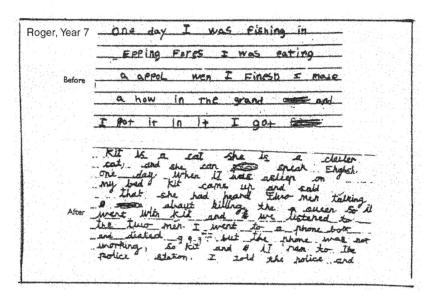

Figure 2.9 Remediation following use of T-HFL

Most right-handers are left hemisphere dominant but may be 'right eyed' and left footed, that is they have mixed dominance. Left-handers, about 12 per cent of the school-age population, also show a tendency to be left hemisphere dominant. Ambidextrous people show a greater tendency towards bilateral dominance.

Mirror writing

This is common in beginning writers and is a sign that lateralisation needs to be readjusted by marking the left-hand side of the writing paper to show where to start and using lines and joined writing to keep the flow going from left to right.

The brain can easily learn to write from left to right, or the reverse, or read and write upside down, so it is usually a matter of light training to settle the system down into the required form.

Writing speed research

In a ten-minute writing speed test, Roaf (1998) found that secondary school pupils who had not reached a speed of 25 words per minute were disadvantaged and failing in all subjects where there was a preponderance of writing. They had lower achievements and poorer self-concepts than other pupils.

Using Middle Years Information Survey (MIDYIS) Lyth (2004) found that when the pupils (N=10,000) in Year 8 were set to write:

> *I can write clearly and quickly all day long.*

for one minute, one sentence per line and only one line each, the mean speed was 29 words per minute. Boys wrote 5.4 lines per minute; girls wrote 5.7 lines. Pupils from independent schools wrote more: boys wrote 6.1 words per minute and girls wrote 6.3.

Writing the same sentence over and over again is easier and speedier than free writing tasks but is a quick way of obtaining an estimate of potential speed and fluency problems as well as giving a sample of writing to analyse further.

Allcock (2001) assessed the writing speed of a large sample of secondary school pupils using a 20-minute creative writing task. She found that very few could write at an adequate speed for their curriculum needs (see Table 2.2).

Table 2.2 Mean writing speeds across the age ranges in a 20-minute test, N=2,701 (Allcock, 2001)

Year	Words per minute
7	13.9
8	14.6
9	15.7
10	16.3
11	16.9

Table 2.3 Differences in speed of writing by cohort and gender from three Year 7 cohorts, N=536 (Montgomery, 2008)

Speed category	School A (N=125)	School B (N=160)	School C (N=251)
Cohort speeds (words per minute)			
Boys	11.84 (N=75)	12.89 (N=61)	11.14 (N=123)
Girls	14.32 (N=50)	14.77 (N=99)	13.69 (N=127)
MEANS	12.78	14.05	12.44
25% below			
Boys	30.67%	44.26%	21.92%
Girls	22.0%	14.14%	10.36%
MEANS	27.2% (N=34)	25.63% (N=41)	32.28% (N=81)
40% below			
Boys	9.33%	21.16%	12.35%
Girls	10.0%	12.12%	3.98%
MEANS	9.6% (N=12)	15.63% (N=25)	16.33% (N=41)

Allcock's test was designed to match the demands made on secondary pupils by subject tutors and the exam system. Thus it was used in the following studies.

The boys overall were slower at writing in all the categories and schools (Table 2.3). In the groups that were 25 per cent slower, the ratio of boys to girls was approximately 2:1. In the 40 per cent slower category, the ratio overall was 1.65:1. Some details were:

- Only one girl could write at a speed of 25 words per minute.
- The mean handwriting speed was 13.09 words per minute.
- 1.5 per cent could write at a speed of 20 words per minute.
- 28.33 per cent wrote too slowly (25 per cent slower).
- 14 per cent wrote slower than 8.3 words per minute (40 per cent slower) and these had distinct handwriting difficulties.
- 32.33 per cent made more than five spelling errors per 100 words. They failed the HMI criterion, to make no more than five misspellings per 100 words (further data is provided in Chapter 3).
- 18.6 per cent made ten or more spelling errors per 100 words (dyslexic zone).

Thus nearly one-third have handwriting speed difficulties and one-third have spelling difficulties. There also seems to be an association between higher socioeconomic status and writing facility.

Because the test is twice as long as Roaf's, in the third five minutes Allcock found the writer slowed to think and then speeded up again for the final section. Thus a speed of 20 words per minute was set as the criterion for effective writing speed. Only 1.5 per cent of the 11-year-olds met this criterion.

The scripts of pupils in Year 7 in School C were given a more detailed analysis. Their mean speed was significantly lower than that of Allcock's sample and the other two schools in the project. School B was a specialist school in a relatively economically advantaged area in Hampshire, similar to Allcock's samples. School C was a in a coastal town. The results were as follows:

Writing in Year 7 – School C (N=251), 2008

- 0.6 per cent (15 pupils) wrote at 20–25 words per minute (3 boys and 12 girls) – fast enough for the curriculum.
- 37.45 per cent (94 pupils) wrote at a speed of 13–20 words (32 boys and 62 girls) – the above average speed range. The obverse is that 62.55 per cent are writing too slowly.
- Underachievement: 19.16 per cent (48 pupils) were writing at significantly slow speeds, 40 per cent below the mean, and can be expected to be failing in all lessons where writing is needed. These pupils appear to have a special educational need.
- Ratio of boys to girls: 35 boys and 13 girls, nearly 3:1, were writing 40 per cent more slowly.
- Three boys appear severely disabled in the writing area. They write at five words or less per minute. They will need laptops and/or scribes and investigation for dyslexia/DCD.

Although the pupils are not selected by ability in this school we can see that approximately two-thirds are not equipped with the basic handwriting skills to cope with the curriculum. Thus two-thirds of the more able potentially have these problems too. School A did select by ability for a fast-tracking class and amongst that group the proportion of slow writers was smaller. Thus by Year 7 some more able pupils were being prevented from accessing more appropriate curriculum provision. When pupils also had spelling problems this slowed down their writing speed by two or more words per minute.

The bigger ratio of boys with problems was not unexpected. Their motor skills tend to develop more slowly than girls and learning disability studies generally find more boys than girls with problems.

Because these researches took place in the month of October just a few weeks after they had entered secondary school, the results of their primary experience are captured. It was therefore essential to examine writing in the primary school.

The writing test was modified to a 15-minute free writing test to be more compatible with the demands and writing development of children in Year 5 in the next project (Table 2.4).

Table 2.4 Writing speed of pupils in Year 5 in three schools

Socio-economic status	Numbers	Words per minute	Coordination difficulties	Spelling errors
School X (Church school)	N=85	10.04	7.0%	8.84
School Y (Rural school)	N=60	8.05	20.83%	9.56
School Z (Coastal estate)	N=52	7.81	36.54%	10.45

Table 2.5 Writing test mean scores for motor skills from eight Reception classes

School	Numbers	Copy writing	Word count 1	Word count 2
School A1/A2 (Council estate)	58	3.52	6.91	5.90
School B (Owner Occ estate)	55	4.18	5.74	5.66
School C (Prep school)	64	5.86	9.5	N/A

N=177
Means: word count 1: 4.57, word count 2: 7.48 (words per minute)

The three schools had different catchment areas and socio-economic status (Table 2.4). Recent Ofsted reports (2013, 2014) have raised concerns about underachievement in coastal towns and this is reflected in the above data. It also shows that Church schools also have a selective effect on their entries.

The very marked differences in coordination skills between schools Y and Z and school X reflect not only DCD and immature development but also a significant lack of practice and perhaps teaching input on motor skills.

The question therefore arose about what was happening in Reception classes where writing skills are first taught, for by Year 5 it may be thought there was no need to teach them any more. This time there were two untimed tests (see Table 2.5): i) copy writing of news, and ii) free writing of news or story task. Scores out of 11 for motor skills were devised (and spelling ability out of 10, see Chapter 3), and a word count was made. The inter-observer reliability coefficients for the assessments were +0.89 and +0.98 respectively.

The tasks had to fit in as closely as possible to the teachers' normal routine so that both teachers and pupils were comfortable and not threatened.

The copy writing and first free writing samples were undertaken in October 2011 and the second sample of free writing was taken in March 2012 five months later. The independent school opted out at this point.

Boys' motor skills were significantly poorer than the girls': boys' mean score was 4.21, girls' mean score was 5.67. The prep school pupils wrote more words than the other class groups and their copy writing skills were significantly better.

In terms of dysgraphia: 35 out of 112 children showed immaturity/difficulties in coordination, that is 31.26 per cent were 'at risk'. The ratio of boys to girls with potential 'dysgraphia' was 4.5:1.

The five classes in schools A1/A2 and B were the feeder schools (N=112) to school C in the previous study of Year 7s in which 29.33 per cent had writing speed problems. These are not the same children but in each case about one-third appear to have problems that are not addressed.

Gifted writers in Reception?

After five months in Reception, 37 out of 112 children had spelling/writing scores between 8 and 10. The ratio of girls to boys was 2:1. But 12 of these children scored 8–10 on entry to Reception (9 F and 3 M, a ratio of 3:1). Are these the future gifted or do they have a home advantage that others will catch up on later? Twenty-five children had moved ahead to score 8–10 during their time in Reception. Are these the potential 'bright' children of the future? They certainly will be at an advantage in reading and writing for learning. It appeared that no attempt had been made to advance the skills with which these 'gifted' children arrived.

It is possible that the 30 per cent of children in the 'at risk' zone will remain six months behind peers on leaving Reception and carry this disadvantage or even increase it throughout junior into secondary school, falling further behind at each stage.

Stainthorp and Rauf (2009) using the Detailed Analysis of Speed of Handwriting test (DASH, Barnett and Henderson *et al.*, 2008) found similar differences in the skills of boys and girls on all subtests. The free handwriting speeds in the 10-minute test in words per minute were: Year 4: 10.62 girls, 9.06 boys (N=168); Year 5: 13.01 girls, 10.28 boys (N=177); Year 6: 15.31 girls, 13.15 boys (N=76).

Writing neatly

Teachers too often pressure pupils to write neatly and in a formal print style when it is inappropriate and with a little effort they could in fact read the pupil's script that is in a fast informal running hand. They seldom seem to know how to help them write neatly. Instead they order them to take more care and write it out again or criticise them for being lazy.

Some teachers become over concerned with neatness at the expense of content, and studies (Soloff, 1973; Sweedler-Brown, 1992) showed that neat writers gained better marks in secondary schools than other pupils irrespective of content, handicapping those with difficulties even further.

At least 10 per cent of the school population according to Gubbay (1975) and Laszlo *et al.* (1988) had handwriting coordination difficulties. The emotional side effects of all of this may be serious and an underachiever can be turned into a disaffected school leaver by constant criticism. The intervention with Mark (shown above in Figure 2.9) occurred because he was becoming very distressed by his teachers' rejection of his work because it was not neat and legible.

Not writing neatly does not mean children are lazy but that their fine motor coordination skills for writing are poor. The reasons may include:

- lack of practice and appropriate time given to learning
- lack of teaching input on an individualised basis to support correct writing skills
- inappropriate teaching strategies used
- writing started when child was developmentally too young – skill immaturity
- the child's own motor coordination difficulties.

The importance of cursive in supporting children with DCD

Each time pupils have to lift the pen from the page and replace it they can have orientation difficulties and difficulties in controlling stroke, shape, position and relationship to other letters. Teaching children with these motor problems to print *can induce learning difficulties* where there need be none.

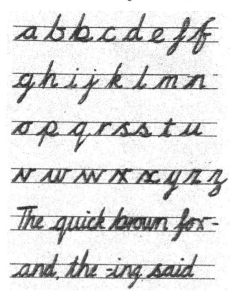

Figure 2.10 Learning difficulties research project: cursive

It is important to start as we mean to go on (Richardson, 1935) and teach one set of motor programmes for writing. Beginning writers really do need lines to aim at. It improves the look, neatness and quality of the written work and does not hamper creativity. It shows little children where to start and place their letters.

Remedial cursive (with lead-in strokes) is recommended for dyslexics and it can also help pupils with dysgraphia because all letters at the beginning of words can begin on the line (see Figure 2.10). Orientation is clear and no restarts and 'in air' time intervene. The joins must be the most efficient line to the next letter.

When cursive was taught from the first days in school good results were achieved for all the pupils (level 6 by most) at the end of Key Stage 1 (Kingston upon Thames project in 16 primary schools, Low, 1990 (see Figure 2.11)). Thomas (1998) described a similarly successful experiment in Kent schools that was modelled on the French system teaching cursive from the outset and spending a significant amount of time on it.

Christensen and Jones (2000) showed that teachers were able to recognise writing problems and learned how to help after only one hour of CPD training. The main difficulty for headteachers is overcoming teacher prejudice (P. Jones, on Kingston project, 2014, personal communication).

Why cursive?

- aids left to right movements in words
- eliminates reversals and inversions

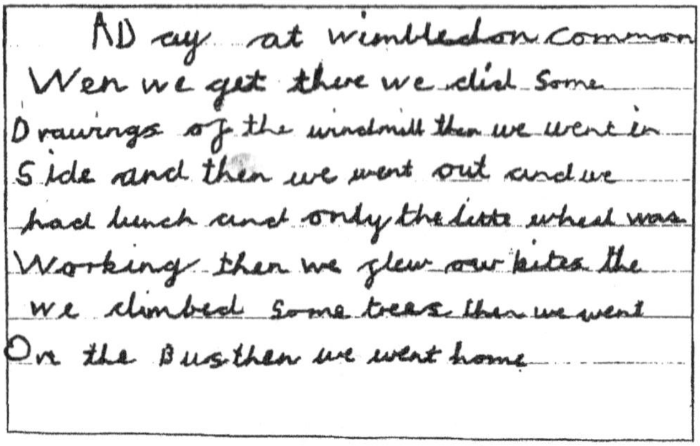

Figure 2.11 Michael's writing, Kingston project

- induces fluency and speed
- spaces between letters and words becomes orderly
- less pain and difficulty experienced
- legibility improved
- programmes for syllables, words and affixes are stored – spelling improves
- reinforces multisensory learning.

Writing needs to be practised until it becomes automatic; intellectual activity can then concentrate on the message.

Motor writing difficulties

Checklist

- Can the writing be felt on the reverse side of the paper? If so, too much pressure and energy are being exerted. Cursive will induce speed and fluency to improve this.
- Is the writing variable in dark and light pressures, being too faint and then too dark?
- Is all the writing too faint?
- Is the writing shaky and wobbly? This suggests coordination difficulty, or tremor and anxiety.
- Is the writing scribbly or spiky?
- Are there rivers of space running down the page? This suggests dyslexic and dysgraphic difficulties.
- Are the same letters variable in form and size?

- The lower case letters w, f, s, and k are particularly difficult to make if there is a coordination difficulty and can be extra large or malformed, or look like capitals in the wrong place.
- A two-fingered grip on top of the pencil may indicate weak pencil hold or bendy joints early on.

If a series of short (5 minutes) daily remedial interventions over a fortnight show a marked improvement effect, this indicates there was a teaching or maturity issue.

No improvement after remedial intervention suggests:

a) a more severe underlying DCD;
b) a resistant attitude that first needs to be overcome (parent's or child's); or
c) the wrong remedial strategy has been used.

Some tests in current use for teachers

There is a range of handwriting tests for teachers to use, some for speed and form have already been illustrated.

1. Sentence test

A classic sentence test item is:

> *The quick brown fox jumps over the lazy dog.*

All the letters of the alphabet are included and it can either be copied or written from memory. Wallen *et al.* (1996) in Australia standardised it for 8–9-year-olds and above but Medwell *et al.* (2008) used it in England with Year 2 and Year 6 children. They had to copy the sentence for 3 minutes. The scores were given in letters per minute (LPM). Year 2 children wrote 9–79 LPM, mean 33.7 and Year 6 children wrote 1 to 113 LPM with a mean of 64.2.

2. The alphabet test

Berninger and Graham (1998) devised an alphabet test format. The subject writes as many letters of the alphabet as possible in order from memory for 1 minute. After 15 seconds there is a ping and a mark is made and only letters to this point are counted and analysed. Christensen and Jones (2000) used a modified version for whole classes so that when they completed 26 letters they continued writing them in upper case. Again LPM was scored.

3. Detailed Analysis of Speed of Handwriting – DASH

DASH (Barnett and Henderson *et al.*) involves the following writing tasks:

- copy best – 'the quick brown fox' for 2 minutes
- alphabet writing – lower case for one minute
- copy fast – 'the quick brown fox' in two minutes
- graphic speed (optional task) – draw Xs in wide circles for 1 minute

- free writing – about 'My Life' for 10 minutes. The test is standardised for pupils from 9.0 to 16 years 11 months. This resembles Roaf's (1998) test.

4. Draw a Person Test – DaPT
DaPT (Naglieri, 2003) is based upon the Draw-a-Man Test by Goodenough (1926), revised by Harris (1963). The tests give examples to support the marking system. Mental age norms are given for figure drawing in the earlier versions but it is significant that difficulties in DCD and spatial body awareness can also be identified. Various forms of the test are frequently used in kindergarten and the Reception year. After the age of 10 it becomes less reliable, for example when some children use cartoon forms and profiles.

5. Evaluation Tool of Children's Handwriting – ETCH
ETCH (Amundson, 1995) is based on the D'Nealian looped script taught in the USA. It is frequently used by occupational therapists.

6. Test of Written Language – TOWL
TOWL (Hammill and Larsen, 1988) provides standardised measures for spontaneous text writing by pupils.

A school cursive handwriting policy

The general curricular provision schools can make is to ensure that there is a handwriting policy requiring cursive from the outset linked with spelling teaching. It should include speech therapy support and training for those who have articulation difficulties and encourage all children to use citation mode for spelling, the very clear, correct and precise pronunciation of each syllable and word.

The motor programmes for spelling words, particularly their bases and affixes, are stored together in the brain (Kuczaj, 1979) and so cursive syllable and word writing can improve spelling accuracy. It also means that a more efficient fluent and personal style can be developed.

In severe cases of DCD it may be essential for the child to use a laptop from Reception onwards but computers are not the answer in all cases. They permit legibility but not necessarily increase in speed, and there is only about a 15 per cent overlap in the skills. When matched for speed and ability, subjects who hand wrote their essays produced a better quality than those using a computer (Oliver *et al.*, 2009).

General educational provision in DCD

Pupils need a DCD-friendly and supportive environment. Teachers need to:

- mark work for content not neatness;
- require less writing; use other strategies;
- give extra time for any copying, or photocopy notes;
- encourage all attempts to learn new skills but give more time for their acquisition.

- avoid being critical of movements but gradually encourage better posture for longer periods;
- not try to change style once established unless child wants to;
- ensure that the pupil has the appropriate strength and the relevant sub-skills to learn a new skill;
- keep pupil close by to ensure attention is properly focused;
- promote information about DCD to help establish the 'DCD-friendly school';
- prevent bullying.

De Nealian is a style and set of training programmes and materials widely used in international schools. It offers a joined looped style as well as semi-joined script and print.

UK programmes, such as the widely used Nelson scheme, offer only semi-joined scripts fitting custom and practice and misplaced guidance from DfE and its previous incarnations. They have quirks such as 'no loops below the lines' and 'no loops above the lines', 'start these letters at the top': a, b, c, g, h, i, j, k, l, m, n, etc., 'teach letters in formation families'.

These 'rules' can be a hindrance to efficient writing. Loops below the line assist joining, that is why they are essential. In full remedial cursive the lead-in strokes enable all letters to start on the line (except those following o, r, v, w and x) so that the dysgraphic can always find the place to start. Loops above the line can cause clutter so are best avoided.

Seven 'S Rules' for handwriting

- *Size* – Letter bodies and ascenders and descenders need to be a reasonable size.
- *Shape* – Correct letter shape is essential for legibility.
- *Start* – Initial lower case letters and single letters should begin with a lead-in stroke (actual or ghost).
- *Space* – Spaces between words and within words should all be regular and be the equivalent of an 'o' not a finger.
- *Seat* – All the bodies of the letters should sit on the line.
- *Slope* – All the ascenders and descenders must slope in the same direction.
- *Speed* – Speed and rhythm are essential so the necessary information can be written down.

Some remedial intervention programmes in DCD

The most important thing is to consult the parents and any therapist involved to obtain advice for the particular needs. Intervention may include programmes run by occupational therapists, remedial programmes implemented in PE, or specialist writing programmes. Swimming is often a recommended sport because it requires contralateral movements, balance and coordination.

Formal diagnosis is also important as the Joint Examination Boards allow 25 per cent extra time for those diagnosed with slow writing and DASH can be used. The *M-ABC Motor Assessment Battery for Children* (Henderson and Sugden, 1992) is still one of the most widely used tests in DCD by clinicians.

1. Dyskinaesthesia intervention

Laszlo *et al.* (1988) undertook extensive studies of clumsiness. Their view was that 10–15 per cent of children suffer from it to some degree but that it cannot be detected until children are about 7–8 years old.

For dyskinaesthetic children each attempt is like the first attempt and so they *cannot improve with practice*. Laszlo recommends *kinaesthetic* training rather than traditional repetitive training in motor skills. This concentrates on the process. The training sessions last from 15–30 minutes daily for two weeks and then twice a week for three weeks.

In this study the children themselves changed. Whereas before they were quiet, subdued, friendless and never part of the team, they suddenly became chatty and outgoing as their success increased their confidence. The training also transferred to an improvement in handwriting skills and spelling thereby improved.

An example of the Laszlo training technique includes the use of large inflated balls. The child is laid backwards over the ball, head and feet dangling down. They are then rocked to and fro for 5 minutes. It looks strange but the purpose is to exercise the kinaesthetic senses and the vestibular system in these unusual patterns so that gradually the child begins to develop a sense of self in space and an ability to use the feedback.

After these sessions Laszlo found that a whole range of motor skills improved. Practice in catching a ball or ball skills, for example, are unlikely to improve until more basic kinaesthetic information can be coordinated. It is presumably why in these cases ordinary practice does not make perfect.

2. Reflex Developmental Patterning

This is Blythe and McGlown's (1979) remedial programme in which motor patterns of feedback are imposed on the brain. More recently such techniques have been linked with Neurolinguistic Programming and Brain Gym.

The 'patient' is allowed to return developmentally to the stages where the reflexes failed to be inhibited, modified and transformed. They are even returned to stages of motor development that may have been missed in part or whole. In this way the person gets a second chance to correct an aberrant pattern and continue development. The technique is claimed to promote measurable neuro-logical organisation within the individual (Goddard-Blythe 2009).

3. Holistic Approach to Neurodevelopment and Learning Efficiency – HANDLE

This approach was developed over the last 40 years by Bluestone (2001, Kokot, 2003: 12–15) working in her clinics with children and adults with a range of learning disabilities. Kokot (2003) is a current exponent of the HANDLE technique. Minimal interventions at the basic balance (vestibular) and coordination levels are claimed to work.

4. Sensory Integration Therapy – SIT

This is a method designed by Ayres (1976) and used by occupational therapists. It is thought to be a useful framework for understanding many of the behaviours exhibited by children with Pervasive Developmental Disorders. For example children who seek excessive sensory input such as spinning and head banging or eating playdough can be understood as needing stimulation through the vestibular (balance and coordination), proprioceptive (muscles and joint sense) or tactile systems; they are not behaviourally disordered or badly disciplined.

A baby normally develops the ability to integrate all the kinaesthetic and proprioceptive information from the earliest days as he or she learns to reach and grasp to pull and push and crawl and walk. There is thus an extensive training/development period through the early years as these skills and abilities unfold and build one upon the other.

The exercises involve tracing the need to the appropriate lower level origin such as the vestibular system and developing exercises and games that provide the foundation experiences thought needed. It was a method designed to help children regain control over their nervous systems and sensory processing input. Sensory integration is developed through five sequential components: registration, orientation, interpretation, organisation and execution of a response.

5. Write Dance

Oussoren Voors (1999) developed Write Dance in the late 1980s and early 1990s in Sweden. She moved to the Netherlands and introduced the method there. It is now used every day as a 'getting ready for writing programme' in schools in Sweden, Holland, Denmark and Germany.

It aims to develop pupils' coordination skills through a combination of movement, dance, music and drawing. The sessions are incremental and combine responses to music to develop large motor movements that are then transferred to paper using both hands. The part of the scheme available in the UK develops pre-writing skills, teaching movements and marks that make up cursive writing.

6. Brain Gym

The Dennisons (1998) developed Brain Gym in the 1980s and 1990s and now thousands of schools and occupational therapists worldwide are reported to be using the system. There are 37 named Brain Gym exercises and there are breakdowns of skills purported to underpin reading, spelling and handwriting. In handwriting, for example, seven subskills are identified that include: postural control, shoulder girdle strength, finger strength, visual and spatial skills, midline crossing and hand–eye coordination.

The idea behind Brain Gym is that the physical exercises are designed to increase the brain's effectiveness and that if the right and left sides of the brain work in unison then the pupil will find learning easier. The teacher is free to choose the exercises she or he thinks would be most beneficial. Three examples are:

- Cross crawl is a contralateral movement. One arm is moved with the opposite leg. Any movement can be made – the most well known is crossing one hand or elbow to touch the opposite knee. It is believed to access both brain hemispheres because it crosses the midline.
- Neck rolls – the head is rolled slowly from side to side to relax the neck muscles and to 'help cross the visual midline'.
- Space buttons involves putting the fingers of one hand above the upper lip and holding the other hand over the tailbone. These are said to be either end of the acupuncture-governing meridian and are linked with the central nervous system.

Experience shows that primary school children involved really enjoy many of the exercises. But there is a lack of evidence for transfer to curriculum tasks other than improving attention. The neurodevelopmental claims appear to have little foundation.

7. Cognitive Orientation to daily Occupational Performance – CO-OP

CO-OP originated in 1977, derived from the cognitive behavioural approach. It is based on contemporary models of motor skill acquisition and focuses on the strategies that are necessary for successful task performance. The traditional model before this was to deal with handwriting problems by focusing on a neuromaturational model of decreasing the motor impairment. Because each child's pattern of difficulties may be different, the CO-OP method is child-centred.

The cognitive strategies are thinking strategies that will help direct the motor activity to attaining the goal. Typically the strategy is based on Goal – Plan – Do – Check (GPDC) and the child self-talks through it, for example:

- Goal: What do I want to do?
- Plan: How am I going to do it?
- Do: I'm doing it.
- Check: How well did my plan work?

The therapist guides the child in the domain specific strategies required and they problem solve together and decide how the strategies may be applied.

After ten sessions of CO-OP, with 15 boys and 5 girls, pre and post testing found that all the children had improved on all three test measures to a significant degree and all the children were pleased with their progress (Addy, 2004).

8. Motorway to ABC – Attention-Balance-Coordination programme

Upton *et al.* (2008) designed a programme to help pupils with DCD in primary schools. At the end of Year 2 all the pupils in schools opting into the programme undertake an ABC PE lesson. The teachers observe and identify the children with problems who might benefit from the programme. They look for children with:

- difficulties in maintaining a still posture
- poor sense of rhythm
- difficulties with spatial awareness

- problems carrying out a sequence of movements
- poor balance
- difficulties controlling direction
- difficulties controlling force.

A regular routine is established that begins with walking along the corridor, settling in the room, dressing and undressing, and listening. Gym shoes are worn or bare feet, sweatshirts and ties are removed and the sessions begin with a 'warm-up' activity and the series begins with 'body awareness' training. One of the series is devoted to fine motor skills. The creativity of the teaching assistants and all involved is encouraged so that new games based on old themes are brought in and adapted so that the children enjoy what they do.

The questionnaires from the children and the staff showed that the programme was successful and raised the esteem and the skills of the participants. The schools have come to value it highly.

These examples show that what most DCD programmes address is the involvement and training of the vestibular system and the strengthening of the cerebellar pathways (Goddard-Blythe, 2009).

Handwriting versus word processing

With the arrival of computers and laptops some people suggest that handwriting is no longer needed, but recent research using fMRI scanning has shown that handwriting is much more important than has previously been thought. For example, Berninger *et al.* (2010) followed children in Grades 2–5. Their study showed that printing, cursive writing and typing on a keyboard were all associated with distinct and separate brain patterns – and each resulted in a distinct end product. When the children composed text by hand, they not only consistently produced more words more quickly than they did on a keyboard, but expressed more ideas. In the oldest subjects brain imaging suggested that the connection between writing and idea generation went even further. When the children were asked to come up with ideas for a composition, the ones with better handwriting exhibited greater neural activation in areas associated with working memory and increased overall activation in the reading and writing networks.

Mueller and Oppenheimer (2012) found that in both laboratory settings and real-world classrooms, students learned better when they took notes by hand than when they typed on a keyboard. This suggests that writing by hand allows the student to process a lesson content and reframe it – a process of reflection and manipulation that can lead to better understanding and memory encoding.

Conclusions

Although writing difficulties are apparent to any casual observer, their significance in academic underachievement has often been overlooked and children may be criticised and even punished for something they are powerless to overcome without support.

General coordination difficulties not only create a loss of self-esteem and induce bullying but also carry with them problems in social interaction, emotional control and can be accompanied by speech and language difficulties. All of these can diminish participation in school life and the curriculum. Thus giftedness in school may go completely unobserved when a child has DCD and is the major cause of their underachievement and ultimate disaffection.

Free-form and cursive handwriting from the outset have been shown to improve early learning potential and aid recovery from dyslexic difficulties in older pupils. This places school handwriting policies at the heart of strategies for overcoming underachievement and promoting learning.

DCD also contributes to other difficulties and disorders making them more difficult to support. Specialist help can improve a situation, but perhaps the most helpful of all is to have a supportive family, a supportive and DCD-friendly school and knowledgeable teachers.

3 Identifying and supporting children with Dyslexia Spectrum Difficulties

Introduction

There has been a vast amount of research and controversy about dyslexia since the problem was first identified and named by Kussmaul in 1877. Initially, because potentially bright children were unable to learn to read and write when less able classmates could, it was supposed that they must be 'word blind'.

When this theory was discounted it was followed by theories about perceptual disabilities, sequential ordering problems, short-term memory deficits and intersensory integration problems – all of which Vellutino (1979) and his co-workers tested but found wanting. He concluded that the inability to learn to read and write was due to a verbal processing problem particularly in the area of phonological processing in the majority of cases. It involved problems in the association of alphabetic symbols with their sounds.

Thus it is that phonological processing deficit over the last two decades has become the dominant theory. It is therefore puzzling that children in schools today are still having problems and dyslexia provision does not seem to be able to help clear it up.

Because children's dyslexic difficulties do not seem to differ in nature from those of other poor readers the notion of the existence of a separate condition such as 'dyslexia' has frequently been challenged, most recently by Elliott and Gregorenko (2014). Once again there is the suggestion that anxious 'middle-class' parents are seeking to gain advantage for their children by claiming they are dyslexic.

Although the preponderance of dyslexics do appear to show phonological difficulties, Stein (2001), for example, has argued for a visual deficit in the magnocellular system in at least a small proportion of cases. Others such as Goswami (2003) have proposed a slowness in auditory processing of phonemes and confusion arising from the several hundreds of sounds associated with the 26 letters of the alphabet. Gathercole (2008) has proposed that dyslexics have working memory deficits and this is popular because teachers find that what dyslexics appear to know one day they seem to have forgotten the next.

A massive industry has been established in dyslexia research, assessment, methods and materials to help remediate the condition. No one wants to give up their definition or their theory. But approached from a different perspective a number of questions must be raised about this current 'zeitgeist'.

The term 'dyslexia' has a medical connotation but simply means 'difficulties with words' (*dys-lexus*), especially in their written form. We know that children across the ability range, not just the more able research subjects, may have 'dyslexic' difficulties.

Particularly problematic it would seem is that most research on dyslexia over the decades has focused primarily upon reading difficulties. For example 'dyslexia' or 'reading disabilities' are taken as synonymous in *Excellence for All Children* (DfEE, 1997). Yet all the hundreds of dyslexics in the researches to be discussed had spelling problems that were equally problematic and most often were more severe than the reading deficits, and that persisted into adulthood even after the reading problems had mainly cleared up.

Researchers tend to undertake their investigations on groups of subjects, dyslexics and controls, and have a hypothesis in mind based upon previous research. Teachers work with individual cases and small groups applying the knowledge from research and from custom and practice, but their theories and practices are often inconsistent.

Bringing knowledge from individual casework in grounded research to the mix is powerful. Multiple cases can then inform research under controlled conditions to confirm or develop new theories. This approach has shaped this chapter.

The nature of dyslexia

Dyslexia is a specific learning difficulty in the literacy area. Slower learners may also have it and it appears to range from profound, a complete inability to read and write, to severe, moderate and mild depending on the response to remediation.

The British Dyslexia Association (2015) and Dyslexia Action (2015) identified 10 per cent of the school age population with such difficulties and 4 per cent of these have severe problems. Most dyslexics do nowadays learn to read to some degree but the spelling problems remain even if reading difficulties clear up.

The incidence of dyslexia is different in different languages with a lower incidence in transparent languages such as Turkish and Italian. These are languages in which there is a close correspondence between the symbols of the alphabet and their sounds.

English is not transparent. There are some phonically regular words with one-to-one correspondence such as bed, cat, dog, went. But it is also a morphemically governed language with spelling based upon the meaning and origin of words. This has implications for remediation programmes and general teaching.

1. Developmental dyslexia

In 'dyslexia' the ability to learn to *both* read and spell is seriously depressed however bright the pupil. In some cases these able pupils also have excellent visual memories. They use it to memorise early texts and their difficulties are not revealed until about the age of 8 years when the range of texts broadens and they have to 'read to learn' rather than 'learn to read'.

2. Developmental dysorthographia
These pupils do not have a reading problem but do have severe spelling difficulties. They have often learned to read self-taught at an early age. Others may originally have had reading problems but by good teaching or great determination have overcome their difficulties. Their spelling difficulties remain into adulthood.

3. Developmental dysgraphia
These children have difficulties in handwriting but the result is they get little practice in writing and spelling and this delays spelling development too. This may mean that their reading is also affected to some degree.

4. Dyslexia with dysgraphia
These children make up 30 to 50 per cent of the dyslexic group and their difficulties can be severe in reading, spelling and writing. The problems with writing hamper the remedial interventions and need to be systematically addressed in the dyslexia provision.

5. Dyslexia with organisational difficulties
In these cases there seem to be deeper dyspraxic difficulties associated with the dyslexia and dysgraphia, taking the organisational problems to an extreme level.

6. Developmental dyscalculia
This is a difficulty in learning arithmetical skills and the concept of number. It is seen in difficulties reciting times tables and undertaking mental arithmetic. A significant amount of the problems appear to be a result of dyslexic verbal processing problems but not all dyslexics have number problems.

Although not necessarily on a continuum there is a spectrum of difficulties, hence the proposed term: *Dyslexia Spectrum Difficulties*. Unfortunately there are some dyslexics who have all the difficulties – reading, spelling, handwriting, number and organisational difficulties – and these may also co-occur with ADHD, DCD or ASD.

Phonological difficulties

The Phonological Assessment Battery (PhAB) by Frederickson *et al.* (1997) consists of eight subtests and two supplementary tests, for example:

- alliteration – segment the initial sound including consonant digraphs (e.g. ph, wh, th, sh, ch)
- rhyme – same end-segments of words –'rimes' (e.g. -ed in bed or fed versus peg)
- spoonerisms – Part 1: 'cat' with a 'f' gives 'fat'. Part 2: King John gives Jing Kong

- non word reading – e.g. prib, nid
- naming speed – pictures
- naming speed – digits
- fluency – e.g. generate /k-/ words (e.g. cat, cap, can, etc.)
- fluency in rhyme – e.g. /-at/ words (e.g. bat, sat, cat, etc.).

The supplementary tests are alliteration with pictures and a non-phonological test – a fluency semantic test.

Non-word reading and speed of naming are found to be persistently difficult even for recovered dyslexics in adulthood and their scores still tend to be lower and slower than controls. This is not surprising since they will have had less practice time over the years (Rumelhart *et al.*, 1995).

What is involved in phonological processing?

According to the theory, phonological processing deficit can give rise to:

- inability to appreciate rhyme
- lack of phonemic awareness
- poor development of alphabetic knowledge
- lack of development of symbol-to-sound correspondence
- lack of development of segmentation skills
- lack of spelling development at the higher levels
- lack of metacognitive awareness of spelling.

These phonological skills and abilities are thought to underlie the development of good spelling and reading and appear to develop incidentally in most pupils during reading and writing, but not in dyslexics.

In PhAB segmenting initial sounds from words – matching 'rimes' as in 'bed' and 'fed', making spoonerisms, non word reading, generating words with initial sound and words with the same 'rimes' – all require secure phonic skills, but these are just what dyslexics find so difficult to acquire. It might be preferable to give them a graduated spelling test that includes regular and then less regular words to uncover just what they know about the alphabetic system. This would be quicker to administer and enable the teacher to target the skills the pupil is lacking.

A spelling test provides a record of what the pupil knows and needs to learn next. Instead children are regularly trained on 'phonological awareness' and 'phonological segmentation' skills abstracted from the skills of reading and writing. The result is that the phonological skills improve but there is little transfer to reading and writing (Helene, 2007). The time would have been better spent on them. Similar criticisms apply to the online variants of such test batteries.

Phonological segmentation and assembly skills are basically spelling tasks and dyslexics have difficulty with them. Thus it can be suggested that phonological deficits like spelling deficits are a result rather than a cause of dyslexia. They could both derive from a third factor and what we see is correlation not causation.

The core difficulties in dyslexia

The core disability/difficulty in dyslexia is a failure to develop sound–symbol correspondence according to Liberman (1973), Golinkoff (1978), Vellutino (1979) and Snowling (2000). Dyslexic beginning readers and writers appear to find it almost impossible to learn the sounds and names of even some of the letters of the alphabet during normal teaching.

So we must ask, why is it that a gifted child at 5 years (Robin, who scored 158+ on WISC at 6 years) who had an encyclopaedic knowledge of the galaxy and prehistoric monsters was unable to learn the names and sounds of 26 letters of the alphabet? Goswami (2003) suggests it is because the actual sounds to be associated with these alphabet letters vary widely and there can be several hundred of them. Even so other much less able children do this easily. Can this really be the cause of the disability? It might make sense in the context of children's reading and reading development but not in their writing acquisition phase and, according to Clay (1975), children's first impulse is to write not read.

Figure 3.1 gives examples of Reception children's writing after just one month in school. Some of them can already form letters and readable words and make a story or tell us their news. By this stage there will have been very little formal or informal teaching. Similar examples were recorded in Chapter 2 on handwriting and DCD.

Compare the writing of dyslexics in Figure 3.2 aged 6–8 years. There is a complete lack of phonic knowledge at 6 and 7 years although the 7-year-old has learned to write some whole common words. David at 8 years has just begun to learn some letter sounds to use in words. These examples were collected in a period when the 'Look and Say' system of literacy teaching predominated. Since that period and the introduction of the National Literacy Strategy (DfEE, 1998) and the Rose Review (Rose, 2006), phonics has been given a greater emphasis but many teachers still prefer to establish a basic sight vocabulary before introducing phonics and letter sound teaching is still too separated from the acts of reading and writing (Figure 3.3).

In a survey of the teaching of reading in Scotland, Clark (1970) found an incidence of 1.5 per cent with dyslexia due, it is thought, to the early emphasis on phonics teaching in comparison with England (which had an incidence of 4 per cent: Rutter *et al.*, 1970). Even if phonics is systematically taught from the outset, 1–2 per cent of children still fail to learn the alphabetic principle (Chall, 1967, 1985; Clay, 1979; Silva *et al.*, 1996). It suggests that whilst early phonics protects some children from dyslexia it does not reach all.

Despite all good intentions the dyslexia count in England has not decreased over the last four decades and has even risen from 4 per cent to 10 per cent to include milder difficulties. This may be because of a better understanding and identification of the condition but it suggests there is still a substantial problem not yet overcome by phonics teaching. In the past most remedial work consisted of phonics but this still failed to bring dyslexics up to grade level and they needed specialist help (Montgomery, 1997).

Many dyslexics like David do finally seem to make the breakthrough and begin to learn. But by then they are up to three years behind peers in literacy

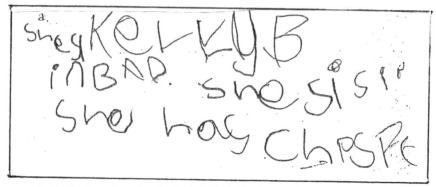

Kelly B.: (My little sister) *She is in bed. She is sick. She has chicken pox.*

Jacob: *I went to bed*

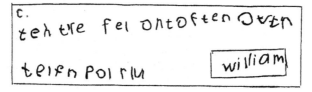

William: *The tree fell on top of the telephone pole wire.*

Figure 3.1 Examples of beginning writing after one month in Reception

and cannot catch up without or even with specialist help in some cases. The normal literacy teaching by this stage is beyond their level and speed. A remedial programme is thus essential. But what should it contain – not more of the same? We know phonics teaching alone does not overcome it nor does multisensory training, for these are the first resort in remedial provision and are now included in all the major programmes. Essential is a remedial writing programme linked to spelling (Berninger, 2008) as found in the Hickey (1977) dyslexia programme and Teaching Reading Through Spelling (TRTS)

a)

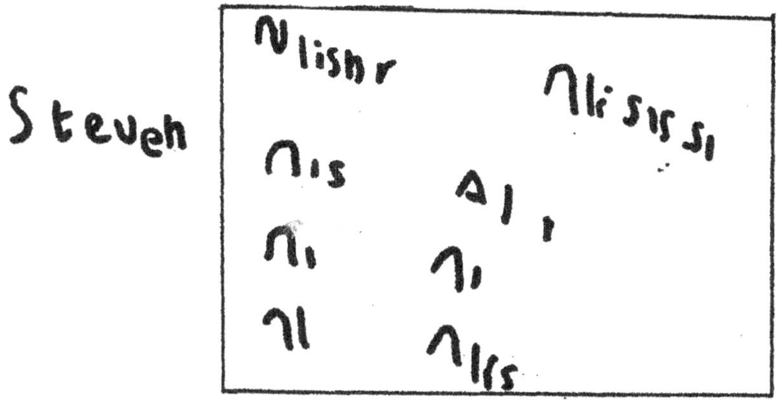

Steven

Steven, 6 years 6 months

b)

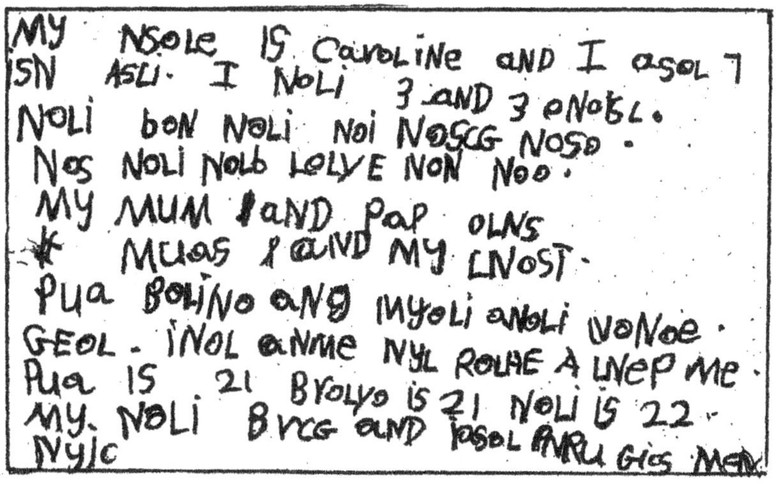

Caroline, 7 years

'My name is Caroline and I am 7 years old. I have 3 brothers and 3 sisters. Some of them live at home and some of them do not. My mum and dad live at home and so do my goldfish. Paul, Breda and Mark still live at home. They are a lot older than me. Paul is 21, Breda is 21 and Mark is 22. My other'

Figure 3.2a Examples of dyslexics' writing after the Reception year

(Cowdery *et al.*, 1994), both of which are based on the original Gillingham and Stillman (1956) programme.

To 'catch up' means dyslexics must progress at *twice the speed of normal* when what we see is that with 'remedial' in class support they 'stick' at a particular level

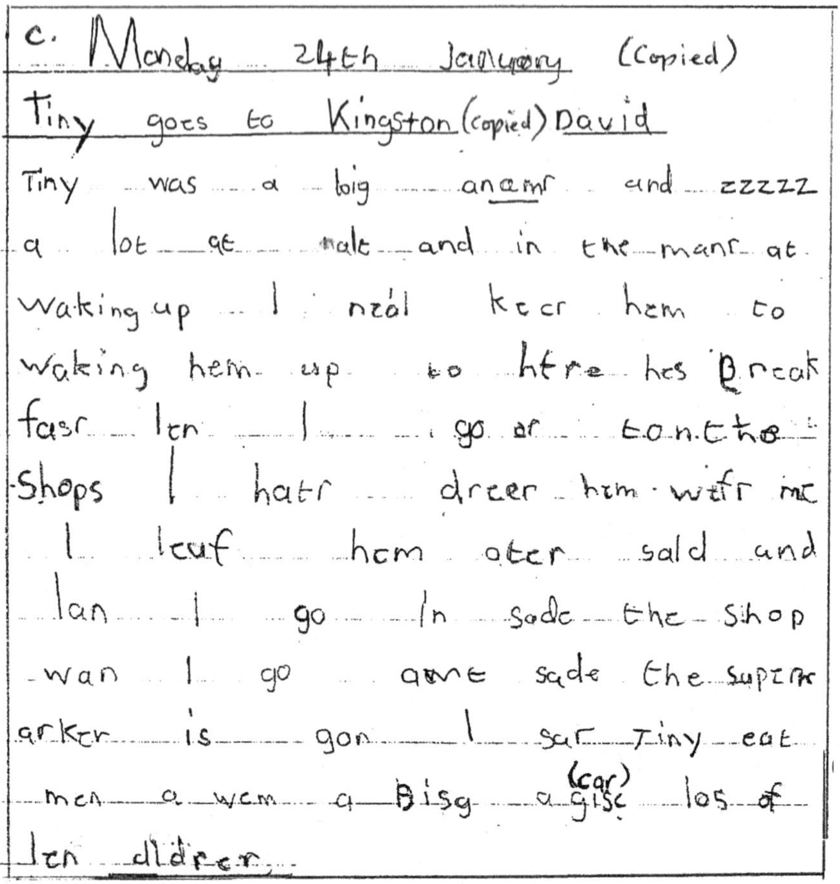

> c. Monday   24th   January   (copied)
> Tiny   goes   to   Kingston (copied) David
> Tiny   was   a   big   anamr   and   zzzzz
> a   lot   ae   nalt   and   in   the   manr   at
> waking up   I   nzol   keer   hem   to
> waking hem   up   to   htre   hes Brcak
> fasr   Icn   I   go ar   to n the
> Shops   I   hatr   dreer   hcm · wttr   mc
> I   Icuf   hcm   oter   sald   and
> Ian   I   go   In   sodc   the   shop
> wan   I   go   ame   sade   the   suprmr
> arkcr   is   gon   I   sar Tiny eat
> mcn   a   wcm   a Bisg   a gisc (car)   los of
> Icn   dldrer

David, 8 years
Tiny was a big animal and slept a lot at night and in the morning I have to keep waking him up. I have to keep waking him up to have his breakfast. When I go to the shops I have to drag him with me. I leave him outside and then I go inside the shop when I go outside the supermarket he's gone. I saw Tiny eat men and women and lots of little children.

Figure 3.2b David's writing aged 8 shows he is just 'cracking the code'

and make little or no progress with the usual methods. Even a 'specialist' level of support may only bring about average progress of three to four months development in three or four months provision. This cannot remediate their condition. It is not surprising that the term 'remedial support' has been replaced by 'learning support': learning support covers a wider range of skills and does not pretend to help the dyslexic learn to read and spell at grade level.

What is observed is that once dyslexics do begin to become literate their progress follows a normal, if delayed pattern, not a disordered one (Bourassa and

Treiman, 2003; Montgomery, 1997). It is probably this that causes some people to think that there is not a dyslexic condition. But something, some deficit, initially stops them from 'cracking the alphabetic code' (Montgomery, 1977).

Beginning writers even without tuition as in the examples in Figure 3.1 show what they know of the alphabetic principle by using 'skeletal' phonics to represent their words. They gradually build on these structures and eventually spell more or less correctly – creative spelling (Read, 1986). Texting is good for spelling development because it reinforces the basic phonic knowledge in skeletal form. Dyslexics follow this pattern but to the untrained observer the beginning writing of a dyslexic 10-year-old looks 'bizarre'.

The potential origins of dyslexia

In English there are 44 speech sounds that are represented by 26 alphabetic symbols and combinations to make up all 44 sounds. The visual symbol for the sound (grapheme) and the sound itself (phoneme) are abstract perceptual units (Ehri, 1980). It is remarkable that any infant can therefore learn them. There has to be some concrete clue that enables them to do this by themselves, something overlooked. The key is that beginning readers and spellers can be observed using concrete articulatory cues to link the consonant phonemes with their graphemes. Vowels do not have such contacts and so appear sporadically in early written work.

In 1917, Edith Norrie taught herself to read her fiance's letters using an articulatory system (Norrie, 1973) and Monroe (1932) and Schonell (1943) were very insistent about the importance of the articulatory aspect of learning to spell.

The alphabetic writing system itself was invented by the Phoenicians in their consonantal language (Delpire and Monory, 1962). They used 22 consonants so to them the system must have seemed obvious because consonants have a particular set of articulatory contacts in the mouth, e.g. the feel of 'l' and 'm' and 's' as we hear their sounds. All children have to do is connect them with their graphemes in 'feel order' to make words, e.g. ws (was), bd (bed), etc. as in Figure 3.1 above and Figure 3.3 below.

However, if dyslexics have some difficulties with articulatory awareness or using this information in learning to read and write (Montgomery, 1981a, 1997, 2007) it could prevent them using it to 'crack the alphabetic' code when it is not explicitly taught (see Table 3.1).

Table 3.1 Articulation awareness and phoneme segmentation test means

Numbers and groups	Chronological age	Reading age	Spelling age	Phoneme segmentation	Articulation awareness	IQ
Controls N=84	7.94	8.63	8.02	11.84	7.75	110.03
Dyslexics N=114	12.90	7.95	7.02	10.27	4.31	110.43
Dyslexic Waiting group N=30	8.96	6.73	6.0	4.13	5.87	112.67

The dyslexics (N=114) were all attending the Remedial Centre twice a week in pairs and had been started on the Teaching Reading Through Spelling programme (TRTS, Cowdery *et al.*, 1994). Despite being at various points on the programme they showed unexpected difficulties in articulation awareness. Their phoneme segmentation scores 10.27 out of a possible total of 15 reflect and correlated positively with their reading and spelling scores. Thus as literacy improved, so did phonological ability. Koppitz (1977) found similar correlations.

In a follow up study only four children out of over 100 tested for articulation awareness in the first month in Reception in three primary schools in the same area were unaware of their articulators whilst making sounds (Montgomery, 1997). Forsyth (1988) found that in an infant screening survey in the same local authority the only effective identifier for their later reading problems at 7 years had been the articulation awareness test.

Visual symbols (graphemes) are processed in the visual cortex of the brain (occipital cortex). The phonemes, auditory signals, are processed in the temporal cortex and linkages between them have been found to take place in the angular gyrus (parietal cortex). This appears to be the intersensory integration area for sounds, symbols and articulations (Galaburda, 1993; Geschwind, 1979).

A dysfunction or dissociation in this region could make it impossible to easily and reliably associate sound with symbol in the absence of their concrete articulatory cues. A heavy retraining system would then be needed to help the regions around the key one take over its function. We know that the brain is capable of this especially in the young. It is also evident that some remedial programmes based upon the Gillingham *et al.* method (1940, 1956) do focus upon such an approach. Once the first few sounds and symbols have been laboriously learned the whole process suddenly speeds up. But the slow systematic start is crucial.

It is important to target intervention in the Reception year so the breakthrough comes at the right time. The delays introduced by following policies such as set out in the *Code of Practice* (DfEE, 2001) must be set aside because of the delays they introduce. For example the pupils must fail three times over about three years before they might get appropriate help. If the pupil begins to make any progress this is regarded as a success and may be continued for years and years but the dyslexic may never catch up to grade level.

Teacher identification of potential dyslexia in Reception

This can easily be undertaken after the first few weeks in school by asking all the pupils to write a message or their news without help in any way they can. The teacher can then note which scripts do not incorporate any of the sounds and symbols that have already been taught. Results from such a study can be seen in Table 3.2 (Montgomery, 2014). They show how particular teachers (A1 and C1) can make a difference. Some examples from the scripts can be found in Figure 3.3 and in Chapter 2.

Table 3.2 Numbers of children in five Reception classes who have 'cracked the alphabetic code' (Scores out of 10; a score of 4 is the critical borderline)

Class	Number	Free writing 1	Free writing 2	Number 'at risk'
A1	17	2.33	7.12	3 + 2
A2	18	2.44	4.3	11 + 3
B1	21	3.24	6.13	4 + 2
C1	28	6.11	6.76	0
C2	27	5.37	6.1	5
Totals	111	4.29	5.32	23 + 7 borderline

Free writing 1: October 2012
Free writing 2: March 2013

The catchment areas of schools A and B were in council estates and school C was set in an owner-occupier estate. This confirms the disadvantages associated with being poor found in The Sutton Trust Research (Jerrim, 2013). The ratio of boys to girls 'at risk' was 1.4:1 respectively and 20.7 per cent of the whole cohort was at risk from potential literacy difficulties after five months in school.

These three schools were the feeder schools to the large secondary school C in the Year 7 writing research project and the spelling results from this Year 7 study are presented following Table 3.3.

These data show that one-third of pupils in the cohorts failed the HMI (2001) criterion and the ratio of boys' to girls' failure was similar. The ratio of boys to girls in the dyslexic category varied between the cohorts. Overall the ratio was 1.2:1 boys to girls, close to Rutter *et al.*'s (2004) survey figures of 1.4:1.0 boys to girls. In other words the traditional figure of a 4:1 ratio of dyslexic boys to girls is challenged. It suggests that girls may not be getting their rightful amount of dyslexia provision and their difficulties are being overlooked. This was confirmed in an earlier study where the referral ratio for dyslexia was 5:1 boys to girls (N=288). Girls were referred a year later than boys with the same level of difficulties (Montgomery, 1997).

School A had fewer in the 'dyslexia' zone and was a school in an advantaged area compared with schools B and C. In secondary school C, 18 per cent fell into the dyslexia risk zone and this was the school the Reception classes fed.

Recent government-funded research at Hull University in 2014 showed that of 1,300 pupils failing SATs at 7 and 11 years over 50 per cent on further investigation showed 'dyslexic type' difficulties (i.e. reading and spelling problems).

In a study of mathematically gifted pupils in Germany, Fischer (2014) found that 35 per cent of the group had reading and spelling problems. When the spelling problems were addressed the reading difficulties also cleared up and they were able to cope better with their mathematics.

(a) Sahana   *I do my homework after school*

I do mr hom
wuck aft Sool

(b) Abi   *I had a Hello Kitty birthday cake*

t d alck

(c) Harry   *Red hen had some bread*

rhe hed
hdsmdh

(d) Devon   *I went to the cinema*

Figure 3.3 Examples of writing in Reception, October 2012 – 'phonics era'

Table 3.3 Percentages of pupils in Year 7 in three secondary schools failing the HMI (2001) criterion

	School A	*School B*	*School C*
	N=125	N=160	N=251
	(75B + 50G)	(61B = 99G)	(124B = 127G)
More than 5 errors per 100 words			
All	31.2% (39)	31.25% (49)	37.05% (93)
Boys	28.0%	29.03%	40.32%
Girls	36.0%	35.03%	32.28%
More than 10 errors per 100 words – dyslexic category			
All	12.80% (16)	22.50% (36)	20.21% (51)
Boys	12.50%	31.10%	20.16%
Girls	14.05%	17.70%	20.47%

B = Boys G = Girls

What counted as a dyslexic problem in School C's written work?

Poor spellers make more than five misspellings per 100 words, the HMI (2001) criterion. The spelling errors from the 251 Year 7 scripts from the large community secondary school C were recorded. As it was a non-selective school it was predicted that 4 per cent of pupils would be in the 'dyslexic zone'. These 'dyslexic' Year 7s were found to make ten or more different errors per 100 words. The errors of all subjects making ten or more errors were then recorded and assigned to the popular diagnostic categories said to be typical of dyslexics. The results are shown in Table 3.4.

Table 3.4 'Dyslexic-type' errors made in School C

Sequencing	*'Bizarre'*	*Omissions*
bronwe (brown)	ckach (chase)	sise (since)
filed (field)	takt (chased)	nity (ninety)
berdy (buried)	janjoys (enjoys)	haging (hanging)
colse (close)	coicens (cousins)	enharse (enhance)
biult (built)	oncl (uncle)	scapering (scampering)
nigt (night)	evetchers (adventures)	whet (went)
aronud (around)	haja (hair)	thigs (things)
pepels (peoples)		

Concatenations	*Basic phonics*	*Reversals*
favote (favourite)	oncl (uncle)	
deiced (decided)	inuf (enough)	
probl (probably)	safen (Southend)	
	coules (colours)	
	thand (found)	
	moe (more)	

Table 3.5 Main categories of CPSS errors made by Year 7 pupils in Schools B and C

Error type	% errors SEN group (N=27) Cohort B	Cohort B (N=160)	Cohort C (N=251)	Total all words
SYNTHETIC PHONICS				
Artic/pronunciation/syll	12.4%	11.9%	12.9%	0.585%
Phonetic/phonic	32.8%	28.7%	29.1%	1.23%
MORPHEMICS				
Baseword/origin	29.2%	30.0%	19.6%	0.83%
Suffix/prefix/vowel rules	11.8%	18.4%	17.2%	0.73%
Homophones	1.4%	3.5%	9.5%	0.40%
Grammatical	13.2%	9.7%	11.7%	0.49%

From the total number of 670 errors made by the 22 poorest spellers (see Table 3.5) it was not possible to identify more than 31 errors that fitted the supposed 'error' categories. Even so most of these demonstrate an inadequate grasp of phonics and syllabification and no reversals such as 'saw' for 'was' and 'on' for 'no'. When these are recorded they usually occur in the scripts of much younger children and demonstrate a visual approach to spelling. Use of articulatory onset cues would correct these.

A more appropriate spelling error analysis was needed, one that also enabled an intervention to be determined. A proposal for such a system was set out under Cognitive Process Strategies for Spelling (CPSS) (Montgomery, 2007).

In a similar study with undergraduates (Montgomery, 1997) the error balance was very different: most were in the morphemic category. This is to be expected as their developmental stage was far more advanced and they were all in the more able category.

Remedial provision in dyslexia

In order for a dyslexic to catch up with peers a remedial programme needs to deliver at least two years' progress in one year. Programmes that so far have been found to do this are detailed in Table 3.6. (Readers are invited to share further data at http://www.ldrp.org.uk)

Table 3.6 shows that A to O, Hickey and TRTS, all based upon the Gillingham and Stillman programme (1956), were capable of being effective in attaining two years' progress in one year when correctly used.

Ridehalgh (1999) examined the results from teachers who had undertaken dyslexia training courses at dyslexia centres. The factors investigated were length of remediation, frequency of sessions and size of tutorial groups in dyslexic subjects taught by three different schemes: Alpha to Omega (Hornsby and Shear, 1978), Dyslexia Institute Language Programme (DILP) (Hickey, 1977), and Spelling Made Easy (Brand, 1998). She found that when all the factors were

Table 3.6 Outcomes from different remedial programmes

APSL progammes progress in 1 year			Non APSL programmes progress in 1 Year		
	R. Prog	S. Prog	R. Prog	S. Prog	Researcher
A to O N=107	1.93	1.95	0.53 N=107 (teachers' phonic programmes)	0.32	Hornsby and Farrar, 1990
TRTS N=38	2.45	2.01	1.06 N=15 (eclectic mix by teacher)	0.16	Montgomery, 1997a
(H & A to O) N=50	1.21	0.96	0.69 N=50 (SME)	0.65	Ridehalgh, 1999
TRTS N=12	3.31	1.85	2.2 N=12 (SME/TRTS)	1.14	Webb, 2000
TRTS N=12	4.04	3.00	(no control group)		Gabor, 2007
A to O N=10	2.4	2.4	Same group, no progress in previous year		Pawley, 2007

APSL = Alphabetic-Phonic-Syllabic-Linguistic
R. Prog = Reading progress
S. Prog = Spelling progress
TRTS = Teaching Reading Through Spelling
A to O = Alpha to Omega
H = Hickey Language Programme/Dyslexia Institute Language Programme
SME = Spelling Made Easy

held constant the only programme in which the dyslexics gained significantly in skills above their increasing age was Alpha to Omega.

However, in a follow-up Ridehalgh found that the users of the Hickey programme in her sample had found it more convenient to leave out the spelling pack work and the dictations! The data also showed that in *paired tuition* the dyslexics made greater gains than when working alone with the teacher. This is an important consideration in terms of the dyslexics' progress and of economics in schools. All the four tutors in the 1997 TRTS study worked with matched pairs of pupils.

Webb (2000) found that she had to cut out the dictations and some of the spelling-pack work because the allocated time for lessons was too short. As can be seen this has had an effect on the spelling results. She also found that in using SME the pupils were not making progress unless she introduced the articulatory training from TRTS to link the sound and symbol. This accounts for the better SME results than for Ridehalgh's groups.

In Gabor's (2007) study at an international school the high progress dyslexics had supportive backgrounds and were encouraged at home to do the homework.

Pawley's (2007) study took place with ten pupils placed in a special school for Emotional and Behavioural Difficulties (EBD). He found that as their reading and spelling improved the incidence of EBD decreased by 30.7 per cent. Before and after the programme the incidence of behavioural problems was independently recorded on the Conners Teachers Rating Scale for EBD (2007).

This data lends support to case observations that many pupils develop EBD as a result of their literacy problems (Edwards, 1994; Kutscher, 2005; Montgomery, 1995). In addition to this, research by the BDA (Singleton, 2006: 119–20) showed that 52 per cent of young juvenile offenders were dyslexic. The incidence in the prison population is three to four times that in the general population.

Dyslexia is thus a very serious problem for society as a whole if so many of its sufferers turn to crime. Being bright and unsuccessful in school can easily lead to alienation and even rage (Miles and Miles, 2001). Thus dyslexics may have to find other ways of being successful and using their gifts. This may mean turning to crime or becoming an independent entrepreneur. Thirty per cent of highly successful entrepreneurs reported they were dyslexic (CBI, 2000).

Developmental dysorthographia and its remediation

Dysorthographia is a severe difficulty in learning to spell in the presence of very good or adequate reading ability. It commonly appears in gifted children who often learn to read self-taught but their spelling is regarded as 'atrocious'. It is also evident in children who are very determined and persistent and go to great lengths to overcome their reading difficulties. Most dyslexics do eventually learn to read with good remedial support but the reading remains slow and their spelling problems persist into adulthood.

Examples of dysorthographic writing

Maria, 5 years 10 months

I wnt to the Titic Esbtnn
I swo srm thes fom the Titic
and srm thes war reil

Translation: I went to the Titanic Exhibition. I saw some things from the Titanic and some of these were real.

Maria is fluent in German and English and was a good reader self-taught at the age of 4 years.

Alex, 14 years
Before intervention:

He eat him, now I'm no exspert but anemals do behve lick that and he did the same to the others but the had difrent larws and the PLeos cort him eath is the most strangest plac I onow
Yors fathly

After several CPSS intervention sessions:

Dear Hoblar

I fanck you for your letter. I looked up your animal consirns and animals on earth have a good reputasn like Robin Hood, the Foxand Bugs Buny. I have beny watching a lat of films and cartoons and I disagree with you. For example police dog's save live's and guide dog's help blind people. I'll meet you at the space café on Wednesday 4th July.
See you soon,
Blar

Alex is a good reader at grade level.

During these investigations it became clear that the APSL schemes catered well for dyslexics who had 'alphabetic problems' but were tedious and lacked intellectual challenge for those who could read relatively well but still had delayed spelling. It was thus helpful to distinguish between first level and second level dyslexics and offer them different programmes. It was the dysorthographics who made this obvious.

Provision for first level dyslexics

These pupils need help in Reception to *crack the alphabetic code* because they have a deficit condition. This is when the sound, the grapheme and the articulatory feel of the sound are connected in normal learners. For some reason there is a disconnection in this area in dyslexics that needs to be remedied.

Children with very good visual memories can learn to read by sight before entry to school but once in school have serious difficulties with spelling. Spelling by sight places too much load on the memory and is a poor strategy. The child needs both sight methods and articulatory phonics in the first stages to lay the foundations of good literacy development.

The implications of this dissociative condition at the neurological level are that areas around the deficit need to be trained to take over the integrative function and this is harder work than if there was no deficit. It involves a process of over-learning for the first half dozen symbols and sounds. This is a crucial period, for total confusion can set in if the pace is forced.

It is essential to follow a multisensory, articulatory synthetic phonics process such as in TRTS. Most remedial schemes now include multisensory training but omit the crucial explicit articulatory-kinaesthetic aspect. Sometimes the synthetic phonics is not correctly developed. It is also necessary to follow the APSL scheme very precisely. When the spelling pack work and dictations were omitted then the results were no better than other schemes.

When APSL programmes are used with first level dyslexics the expected progress rate is two years progress in each year with two 50-minute sessions per week for matched pairs of pupils.

Provision for second level dyslexics and dysorthographics

Most bright dyslexics are discovered late and are able to read slowly but write and spell very poorly. They need second level intervention with a *strategic approach* to spelling that will also transfer to reading, This was called Cognitive Process Strategies for Spelling (CPSS) (Montgomery, 1997) and two years progress in each year can also be expected.

When CPSS was implemented with second level dyslexics (Montgomery, 2007, 2012), as with the APSL programmes, they were found to be able to advance the spelling and reading skills by at least two years in each year but with only a few minutes input each day. In fact two years progress was achieved within a semester by some pupils. The essence is to use one of the 12 'engage brain' strategies to correct the misspelling in the lexicon and a linked cursive writing strategy to lay down a new memory in the motor memory store. Look-Cover-Write-Check, the major remedial strategy used in schools, on its own does not work because it does not 'correct' the error in the lexicon. The CPSS strategy lays down a new correct memory in the lexicon and gives it a higher profile for recall than the old one that is gradually suppressed.

The advantage of CPSS is that it can be used with all pupils in the form of mini-lessons or asides in any subject involving writing. Parrant (1986) compared a class of 27 primary school children given CPSS over a six-week period with a class of 26 controls receiving Look-Cover-Write-Check spelling intervention. The same dictations and tests were given pre and post intervention. The control group's error scores decreased pre and post training but not significantly, whereas the experimental group's errors after CPSS dropped significantly from 273 to 162. A change in attitude was also reported in the experimental group from learned helplessness or neutrality to positive interest and an increase in self-esteem and feelings of competence.

12 Cognitive Process Strategies for Spelling

Lower order strategies

- *Articulation* – The misspelled word is clearly and precisely articulated for spelling: citation mode.
- *Over articulation* – The word is enunciated with an emphasis on each of the syllables or unstressed sound, e.g. parli (a) ment, gover (n) ment, w (h) ere.
- *Cue articulation* – The word is pronounced almost incorrectly, e.g. Wed - nes - day, Feb - ru - ary.
- *Syllabification* – The word is broken down into syllables, e.g. misdeanor: mis / de / mean / our, criticed: crit / i / cise / d.

- *Phonics* – A comprehensible articulatory skeleton or word scaffold is made to build upon, e.g. km, cm, then cum, may appear before come.

Higher order strategies

- *Origin* – The word's root in another language may give clues, e.g. op / *port* / unity: an opening, a *port* or a haven means the pupil has a strong clue to the spelling.
- *Rule* – A few well chosen rules can help unravel a range of spelling problems, e.g. the l - f - s rule: these are doubled in one syllable words after a short vowel sound, e.g. ball, puff, dress. The seven exceptions are made into a sentence, e.g. 'YES, the BUS runs on GAS PAL. THUS IF you pay NIL you get nowt.'
- *Linguistics* – Syllable types open, closed, accented and unaccented need to be taught as well as the four suffixing rules which govern most words, e.g. add, double, drop, change.
- *Family/base word* – Family helps reveal silent letters and correct representation for the 'schwa' unstressed vowel, e.g. Canada, Canadian; bomb, bombing, bombardier, bombardment; sign, signature, signal, resign. Basewords can make families of words, e. g. form, reform, forming, deform, reformed, formation.
- *Meaning* – Separate is often misspelled as sep / e / rate. Looking up the meaning in a dictionary shows it to mean to divide or part or even to pare. The pupil then just needs to remember 'cut or part' and 'pare' to separate.
- *Analogy* – This is the comparison of the word or a key part of it with a word the pupil does know how to spell, e.g. 'it is like boot – hoot, root' or 'hazard' is one 'z' like in 'haze' and 'maze'.
- *Funnies* – Sometimes it is not possible to find another strategy and so a 'funny' can help out, e.g. 'cess pit' helped me remember how to spell necessary.

Note: Mnemonics are no part of CPSS: they do not generalise to new words and are laborious.

The seven-step protocol for using CPSS

Younger pupils and those with poorer spelling will need more of the first five CPSS strategies and little or no dictionary work to begin with.

1. The pupil selects *two* misspellings to learn in any one session.
2. The pupil identifies the *area of error*, usually only one letter with the help of the teacher or a dictionary.
3. The pupil puts a *ring around* the area of error and notices how much of the rest is correct.
4. The pupil is taught (later selects) a *cognitive process spelling strategy* to correct the misspelling. A reserve strategy is also noted where possible.

5. The strategy is *talked over* with the teacher and is used to write the corrected spelling.
6. The spelling is *checked* to see if it is correct – the dictionary can be used again here.
7. If correct, the pupil covers up the spelling and writes the word three times from memory in *joined-up/full cursive* using *naming* the letters (Simultaneous Oral Spelling, SOS). It is especially important to use the joined script over the area of error if full cursive presents a problem.

SOS was first described for dyslexics by Bessie Stillman (Gillingham *et al.*, 1940). CPSS starts correcting the lexicon and SOS modifies the motor programme. A new dictionary containing intervention strategies for hundreds of misspelt words, *Spelling Detective Dictionary* (Montgomery, 2012), can be found at http://www.ldrp.org.uk

Different dictation effects

Myklebust (1973) found different effects on a 15-year-old dyslexic's spellings as follows:

*   *writing spellings from own head*: cabinet – kntrs; window – wror; recorder – rkrrd;
*   *words dictated one syllable at a time*: hundred – hundred; indent – indent; represent – represent;
*   *words dictated normally*: pencil – pnsl; manufacture – mufnctur; candidate – cndati.

This indicates the power of syllabification and citation mode as part of developing good spelling. Encouraging oral work, clear presentations and pupils reading their work to each other all contribute to better spelling. No mumbling!

Developmental dyscalculia

In popular terms 'developmental dyscalculia' is a relatively 'new' learning difficulty and refers to 'dys': a 'difficulty', with 'calculus': number operations. However, the condition has been known for almost as long as dyslexia but has not raised the same interest until recently.

Dyscalculia is defined as a specific learning difficulty affecting a person's ability to understand and/or manipulate numbers. It is often used to refer specifically to the inability to perform operations in arithmetic, but it may also be used to describe the more fundamental inability to conceptualise numbers themselves as a representation of quantity.

According to APA, *DSM-IV* (1994) dyscalculia is assumed to be present when there is a marked discrepancy between a pupil's mathematical developmental level and the general cognitive ability giving due consideration to age, education and reasoning ability. We could also add that it may be present in the absence of dyslexic difficulties that may also cause number difficulties.

The relationship between dyscalculia and dyslexia is still not clear. Statistics vary widely and studies looking at the percentage of dyscalculics who are also dyslexic range from 17–64 per cent (Lewis *et al.*, 1994). The International Dyslexia Association (2003) suggested that 60 per cent of dyslexics have some difficulty with numbers or number relationships, whereas Miles (1993) found that 96 per cent of his sample of 80 9–12-year-old dyslexics found difficulty in reciting the 6, 7 and 8 times tables. However, it can be argued that this problem was a result of their verbal processing difficulties as reciting the tables muddles them but they can frequently give the pattern e.g. 7, 14, 21, 28 in the 7 times table.

Reading problems on mathematics tests

An analysis of mathematics and reading was undertaken by Shuard and Rothery (1980) and it was found that many of the pupils' difficulties were unrelated to the mathematics but arose from the reading, language difficulties and the specialist language demands of the subject of mathematics itself.

They found the seven following factors affected performance on mathematics tests:

- *Vocabulary* – Some words (e.g. hypotenuse, coefficient) are only used in maths, but others have a special maths meaning and a general meaning (e.g. product, field).
- *Symbolic language* – 'x' means times and 'x = 3' means 'x replaces 3'; 'xy', means 'x times y'.
- *Sentences and their structure* – They follow English grammatical conventions but often refer to other sentences, e.g. 'Applying the above rule…'
- *Flow of meaning in text* – Not all the meaning units are in the text but have to be inferred or questions are asked about them.
- *Special reading techniques required* – Not only do we have to read the symbols, we have to have the spatial awareness to appreciate the full meaning (e.g. use of brackets).
- *Appearance of the text* – Clear layout and pleasing appearance can increase readability and motivation to read.
- *Ambiguities in the text* – The response required is not clear, e.g. 'Do you know another way to construct a right angle?'

Dyslexics would be highly likely to have problems with all of these.

Poor teaching and mathematical difficulties

Despite many attempts to improve the quality of teaching and learning in mathematics, there is as yet no consistent evidence that the situation has improved. For example, Hodgson *et al.* (2009) found that in 2009 pupils were no better at mathematical reasoning than they were 30 years previously when 3,000 pupils were given the same tests as a similar sample in 1976. Pupils in 2009 were better at decimals and poorer at fractions, but overall there was no sign of the expected 'step change' improvement.

Classroom observations (Montgomery, 2002) have shown that children can still work through pages and pages of individualised or class mathematics work and at the end are unable to demonstrate they have understood what they have been doing. Skills in the hierarchy may still be missed through absence or poor teaching and can then undermine later learning.

Unquestionably, however, it is also *teachers' attitudes* to teaching number that needs addressing. Over the last 15 years teachers studying a dyscalculia module in their MA SpLD programme have written about their former maths teachers. No teacher out of hundreds has ever said they could *not* think of a teacher who had hindered their progress. Some sadly could not think of one who had helped them.

Sometimes the teachers who have the highest qualifications in mathematics and never had problems themselves were the least good teachers of maths to children. They frequently could not understand why they needed to teach more slowly or carefully, not necessarily because children were less able, but for all or many of the issues identified above.

Typical teacher stories

Story 1

The one who hindered me the most was the teacher I had for two years leading up to O level. This teacher only taught the top end of the class and did not offer any support. The teaching was all teacher-directed and we were expected to work individually from textbooks. Moreover the teacher only interacted with the boys and the very confident girls. I seemed invisible and was ignored for two years. I was extremely quiet, completely self-effacing and never volunteered an answer. I hated and dreaded maths lessons more than anything else at school. I spent two years day-dreaming and copying (including all homework) from my best friend who seemed to know what was going on. I obtained a grade E at O level–I was quite pleasantly surprised by this. I had expected a U grade as I had done no revision whatsoever and expected to fail. I did not want to waste time revising to the detriment of my other subjects that I enjoyed.

Story 2

I cannot think of a single maths teacher that I would have considered being helpful in my mathematical development. I have a clear vision of a very calm, approachable male teacher who was very patient with me during my time at secondary school, who would spend a lot of time verbally trying to explain the task in hand but his one common phrase would be to 'guess a number that you think may work' and this was a leap too far. I did not have the confidence in maths and so to ask me to work on a trial and error basis or estimation was a nightmare because I always expected my answers to be wrong.

Story 3

In lower secondary the deputy head was my teacher so you would be scared to ask for help. He provided us with textbooks to work through on our own and if you did ask a question his response would always be, 'Try and think for yourself'. Fortunately the answers were in the back of the book so we just used to blindly copy them down with little or no understanding and he would tick them; very little feedback or understanding occurred.

The MA teachers were next set to identify and help a child with number difficulties. They found children today equally frightened and lacking in confidence and basic skills as they had been. First they analysed the child's mathematical difficulties using a miscues analysis (below) and were then set to design a series of tutorial sessions based upon Mary Kibel's work (2002) using a concrete and 'sum story' approach to overcome the problem. All of these interventions proved highly successful and the teachers were able to use their creative skills in designing and implementing their mini-programmes.

Miscues analysis in maths

Most computational errors that children make are systematic with a few random and careless errors thrown in (Ashlock, 1982). This means that the teacher can usually work out what the error is, e.g. miscounting, basic tables wrong, misapplication of operations, errors with zero, errors in regroupings, e.g. place value, procedural mistakes, use of meaningless symbols or numbers, failure to answer, failure to understand fractions especially more complex ones, failure to understand decimals (see Table 3.7).

In addition to these common problems there are also:

- language and symbolic misconceptions;
- failure to understand the concepts despite being able to go through the operations and find the correct answer most times;
- failure to grasp the principles of estimation and use these in checking computation;
- failure to hold several operations in the memory whilst computing;
- failure to rectify solutions and check for errors.

Table 3.7 Examples of systematic errors

	(a)	(b)	(c)
1.	83	35	43
	+ 49 +	67 +	72
	———	———	———
	1212	912	115

Does not understand place value and how to carry over into tens column

	(a)	(b)	(c)
2.	46	372	154
	− 39 −	295 −	86
	———	———	———
	13	123	132

Deducts smaller number from larger ignoring positions and meaning of the sums

	(a)	(b)	(c)
3.	$22 \times 3 = 66$	$43 \times 5 = 205$	$29 \times 6 = 484$

(b) Multiplies correctly but fails to carry over to the tens. (c) Carries 50 over to 100s column and deducts $6 \times 20 = 120$ from 504

	(a)	(b)	(c)
4.	$\underline{1} + \underline{2} = \underline{3}$	$\underline{3} - \underline{2} = \underline{5}$	$\underline{3} \times \underline{3} = \underline{6}$
	5 5 10	7 7 14	4 5 9

Simply adds numerators and denominators across, also ignores signs in (b) and (c)

These error types can be found in dyslexics and poorly taught children across the ability range. They need concrete examples and practice to build concepts and overcome errors.

Learning styles: inchworm or grasshopper?

In a paper entitled 'Mathematics and the brain: A tale of two hemispheres', Loviglio (1981) hypothesised two learning styles based on the differences between the functioning of the two hemispheres and frequently encountered in children learning maths: she called them inchworm (left hemisphere style) and grasshopper (right hemisphere style).

* *Inchworms* are better at counting forward, understanding additions, subtractions and multiplication, and following a recipe approach step by step.

They seldom estimate, remember parts rather than wholes, have a strong need to talk themselves through the procedures, and arrive at the correct answer but are unsure of the logic behind it.

- *Grasshoppers* are good at counting backward and understanding division. They are impatient with step-by-step procedures, are good at estimating and may give the correct answer without knowing how they got there. They are good at seeing the overall pattern, and are especially good at visualising and picturing situations and configurations.

It would seem that to be good at maths we need to operate in both styles as appropriate, but may have developed preferences. For example, when setting up a new gadget or doing a jigsaw some prefer to read the instructions first and follow them step by step. Others have a go and only refer to the instructions when they get stuck. Rigidity in either area could indicate a problem.

Dyscalculia as a specific learning difficulty?

The term 'developmental dyscalculia', referring to a neurological disorder affecting mathematical learning, appears to have been popularised by Kosc (1974). He identified six types of developmental dyscalculia and although subsequently validated they do need some reconsideration. His varying subtypes have subtle but characteristic differences in their mathematical difficulties. Those with verbal, lexical and graphical dyscalculia have difficulties in recognising numbers and therefore may be unable to compare and contrast quantity or number. Ideognostical dyscalculia presents more conceptual difficulties in understanding the nature of quantity. Operational dyscalculia is a difficulty in using the correct procedure when solving mathematical problems and unsuitable methods may be adopted or regression to using immature, time-consuming techniques occurs.

In rare cases, the dyscalculia may be accompanied by dysgraphia (writing difficulty), right–left orientation and finger agnosia. In these cases, the difficulty is more complex and is called Gerstmann Syndrome (Gerstmann, 1940), although evidence is disputed.

Butterworth (2010) claimed that we have an innate mathematical ability just as we have for learning language. He said that the degree of that ability varies with the genes and is further shaped by life experiences and educational opportunities. The result is a range of mathematical abilities as wide as the factors that combined to produce them.

Both Kosc and Butterworth estimated that the incidence of developmental dyscalculia was approximately 6 per cent. In the US Sharma (2003) suggested it was about 4–6 per cent.

In 1994, Lewis *et al.* undertook a study of 1,056 English children and found 1.3 per cent of the sample had specific arithmetical difficulties, and a further 2.3 per cent had difficulties in both reading and arithmetic. The children with arithmetical difficulties were equally divided as to gender.

Butterworth suggested that the area of the brain responsible for processing number information was found to have two separate specific functions, one for counting 'how many' and the other for knowing 'how much'. The research included experiments using a functional MRI scan to examine the intra-parietal sulcus.

The first test analysed brain activity when the subjects were counting and the second looked at activity when they were assessing quantities. This involved showing the subjects coloured squares, first in sequence and then presented all at once. Both ways of counting were found to use the same area of the brain. However, in the second test the subjects were shown changing squares and merged colours. This type of counting relied much more on estimation skills and activated different areas of the brain. Control subjects could naturally apprehend groups of three or four items but dyscalculics had problems and showed a more limited grasp of number. Butterworth concluded that there was a brain network that underlies arithmetic and may be abnormal in dyscalculics, and that training on extending these abilities could prove effective.

Some specific cognitive difficulties found by Sharma (2003) were:

- *Semantic versus rote symbolic processing* – Many students with dyscalculia may find it easier to compare the size of numbers than understand arithmetic symbols.
- *Arabic number reading and phonological recoding* – Being able to comprehend a mathematical symbol is a key factor in mathematics. It is a vital aspect of learning to read and write the symbols and part of this is the process of verbalisation (transcoding). Those with dyscalculia like dyslexics may experience difficulty with transcoding.
- *Sequencing difficulties* – Linking data in a sequence or using sequence to identify the item that 'comes next' are critical aspects of mathematical learning and thinking. These difficulties often co-occur with dyslexia, dysphasia and/or dyspraxia. Children in the early stages of learning to count show similar errors.
- *Cardinality difficulties* – Cardinality is an understanding of the number of items in a set – and the inherent value of quantity associated with that number. This understanding allows pupils to comprehend both quantity and number.
- *Difficulty recalling number facts* – Many dyscalculics (and dyslexics) have difficulty in the automatic recall of basic addition, subtraction, multiplication or division number facts. To compensate they will resort to skills such as counting aloud or using their fingers.

As can be inferred from these 'special difficulties' they can equally be caused by the verbal processing deficits already identified in dyslexics and are also found in poorly taught subjects.

Current educational provision for dyscalculics

The question that arises in schools is whether or not to separate those with diagnosed dyscalculia from those with low mathematical ability due to other reasons.

Those who advocate this latter approach suggest that dyscalculics need training on very simple number concepts that other people (including those who have low mathematical ability for other reasons) take for granted.

Other specialists in dyscalculia advocate withdrawal from the main teaching group because children with dyscalculia have a special need to be taught differently, and to learn coping strategies. Diagnosis of the errors is the first step in this process.

Current remedial intervention strategies for dyscalculia strongly feature a multisensory approach. This approach was developed through the study of dyslexia and may be of questionable value in addressing dyscalculic or mathematical problems except in so far as numbers need to be written accurately. The concretisation of the strategies used and story sum approach seem to be most helpful with pupils with the verbal processing deficits and difficulties. More research is needed on the concept of quantity procedures and remedial success.

Conclusions

This chapter has been a summary of some key aspects and issues from this large and important area. The conclusion is that we should give more attention to the contribution of spelling and handwriting in reading acquisition and development and even consider that spelling, not reading, may be the core difficulty in dyslexia.

In the researches discussed, the very bright dyslexic made up 10 per cent of the dyslexic groups. They had IQs 130 points and above and 34 per cent of this group of 288 dyslexics had at least one IQ scale of 120 points and above (Montgomery, 2007). Given the disadvantaging nature that dyslexia has on test scores these children were even brighter than the scores portrayed. Many such bright children are regularly denied the support they need by the application of the 20 per cent decrement criterion.

This criterion has become widely used in many countries to determine dyslexia provision. Typically the pupil with learning disability is required to have a decrement of at least 20 per cent between reading skills and chronological age, with reading the lower score. This means that at age 10 years the reading score must be at 8 years or lower. This brings about problems for our 'Gifted Learning Disabled' (GiLDs):

- As gifted children have good intellectual comprehension skills they can boost their scores on many reading tests and so they are not identified as dyslexic/dyscalculic.
- Using chronological age rather than mental age based on IQ is also wrong for gifted dyslexics, who will often read at the level of peers when we should expect them to be reading well above this. Many gifted children without dyslexia have reading ages five years above their chronological age level.
- Using only a reading test rather than a reading *and* spelling test decrement is also problematic, as many gifted dyslexics learn to read well enough but

still have severe problems with spelling that will hamper high achievement in written work.

- Having a numerical value such as 20 per cent encourages many to believe that rationing resources is a true or valid strategy rather than an administrative convenience.
- If not given remedial help, a child with a decrement of 10 per cent at 6 years will have a decrement of 5 years at 15.

If we consider the other learning disabilities such as ADHD, DCD and ASD it is only the dyslexics whose problems are dealt with in this way. To get help they must pass a double standard detection system, both of which are inadequate and discriminatory in the disadvantaging sense.

The others are exposed to clinical assessment using a checklist system and clinical observation. Although this too is not entirely reliable it does take into account the severity, individual and changing nature of the conditions.

4   Identifying and supporting children with High Functioning Autism – Asperger syndrome

Introduction

In the 1960s the condition of autism was not widely known although psychiatrists were regularly dealing with such cases. They were generally labelled 'childhood psychoses' and 'childhood schizophrenia', even though Kanner (1943) in Germany had identified autism as a separate clinical condition from childhood schizophrenia and other childhood psychoses. He first described the condition as a clinical syndrome involving 'Autistic Disturbances of Affective Contact'. The characteristics were:

- *An inability to relate themselves in the ordinary way to people and situations from the beginning of life* – The children showed no anticipatory posture on being picked up; no moulding into arms when picked up; and appeared to be 'good' – too good.
- *Failure to develop language* – either totally or simply parroted what they heard showing good rote memory – 'echolalia'.
- *Anxious and obsessive desire for sameness* – They lacked spontaneous activity; engaged in ritualised behaviours such as always walking on tiptoe, in a straight line, continuously flushing the toilet. When stopped in a ritual, they were subject to panic rage attacks.
- *Fascination for objects* – The slightest change of place or position of familiar objects was noticed and could provoke rage.
- *Good cognitive potential on some tests* – Memory feats and performance on non-verbal tests were above age level (in those that were testable).
- *Family background* – Intelligent parents, social class 2 prevailed; 'marked obsessiveness and coldness' observed in the parents. Cause or effect was not established but soon the parents were blamed for the child's bizarre behaviours because of being aloof and engaging in 'cold parenting'.

This was still a commonly held view well into the 1970s and very distressing so that some parents were made psychologically ill by these accusations and came for counselling not only to cope with their child but for themselves.

The condition became known as 'Early Infantile Autism'.

In 1944, Asperger (1979) identified a separate but seemingly autistic group with higher intellectual potential and less severe disabilities. He chose the name 'autistic psychopathy' but later the more neutral term of Asperger's syndrome was used and then Asperger syndrome (AS).

In the 1960s in London a clinical research group developed that pursued studies into these disorders and one of its leaders had an autistic child. Their work formed the basis of much that we now know about Autistic Spectrum Disorders (ASD). In that period the National Autistic Society began to set up special schools and units to help educate autistic children rather than confine them in secure units and mental hospitals.

In a long-term follow-up study of 100 children with autism, Rutter *et al.* (1970) at the Maudsley Hospital found that only 30 per cent had IQs in the 70–100 range. Very few were in employment. Half of them were in a 'mental hospital' and 70 per cent were doing badly by adolescence.

In 1981 the *Autistic Spectrum of Disorders* (ASD) was identified by Lorna Wing to encompass the ever-widening group who had some aspects of the autistic condition. In her studies she found individuals with IQs up to 111 and identified the Triad of Impairments.

The Triad of Impairments

*   *Social interaction* – difficulty with social relationships, e.g. appearing aloof and indifferent to other people, failure to follow social rules.
*   *Social communication* – difficulty with verbal and non-verbal communication, e.g. not really understanding the meaning of gestures, facial expressions or tone of voice.
*   *Imagination* – difficulty in the development of play and imagination, e.g. having a limited range of imaginative activities, possibly copied and pursued rigidly and repeatedly; literal comprehension.

These impairments are most frequently accompanied by a limited, narrow, repetitive pattern of behaviour. It is the problem behaviours and poor social skills that teachers have most difficulty in managing.

Although Rutter (2005) found that a faulty gene transmitted ASD, it appears that the three different characteristics are caused by distinct genetic and environmental causes (Ronald, 2014) and can appear separately: the 'fractionable autism triad' hypothesis (Happe *et al.*, 2006).

Eighty-nine different, mostly rare, conditions have some autistic characteristics e.g. Fragile X and Tourette's syndrome.

The American Psychiatric Association *Diagnostic Manual DSM-IV* (APA, 1994) included AS distinct from autism, but *DSM-V* (APA, 2006) identified ASD as Pervasive Developmental Disorders (PDD). The condition formerly known as Asperger syndrome in *DSM-IV* was included as High-Functioning Autism (HFA) on the autism continuum or PDD-Not Otherwise Specified (PDD-NOS). In this text three clinical patterns are the targets for educational intervention (see Figure 4.1).

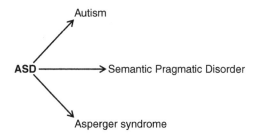

Figure 4.1 The main Autism Spectrum Disorders

Comorbidity and therefore dual diagnosis was finally recognised in APA *DSM-V* (2006) so that an individual with AS may also be diagnosed with Attention Deficit Hyperactivity Disorder (ADHD) or other disorder. Rommelse *et al.* (2010) found that 30–80 per cent of those with ASD had co-occurring symptoms of ADHD and 20–50 per cent of individuals with ADHD also met the criteria for ASD.

ASD and ADHD are both developmental disorders in that they begin in childhood and persist throughout life. They both occur more frequently in males than females and in individuals with any level of IQ. ASD is characterised by impairments in social communication, imagination and restricted, repetitive behaviours and routines, whereas ADHD is characterised by impulsivity, hyper-activity and inattention.

Twin studies show that these two conditions are highly heritable because they share a common genetic pathway (Ronald, 2014). It means that a parent having one child or partner with one condition is likely to have an increased chance of producing future children with either condition.

Neither ASD nor ADHD are 100 per cent heritable and environmental risk conditions also operate. It is known that smoking during pregnancy is a risk factor for ADHD but not in ASD. In ASD a risk factor is higher paternal age but not for ADHD (Gabis *et al.*, 2010).

Although anxiety and ASD co-occur in 84 per cent of cases, genome-wide association studies (GWAS) show that they do not share a pathway. Instead the anxiety mainly occurs as a result of the social interaction difficulties and problems caused by the rigid routines (Hallett *et al.*, 2010). Thus interventions need to help reduce the need for the routines and promote better social interaction.

Asperger syndrome or High Functioning Autism

What we now know is that many High Functioning Autistics were missed in surveys because they were able to maintain a place in school to some degree and were often highly verbal and had compensatory attributes that at least in elementary or primary school might cause their problem behaviours to be tolerated. Autism and Asperger are the most similar and prevalent of the Autism Spectrum Disorders with an incidence of 1 per cent. They share many characteristics so that some argue they are varieties of the same underlying condition on a continuum from mild and moderate to severe and profound. Others such as Frith (2014) prefer the categorical clinical distinction of AS.

Asperger cases would be found at the upper, more able end of the continuum, but no precise cut-off points can be determined. The condition also appears to shade off into the 'eccentric normal' range, supporting the notion of an ASD continuum rather than a clinical categorical one. However, Asperger cases do have their own clinical pattern.

It was not until the 1990s that the needs of children with AS became more widely known in educational circles through the work of Frith (1991). By secondary school stage they were frequently to be found in special units attached to mainstream schools. Although some still finished up in Pupil Referral Units (PRUs) or special schools for children with emotional and behavioural difficulties. Others were 'home educated' when their problem behaviours caused them to be excluded.

Asperger had noted that the condition was much more common in boys than girls. He found it was not usually identifiable before the age of 3 or even later; however, autism was most frequently identified around the age of 2 years. Researchers have now identified the conditions within the first few months of life using gaze avoidance and brain scan studies, but the average age of diagnosis of AS in the UK is 7–9 years and many may not be diagnosed until adulthood if at all (Hattersley, 2010). Jenkins (2014) reported a 40-fold increase in diagnosis of AS in the last few years. In the popular media there has been a corresponding interest shown in the condition.

If a 6-year-old throws a temper tantrum or screaming fit in class it can be managed and understood, although such behaviours are more typical of a 2-year-old. However, when a 16-year-old does the same it is not manageable or understood. It is not normal behaviour and if it happens frequently the pupil is soon excluded or sent to a special unit or school for the behaviourally disturbed.

Case example – Angela

Angela was a beautiful, blonde-haired 15-year-old in the 'top set' in a comprehensive school, but her reputation frightened her teachers. She was frequently absent from school and they found this a great relief. If mildly provoked or prevented from doing what she thought she would, usually talking or asking questions when asked to be quiet, she would throw herself on the floor and thrash about, screaming and often connecting with a victim's legs. She would go red then blue in the face. The Deputy Head Pastoral Care had to be sent for and, when Angela calmed down exhausted, she would be escorted to the medical room to lie down. Her parents would be 'unavailable'.

Angela seemed to have no close friends and apparently had a 'nightlife' that earned her money and the school longed for her to become 16 so that she could leave. She decided to attend every biology class I gave; I was anxious. Fortunately she did not throw one wobbly. When she seemed ready to flip I tried some nonverbal warning cues and it seemed to work. She would settle down again and it became a sort of game between us and we chatted a bit on the way from class. Looking back now, I wonder if she was on the autistic spectrum. She was certainly bright and did not suffer fools gladly, telling teachers as well as peers exactly what she thought of them. She would loudly point out their most unattractive features.

Case example – Tom

Tom was a 15-year-old diagnosed with AS. He attended regular school and was accelerated in maths, physics, biology and modern foreign languages. In Year 8 he took GCSEs in physics and maths and obtained 'As' in both and passed the extension paper in maths. He was able to follow the 'A' level and scholarship-level work with the support of a lecturer from the local university, and staff from the school provided enrichment programmes so that he gained an 'A star' in biology and an 'A' in French.

Although he was capable of advanced work in these academic subjects his social and behavioural skills were a cause of much concern. Staff had referred to his frequent interruptions of lessons. He asked many inappropriate questions, not accepting a conversation with a teacher was finished when it was. He had difficulties remaining in his seat and problems working in a group.

At the beginning of Year 9, his teacher (Barber, 1996) decided to develop a special programme to teach him how to take a bus to the nearby city, to begin to prepare him for going to college. On the first visit she paid the fare. They took an agreed route through the city centre and planned what to say if someone asked for directions. The next time, Tom paid the fare and took his tutor on the journey. On the next occasion he went alone whilst she followed the bus in her car and finally he went through the whole process on his own. In his evaluation he wrote: 'This was useful as it helped me to gain independence and I learned how to use the bus service. I would like, if it were possible, to do this again, over a longer distance.' (p. 21)

Barber went on to develop a behaviour management programme to stop him making a fuss, grumbling under his breath, looking as angry as he could and even screaming when asked to do something he did not want to do. When asked why he behaved in this way he said that it was because of his 'urge to learn' and because the teacher often covered work that he already knew. Barber's future plans for him were to target skills in shopping, planning a meal and using a telephone.

There is an extraordinary range between high abilities and deficits in Tom's case. The deficits are in life skills areas that pupils at a much younger age would normally acquire without being directly taught. They are capable of incidentally learning all these necessary social and life skills whereas pupils like Tom may need specific step-by-step instructions. If his parents had been better supported they might have been able to help him at a much earlier stage. He was fortunate to meet a well-informed teacher-mentor who clearly helped him.

He is also fortunate that he has 'special talents'. These can protect pupils with AS from being excluded or sent to special schools for EBD. Unfortunately there may be only one in ten with AS who have such high ability and special talent.

Case example – Peter

Peter, aged 18 years, was in Year 13 in a small comprehensive school. He was from a disadvantaged city background. Neither parent had ever been in work or had any form of advanced education.

Peter has mild AS showing clumsiness, poor social skills and literal comprehension. He finds it difficult to adapt to any new situation or change in routines but these circumstances do not now provoke strong behavioural outbursts. At GCSE (Year 10) he achieved nine A stars, two As and a B. In Year 12 he gained an A in maths. His maths teacher-mentor (Teasdale, 2000) determined he should apply for university, although many others who had taught him were against the plan. They said he would not cope in an open learning environment and one so full of new and different experiences and social demands.

Peter refused to go on the school's week study tour of a number of universities. He was, however, finally persuaded to go on a residential visit to one university. The whole sequence of buying tickets, journey planning, accommodation and transport to and from the railhead were gone over in detail and executed with his tutor. He had never been away from home and his parents were against the university project. However, Peter was impressed with the place and the facilities.

With intensive training he managed to fill in the UCAS (Universities and Colleges Admissions Service) form, finding the business of writing, acquiring stamps, cheques, photographs, photocopies and envelopes extremely frustrating. His first trip and interview went well but he was not offered a place. However, it boosted his confidence to have succeeded in making the trip and finding he could master it all.

At his second and third choice universities he was offered a provisional place depending on gaining good grades – AA BB, which in due course he did. He accepted a place at the campus university that his mentor thought more suited to his needs. His mentor arranged with Student Services to offer him support as soon as he arrived and that his new maths tutor should also be involved to engage with his needs.

Semantic Pragmatic Disorder

Semantic Pragmatic Disorder (SPD) is identified as a separate condition (Bishop, 1989) on the ASD continuum in which social and behavioural skills and abilities are not markedly deficient, illustrating the fractionating hypothesis. Dehaney (2000: 36–7) identified the following features of the condition:

- speech is fluent but lacks content and direction;
- explanations and answers to questions are not specific;
- comprehension is poor, particularly of abstract concepts and understanding is often literal;
- interactive and imaginative play is poorly developed;
- difficulty in recognising and expressing emotion;
- difficulty following the unwritten rules of conversation, such as turn-taking, appropriateness and non-verbal language;
- weak temporal concepts causing confusion in school routines and chronological events;
- auditory memory is poor but rote learning is often a strength;
- poor attention skills, erratic motivation and distractibility;
- rarely asks for help or seeks clarification;
- behaviour is naive or eccentric;
- mechanical reading skills are good but comprehension is limited;
- self-esteem is low as a result of the problems and the difficulties caused by them.

Dehaney concluded that in methods for teaching English the pace was too fast and the emphasis on oral and listening skills meant there was a failure to comprehend before the lesson moved on. Even simple stories required imagination or seeing things as others do and this was beyond these children.

Despite these language impairments they can be helped to succeed in school subjects. Even so, there is a tendency to focus upon what the child cannot do rather than find what they are potentially good at. It is always possible to find something to connect with them and an interest they might have such as collecting stamps, playing chess, or a sport that does not require abstract language competencies. This is where extra-curricular activities, school clubs and societies can be useful.

Gender issues and AS

The recorded ratio of boys to girls with the condition has varied from 9:1 (Wolff and Barlow, 1979) to 4:1 (Wing, 2008). Over the last few years the number being diagnosed has stabilised after the increase and now is 3.8 per cent per 1,000 for boys and 0.8 per cent for girls. The likelihood of a child diagnosed with AS arriving in a class is thus about 1 in 100 but Attwood (2008) claimed 1 in 29 men have AS.

The gender ratio of 4:1 raises the question that there could be a failure to identify significant numbers of girls with Asperger just as there has been with dyslexia where the historical ratio was also 4:1.

Those responsible for referring children for diagnosis are perhaps handicapped by prevailing stereotypes, for example the 'geek' or 'nerd' addicted to computer games, football facts and so on are all associated with boys' behaviours. Meanwhile it is frequently ignored that girls with total commitment to celebrity, shopping, horses, make-up, or soap operas on TV may be exhibiting their form of Asperger rituals and routines and need further investigation and support. Boys are also much more likely to 'act out' in overt anti-social behaviours whereas girls are more likely to 'act in' and be more passive and depressed.

Gould and Smith (2011) suggested that girls with AS learn to mimic social interactions and communications more easily than boys and learn to act in social settings. Diagnosticians therefore see someone who appears capable and who has reciprocal conversation and uses appropriate affect and gestures. Thus these girls do not appear to fulfill the criteria in the international classification systems and a diagnosis is missed. A checklist is not sufficient to diagnose their needs; a case history and wider exploration of actions is needed, including their devotion to an interest that is intense and beyond the normal range. If they do attract attention it is likely that their diagnosis will be Oppositional Defiant Disorder (ODD) rather than AS, as Smith (2002) found, her bright Asperger girl was in a special school for EBD.

Talent in memory feats and school subjects

AS received particular attention from those concerned with research in gifted education when it was realised that a significant number of gifted individuals also displayed Asperger-like symptoms, e.g. their intense desire to do nothing but read about their special interest, or practise on their musical instrument for hours on end. Others practise their football skills all day long when free of school or study karate moves to the exclusion of everything else. However, such tendencies can appear in other forms that are not so valued by society such as 'addiction' to the learning of the working of bus or train timetables, naming all the players in the football teams past and present and the goals that were scored in matches, or reciting every song from memory that they have ever heard.

Because individuals with AS and high abilities may have talents in areas involving memory feats and literal activities, studying school subjects requiring more conventional factual knowledge rather than abstract understanding of ideas can enable them to achieve high scores in examinations. This is until they meet the need for more complex abstractions, perhaps at university level. Even then they can navigate their way through to high achievement by memorising different abstract positions.

It became clear that individuals with AS needed support both for their type of giftedness and their special needs. In Chapter 2 on DCD it was noted that Henderson and Green (2001) found that over 90 per cent of those with AS had an additional need in the form of handwriting difficulties. This can radically affect compositional and spelling abilities and success in school, and teachers are generally very unsympathetic to poor or illegible writing. Pupils with AS therefore

Table 4.1 Similarities and differences between giftedness and AS

Factors that can be the same	Factors that are different in AS
Verbal fluency, or precocity	Pedantic seamless speech, lacks appropriateness, understanding is literal
Early reader, often self-taught	Mixes fact and personal details
Excellent memory	Low tolerance to change, screams if change made, may ignore class or school routines completely
Fascination with letters or numbers	Does not understand humour, irony or fables
Absorbing interest in a specific topic	Lacks insight and affective understanding
Memorises vast quantities of information	Clumsiness in 50 to 90 per cent
Annoys peers with endless talk of interest	May especially have handwriting difficulties
Asks awkward questions	Frequently has stereotypic behaviours or rituals, screams at loud noises, refuses to eat this or wear that
Gives lengthy discourses in answers	
Hypersensitivity to sensory stimulation	
High level of skill in one area, average in others	

become multiply disadvantaged unless they find an AS-friendly school and a supportive mentor.

Because providers were becoming confused between what was idiosyncratic gifted behaviour and what was disordered, Niehart (2000) offered the guidance given in Table 4.1.

Typically those with AS may have certain areas of skills such as excellent rote memories and intense interest and knowledge in one or two subjects. In contrast to the gifted child this interest is to the exclusion of all else; those with AS talk about it endlessly even when the listener is uninterested and shows or even says this. Some less intellectually able individuals with AS may fail to understand the meaning of what they recite. Also noted is the apparent lack of empathy that they show for other people's distress. This has been explained as a lack of 'theory of mind' (Baron-Cohen *et al.*, 1985) or lack of insight into the feelings and motivations of other people.

In a press release dated May 2014, researchers at the University of Glasgow reported that in a study of over 50 serial killers 29 per cent had a diagnosis of ASD and 21 per cent had brain injury. However, there were other important factors contributing to their criminal careers: histories of child abuse, early parent death and serious bullying.

Although most pupils with AS experience some bullying, at secondary school especially, school bullying policies have provided a means for dealing with this. The Glasgow research shows how important it is for those policies to be fully implemented.

With two disabilities in literacy and pragmatic language it is not surprising that Jake was making slow progress in school, where these skills and abilities are dominant (See page 84). He is set to underachieve. It is important that the wider

Case example – Jake, 11 years

Jake was diagnosed with both dyslexia and AS at 7 years. He was repeating Year 6 in mainstream in an International School because the secondary school would not accept a child who needed a learning support assistant (LSA) and the primary school felt he was not ready to go to the secondary school.

He had very literal comprehension and did not understand jokes and sarcasm. This made him vulnerable in the playground where he had many altercations. He had difficulties interacting socially and making friends. His behaviour was noticeably immature for his age and he tended to play with younger children. When observed in the classroom it was noticeable that he quickly tended to become overexcited. He also found it difficult to modify his behaviour and adapt to different situations.

When asked what he did when the family went on a camping holiday, he said 'I went to bed, I ate breakfast. I got dressed'. On another occasion he told a story about how his parents were angry with him after he had cleaned out the goldfish bowl. He had emptied out the fish too and that killed it. He was not upset about this and could not understand why his parents were angry.

Jake liked routine and became very upset if the timetable changed or a new teacher appeared without notice. When he visited the special educational needs coordinator's room the first thing he did was check that the date had been written on the top right-hand side of the board. If it was not he would become very agitated and refuse to begin the lesson until she wrote it there.

Although Jake needed a great deal of support he often refused to take it. Sometimes he refused to cooperate or listen. He would know what he wanted to do which was not always what the teacher wanted him to do. It was then very difficult to persuade him that it was necessary for him to do as he was told.

curriculum, perhaps beyond the school, offers him an opportunity to specialise and find a talent to focus upon or to use his perceptual abilities to find an outlet for his abilities.

What we can observe in the goldfish incident is the lack of empathy, the focus of great attention to the particular and the lack of ability to see the configuration or the bigger picture. This is often why things go wrong and why adults fail to understand the 'misdemeanours' and the apparent lack of commonsense. Part of the support system needs to include explanations of this focusing ability, which would help remove a lot of the anger and frustration that the strange acts can engender. Opportunities for employment can be found that will capitalise on such abilities.

Donna Williams (1996), a high-functioning adult with autism, explained:

> I am diagnosed as having autism … If you ask me what the word means, I would tell you that, for me, it is about having trouble with connections … this also causes trouble with tolerance and trouble with control… (p. vii)

She attends to parts rather than seeing the whole, seeing but not hearing or being able to listen at the same time. She accumulates information but does not organise it. She has problems in sensory and emotional hypersensitivity, making input unpredictable and overwhelming. She sometimes fears her own voice or other people's. She has problems with compulsions, obsessions and acute anxiety, so may rock to calm herself down.

This phenomenon of enhanced perceptual focusing can be explained by the suggestion that 'neurotypicals' have evolved the ability to inhibit raw sensory input in order to form concepts and make decisions more quickly, whereas those with AS do not have such an ability. Creativity could stem from freeing ourselves from these 'top-down' interpretations and gaining access to another level of 'bottom-up' processing, in the same sort of way as perception operates in people with AS.

Case example – Susie, 4 years

Susie is in Reception and has had a difficult first term adjusting to the routines and other children. She is now settled at her favourite activity – painting complex swirl patterns. The teacher has a visitor and they are looking at the children's work and discussing it.

Suddenly terrified screams come from Susie at the sink in the corner. She had gone to wash out her paint pot, plunged her arms into the murky water and her hands 'disappeared'. (She thinks they have been cut off!)

Children with AS appear eccentric at school and may be badly bullied and become anxious and afraid. They are unsatisfactory pupils because they follow their own interests regardless of the teacher's instructions and what the rest of the class is doing. There are clues for identifying AS when individuals are involved in playing with a favourite toy or a computer game. If the teacher or parent calls to them by name they do not turn their heads even in a minor social way to signify they have heard. A normal response is to turn and respond or at least move the head and glance towards the adult. Such focused attention can be an attribute in a noisy work setting, but dangerous in a hazardous one.

In adolescence many do become aware of their difficulties, but they may then become over-sensitive to criticism and appear very vulnerable and pathetic or childish. Later it may lead to depression.

Wing (1996) concluded that good self-care, a special ability that can be used in some form of paid employment and a placid nature are required if the person with AS is to become socially independent.

Using a collaborative game to observe and plan intervention

Case example – Josh, 7 years

Josh (JS) was fairly new to the Year 2 class of 7-year-olds. He had been diagnosed with mild AS and had been assigned some LSA time. With her help he was prepared as far as possible for the collaborative game that was to be a change from the usual class routine. He was told the activity would be doing puzzles instead of writing.

Josh had a number of eccentric habits that greatly entertained his peers. He used a number of invented words when fussed about a change in activities or in answers to questions from the teacher. Jaw clicking, finger clicking and hand flapping would accompany this.

At other times he would perform a whole section of his favourite TV programme, 'Fawlty Towers', in the voice and mannerisms of Basil Fawlty. These were very lifelike and funny. He was capable of rerunning a whole programme that he had memorised. Instead of keeping this for playground entertainment he would suddenly start performing as Basil at inconvenient times during lessons. Telling him to stop had little effect. The teacher had to move in close, talk to him in a quiet and calming manner and distract him by showing him an interesting object or new activity. (A picture cueing system was recommended to help in this.)

The collaborative game, 'The Egg Race', had been selected from Bowers and Wells (1988) for Josh's class. Four different egg characters had been cut into pieces and each child was given an envelope with a different number of pieces from different eggs. The group was told that the puzzle pieces fitted together to make four different 'egg faces' but they did not necessarily have all or some of the pieces for one puzzle. Their task was to assemble puzzle pieces to complete all the eggs correctly. The rules were:

- no talking or use of sign language
- no taking pieces from others' puzzles
- you can offer pieces to someone
- you can accept a piece offered to you.

The observation session with Josh's group

Initially, all the pupils just looked at the pieces in front of them and pushed them around without even trying to put them together. They remained totally focused on their own and ignored other people's pieces.

Inevitably JS found the situation difficult. He sat rigidly clicking his fingers, repeating loudly and repetitively, 'Hot king's rock', 'Hot king's rock'. After the boys had watched JS for a few minutes they began looking across at each other's pieces. These three boys, AR, FL and MN, had puzzled frowns and kept looking at the teacher enquiringly as if they wanted her to tell them what to do.

Pupil AR noticed that JS had a piece that he needed and reached across the table to take it. He was reminded that he could not take a piece but had to wait until it was offered to him. JS's response was to pull all his pieces close to him and cover them possessively with his arms, repeating loudly, 'Spemily! Pyloff!'

Eventually FL noticed he had a piece that AR wanted and offered it to him. AR took it but could not work out which piece it fitted with. After several tries with all the pieces he handed it back to FL. FL shook his head and refused to take it back. AR shrugged his shoulders and kept the piece but left it to one side.

MN had watched this exchange and kept looking at his pieces and everyone else's pieces until he realised that he needed to offer FL a piece. This was received with a grin and fitted immediately to correctly form part of an egg. Once AR and MN saw how FL had fitted two pieces together, they looked more carefully at their own pieces and realised that some went together.

Throughout these exchanges JS kept his eyes averted from the others and focused on two of his pieces, intermittently clicking his jaw. The pieces did not fit together but he repeatedly pushed the two together and pulled them apart, whilst kicking his foot against the chair leg and shouting from time to time his made-up words or lines from Basil Fawlty.

By now the other three boys had worked out what they needed to do and were actively looking at each other's pieces and trying to see what they could offer to someone else. The three also used eye contact to communicate their needs. Both FL and AR offered pieces to JS, but he refused to take them despite their desperate attempts with facial expressions and head movements to encourage him to accept them. At no time did he make any attempt to offer a piece to the others, although they were eyeing them longingly.

AR, MN and FL swapped pieces amongst themselves until both AR and MN had completed their eggs. FL could not complete his egg because JS had his missing pieces. He also had pieces that JS needed but had refused to take. The group sat watching JS for several minutes but he did not offer any pieces. FL realised that they had reached a stalemate and so he pushed all his pieces over to JS so he could complete two eggs. He ignored them. The puzzle game took 20 minutes to complete.

This is a characteristic response from children, and also adults, with AS. With adults the game is more complex and consists of 'Broken Squares' but the responses are similar. There is a detailed focus on their pieces and a failure to interact or see the bigger picture. It is a revealing game to use in suspected cases of AS.

Case example – Mary

In a professional development MA class for teachers, a recently appointed primary head tackling the 'Broken Squares' task behaved just as JS had done. Then she became very angry about the 'ridiculous' task they had been set to do. She left the room abruptly and colleagues confided that she was having management difficulties with her staff and that they had been surprised by her appointment because she had a history of relationship problems.

What can be done later is to rerun the game and sit alongside the child with AS and quietly step-by-step pre-programme the behaviours. This involves teaching him or her: 'First look at your pieces – try to fit them together. Now look at AR's pieces – does he need one of your pieces? Now look at MN's pieces ...' and so on. In a second rerun it can be possible to introduce: 'Look at AR's face – is he smiling at you? Yes? It means he wants that piece – give it to him.'

The game strategy can then be used as a protocol to help the child generalise to other situations and develop some social skills, e.g. 'Do you remember the game? First I must check what I have got. Then I must look around to see who or what might help me...'.

Thus far there seems to be no single best fix intervention that can be applied to all children with AS. Their different personalities, home circumstances, experiences, learning histories and abilities make it important for interventions to be more personalised. In addition, it is often the school itself or the pedagogy that needs some modification to create an 'Asperger-friendly environment'.

Vulnerability in AS

Not only are people with AS vulnerable to bullying because of deficient social skills, they can also become caught up in crime. This may occur inadvertently because of, for example, a special intense interest in locks or fires, strong dislikes, inappropriate touching, stalking someone they become infatuated with, peeping into windows and all sorts of other behaviours that might be tolerated in young children but are seen as bizarre in youths or adults (Howlin, 2006).

Case example – Darren, 15 years

Darren was referred with ADHD but his case history revealed he really had dyslexic difficulties and AS. He was banned from the home of one set of grandparents because at 7 years the last straw came when he climbed onto their garage roof and, when told by the grandfather to come down, he told him where to go and what to do with himself in very abusive language.

Darren, like many with AS, was guileless and did as his 'friends' told him. He began stealing sweets in primary school to give to them to make friends and then later other goods to be a member of the gang. At secondary school he was continually set up to misbehave by his peers and was excluded from three schools.

After several cautions he was arrested for theft and 'freaked out'. He had to be restrained. By 15 he had been locked in a secure youth detention centre for behavioural disorders and criminal activity for 18 months. This is over 200 miles from home. When he comes out he will be 16, with a criminal record and little support or understanding of his problem except by his mother. Now he is too big and disturbed for her to manage.

All the attention Darren received at school was focused on his difficult behaviour not his educational needs.

Preoccupation with children's difficult behaviour to the exclusion of other diagnoses is not a new problem. Pawley (2007) identified ten such cases in Year 7 in his London special school for EBD. They all had diagnoses of ADHD and Conduct Disorder but when their literacy difficulties were addressed the problem behaviours diminished by over 30 per cent in one semester. We can only hypothesise that if Darren's dyslexic problems had been addressed in the infant school his Asperger condition would have become more easily manageable and he would have had a better future. His report showed he was in the above average range of ability and except for this dual diagnosis of disability he might be in the 'bright range'. Somewhere there is latent ability but Darren only feels that he is a failure with a profile of low achievement.

Case example – Karen

Karen is 18 and still in education, studying biology and chemistry at A level. She has a 'boyfriend' who is at work and several years older but no circle of girlfriends at school. When asked about friends she says she has lots – she has 500 friends on Facebook and is quite convinced they are real friends.

Her mother is concerned about the future. She knows exactly what goes on sexually between her daughter and the current 'boyfriend' because when she asks, Karen tells her quite literally and in detail. When the young man tires of the relationship Karen will not react well and could become vulnerable to sexual exploitation because of her naivety in relationships.

'The time bomb'

Some children with AS go undetected in school but parents reported to the National Autistic Society (Hattersley, 2010) that the stresses they had to withstand during the school day built up huge pressures. When they arrived home at 3.30 pm they 'exploded' and took out their distress on parents and siblings. They became unmanageable and inconsolable. Greater cooperation between schools and parents is therefore essential to ameliorate these problems.

Schools need to have a time-out area for children with AS. Pupils need to be able to use a cue card ('Get out of Gaol') that the teacher recognises, so that they can escape to the quiet room to calm down. Ordinary classrooms can at times be just too overstimulating with noise and bustle for a child with AS.

Transition times

Some of the most difficult management times in AS occur when there is any transition from one situation to another and there can be many of these in the school years. The screaming fits and excessive rituals can occur when the child moves from home to pre-school or play group; from kindergarten to Reception and so on.

Changing schools can be traumatic for any child who is ill prepared but with the Asperger need for sameness and predictability, transitions can be excessively disturbing. It is essential that the child is very well prepared with visits, explanations, photographs of places and personnel, and that they are allowed time to settle. Teachers and other staff also need to be well prepared. Even the move to a new class and teacher can be difficult to cope with. This can be particularly problematic in secondary school with the ever-changing rooms, subjects and teachers. This is why specials units within schools can be helpful. They can provide a place of safety, sameness and mentors to help cope with issues as they arise.

Teen troubles – A group of Year 11 boys' teenage needs

A typical problem identified by a group of Year 11 secondary school boys with AS was that they were desperate to learn how to 'chat up' a girl they would like to have a date with. They just did not know how to go about it.

Their special teacher/mentor with the help of colleagues in English and drama designed some role-play situations that began with a simple meeting and greetings taking place between two people. The teachers modelled the behaviour, video clips were shown of others' meetings, and the boys practised the sequence and were coached. They learned to make eye contact, smile a little, lift their eyebrows in recognition and offer a standard greeting. They were encouraged to practise this in the corridors at school with people they knew.

They progressed from these scenes to learning to make a short set of interactive statements that might encourage a potential partner to meet them again. They learned how to stand and not confront, not to touch or stand too close. All of this was reinforced in role-play and a group of girls joined in to act as 'buddies' and give feedback and help.

The boys all found this approach helpful. Their teachers felt that their social approaches had improved but their use of the conversational protocols was somewhat rigid in 11 out of the 12. They hoped that with experience these would loosen up a little and be used more flexibly. As can be imagined this would be extremely difficult for most of the boys.

Effective interventions used in AS

According to the National Autistic Society there have been over 55 interventions proposed in ASD. Some of the most effective in AS follow:

1. Applied Behavioural Analysis

This was originally called Behaviour Modification (Skinner, 1958) in Learning Theory studies. It is used to address the ritualistic and antisocial behaviours. The techniques need to be shared with the parents so that they are applied both at home and at school.

Positive reinforcement is widely used to reduce conduct problems in classrooms. It works best when applied to specific and small events such as remaining in seat, stopping talking and keeping still, and stopping hand flapping. Primary reinforcements such as food and drinks may work better than verbal and social reinforcements with children with ASD when they are young. Teacher approval and praise becomes significant as they mature.

Cognitive behaviour management strategies include a discussion with the learner of the means and the ends in managing the problem behaviours. Cognitive Behaviour Therapy (CBT) is widely used in helping children and adults with emotional and behavioural difficulties and illnesses (see Chapter 6).

Time out is commonly used when behaviour looks likely to disrupt the concentration and learning of other children. A 'time-out' routine can be used to establish calm and quiet. There needs to be a time-out place, chair, carrel or even a room where the child can be taken and allowed to calm. Time out in class should be for as short a period as possible (30 seconds) and the purpose is explained. It can be augmented with a picture cue card system (see below). In the early years a time-out corner and big cushions are an essential.

Modelling: The teacher points out desirable behaviour in a peer and positively reinforces successive approximations to it by the AS learner. The pupil with AS may need steps towards achieving the correct behaviour to be made explicit ('I want you to …') and then have them reinforced when each is adopted.

2. Life skills training

These need to be begun by parents in preschool and continued in school as age appropriate. Barber's case study of Tom illustrates these points. As pupils with AS do not pick up life skills incidentally they need to be explicitly taught. The skills can range from self-care in dressing, hygiene and feeding, to preparing food, keeping it in good condition, using local shops, travelling on public transport and so on.

Self-care and life skills need to be built up over time so that by secondary school a pupil does not need to learn how to make a cup of tea and buy sweets in a shop or go on public transport alone. It has to be remembered that each activity has to be broken down into small manageable steps and practised until they can be completed independently. It can be wrong to assume a gifted child with AS will learn these things independently. Regarding them as stupid if they have not learnt them is misguided.

Busy parents may need support in helping their children learn life skills and the school can design complementary experiences or use LSAs to reinforce particular skills.

3. Social skills training

In a meta-analysis of 79 studies Schneider (1992) found social skills training (SST) moderately effective in increasing social competence in natural settings with socially withdrawn children. But problems arose in the generalisation and transfer to new settings, and this is particularly true in AS. Blagg *et al.* (1993) found programmes using modelling and coaching were the most effective. For example, following the 'good shepherd' theory transfer does occur if it is shepherded, nurtured and mediated by specific teaching and learning activities. In AS the social skills training is now frequently incorporated into the Social Stories approach outlined below. When it is not, the social skill needs to be made explicit – clarity, overtness and explicitness may seem peremptory to non-AS learners but are essential in AS. They cannot read facial expression, attitude, affect and implicit techniques.

4. Augmented Visual Communication Systems

Symbol systems work with the tendency for people with ASD to be visual learners. They provide visual support for communication in the form of objects, photographs, pictures, gestures or line drawn symbols. They are usually paired with the words they represent so that a basic vocabulary can be built for communication purposes in severe autism, e.g. MAKATON.

Briefer versions can be used very effectively in AS to gain and support behaviour control and social interaction. People in conversation use many gestures, signs and facial expressions to support their communications and these can all be taught by using the cards and games in, for example, Picsyms from Speechmark.

Football cue card system: Red and yellow cue cards can be used by the pupil with AS to warn the teacher that the pressure is becoming too strong and he or she is suffering distress. Red can be the exit card to go to 'time out' and yellow the warning to 'cool it'. Sometimes they cannot find the words to express these feelings but feel the build up.

Reducing sensory input: Because pupils may be susceptible to overstimulation, sound damping can help, sunglasses might be allowed and headphones might be used at times to cut down input. Eye contact and touch may also be problematic, so sitting alongside may help as can writing notes rather than speaking directly to them when they are stressed. Group work may become overstimulating too.

Picture stories: If verbal instructions to tidy their desk (or room) have little impact, try showing a photograph of a tidy desk. A sequence of pictures showing a routine may also be more effective than explicit verbal instructions.

5. Theory of Mind and Social Stories

Baron-Cohen *et al.* (1985) proposed that the autistic individual lacked a 'theory of mind'. They showed it was a cognitive deficit that could be observed reliably across a series of studies and that resulted in the disorders found in the development of social and communication skills and abilities. They identified 'mind blindness' in autistic individuals as a delay in the development of ability to impute mental states to themselves and others. As a result they find other people's behaviour particularly confusing and worrying.

This was illustrated by Baron-Cohen *et al.* as follows:

> Two people stop and look in a shop window, one points at something in it, the other nods and they go into the shop. Shortly after one of them comes out and looks in the window again and goes back inside the shop. Then they both come out again, one with a plastic bag of something.

The normal onlooker *infers* that the two people are out shopping, see something one of them might *want* in the window and go in to buy it. The shop assistant *wishes* to know where it is in the window and they cannot *remember* exactly, so one comes out to check and then goes back inside to tell the assistant. We *believe* the object is bought and put in the plastic bag and they leave.

If we had no theory of mind about what other people were thinking and doing, all this running in and out of a door in ones and twos would seem very peculiar. A theory of mind gives us a device for understanding social behaviour and ways of interacting and communicating appropriately with others. Without it, life would seem very chaotic, even frightening, and might cause us to withdraw or react in social circumstances in very peculiar ways as though people were objects. This is how it is believed people with ASD experience social situations.

It is noticeable and perhaps not surprising that in spoken language individuals with AS seldom use the words 'know, believe, think, pretend', as many teachers will be aware. It becomes particularly obvious in the early years play and later in English lessons in role-play and imaginative writing. The mental state of attribution is necessary if in our talk with others we are to respect the conversational rules of pragmatics – if it is to be appropriate and relevant to the social context.

The 'mind blindness' aspect of autism may enhance some talents because autistic individuals do not see the configurations that 'neurotypicals' do. Baron-Cohen (2008) went on to develop the theory of a cognitive deficit to include a deficit in social empathy and an above average ability in systematising (imposing order and structure) to account for the triad of impairments.

Social Stories

These are short stories developed by Gray (1990, 2003) in the US that describe social situations in terms of relevant social cues and effective responses. They are often colourful and visually illustrated to clarify the meaning of communication, conversations and social situations.

The stories try to give the children the reason why things happen and direct them in understanding how they should react in a particular situation, what they should say and what they should do, and then explains why. The purpose is to make social rules and conventions explicit to the child with AS, whereas other children infer these principles and procedures. The stories are very short and give the child a protocol of four types of sentence:

- Descriptive – explain where and what.
- Perspective – explain feelings and behaviour of others.
- Directive – state what the child is expected to do.
- Control – strategies the child can use to remember.

In using the protocol Gray advised using one directive and/or control statement to every two to five descriptive/prescriptive statements. The method works in the following way:

- Sometimes my friend Tom tells me to 'chill' (descriptive).
- This means I am getting loud and bossy (descriptive).
- Tom does not want to sit with me when I am loud and bossy (perspective).
- I will lower my voice when Tom tells me to chill (directive).
- When Tom tells me to 'chill' I can imagine putting my voice on ice (control).

(Gray, 1990: 223)

Gray's original comic strips and stories are now enhanced by DVDs. The books and materials may be obtained from http://www.speechmark.net

6. Understanding and counteracting curriculum difficulties

Where curriculum subjects are confined to the literal and factual then pupils with AS will do well, but subjects like history and English are more problematic. This is because tasks require them to 'imagine' or 'think why' people did this or said that.

Difficulties may also arise in some of the practical subjects such as Science and Design because of the inherent coordination difficulties. More problems can result from subjects requiring a lot of handwriting. Word processing may be easier and should be encouraged. Pupils with AS may need extra time in examinations.

When the children are asked to imagine that they are in novel situations or in a different time or place, the pupil with AS will find this task impossible and not know where to begin. In this situation some tasks can be modelled in a concrete way. For example:

> Imagine that you get up one morning and find you are only 25 cm tall. Describe what happens to you during a school day.

This is a typical task that might be set in primary school. After a brainstorming session most pupils will find a way to start on their stories. However, younger children and the pupil with AS may need to make a manikin and walk it round the room to see the concrete difficulties encountered. When teamed up with a 'buddy' each can tell the other what is happening at different stages on the journey.

The key events can be recorded like a scientific experiment as they happen to the toy. Toys and finger puppets can be extremely useful to model what otherwise would be imaginary activities.

How do you think you would feel if … ? This is another problematic area. In a similar fashion, children engaged in role-play can 'see' important scenes played out that enable them to write about them. Video clips, pictures and playlets depicting important subjects will help because they provide the visual support the child needs to understand the world.

Debriefing is an important part of teaching and learning. It is especially important for pupils with AS, as they need attention directed to the key points and the deeper meaning of many events and actions that would otherwise pass them by. They will also need to be shown the overall pattern into which events and actions fit.

Why questions. Because pupils with AS lack a 'theory of mind' they find it hard to move from the literal to hypothesise about ideas and events.

Scaffolds. These can be particularly helpful in guiding pupils in their composing and writing tasks. The scaffolds can be presented in the form of a series of pictures or cartoons, or as short sentences that guide them through typical tasks. The simplest one used with young children in story writing is that stories have a beginning, middle and end. We might give them the scaffold in a series of boxes (visual organisers) in which they can write notes preparatory to writing the story or narrative.

Story schema can be developed by identifying types of beginnings in stories such as:

- Atmosphere – It was cold and dark, the fog just began to drift towards…
- Place – The house was small and stood in a corner of the square…
- Time – It was very early, the sun was just up…
- People – Jane was small and sturdy…
- Period – The harbour was full of sailing ships preparing for…

Thinking Actively in a Social Context (Wallace, 2000): The TASC wheel is a widely used resource scaffolding for creative problem solving. The eight steps are:

1. Explore knowledge
2. Identify the problem
3. Generate ideas
4. Decide on one
5. Implement
6. Evaluate
7. Communicate
8. What have I learnt?

An experimental intervention in the English curriculum

Harbinson and Alexander (2009) identified 12 pupils in their secondary school with AS statements. They gave the pupils an imaginative writing task to establish a baseline before their interventions and analysed previous work.

Their analysis of examples from a Key Stage 3 (14 years) exam illustrated the problems pupils with AS would face even though they had an option to describe a real event, e.g.

> Write a story describing a frightening experience. This may be based on a real or imaginary experience. It may be serious or amusing. In your story you should give information and describe...

They observed that even if the pupils could make a response the mark scheme would discriminate against them. They would be unable to attain the higher levels in the marking scheme such as:

- presents reflections on feelings
- shows development of a personal style
- engages the reader's interest. (p. 12)

Equally difficult were the inferential reading skills required in questions such as:

> What do you learn about Darcy from reading lines 21–69 in the passage?

Here, at the higher levels the mark scheme required:

- analysis of aptly selected references (connections difficult to make in AS requiring generalisation from parts to wholes)
- presents convincing insights (insight into own and others' actions and ideas is absent)
- offers perceptive understanding (mission impossible!). (p. 13)

The word 'imagine' may have aversive connotations for a pupil with AS from past difficult experiences. Some learners with AS even regard imaginative stories as 'telling lies'. Others may have learnt to rely entirely upon an LSA to guide them through the task. Now in a large inclusive classroom there may be shared or no support.

The research programme ran over 16 weeks, cut into two 8-week blocks: section one of whole-class teaching and section two in which the pupils with AS were withdrawn in groups of four for one hour a week for the intervention. Then there was a post-test. The programme involved two types of input:

1. A specially designed creative writing framework – Who? When? Where? What? Why? – with visual cues and prompts.
2. An inferential reading skills scaffold in three sections: 1) What did he say? What did he mean? 2) What did he do? What does this show? 3) How would you feel?

The result was that in the first eight weeks, despite the scaffolds being taught to and used by the whole class including the pupils with AS, no progress was made. In the second eight-week period the intervention in groups allowed more interaction, and informal talk about the tasks and where stories came from and so on. This was a little more successful.

The three English teachers involved in the study identified the following range of problems in the pupils with AS:

*   engaging in talking and listening
*   inferential reading
*   decoding figurative language
*   empathy skills
*   starting new tasks that expect imagination
*   analysing a character in a piece of fiction
*   knowing how to deal with a mistake. (p. 14)

These pupils needed the preparation to begin in primary school and be reinforced across the curriculum for it to be internalised, that is, following the 'Good Shepherd' approach. The suitability of the 'training' scaffolds also needs to be questioned. Many schools embrace the policy of inclusion but do not action it or train their teachers appropriately.

7. Dietary interventions

Casein and gluten: Reichelt (2001) and his colleagues screened 2 million children over a period from 1979–2001 in Norway. They found that as a result of a malfunctioning gene, casein and gluten peptides in milk and flour respectively cannot be properly broken down. This results in abnormally high opioid peptides being found in the urine. The opioid properties lead to the sensory and perceptual disturbances reported by people with ASD and the behavioural disturbances reported by parents and teachers.

Parents had to keep food journals and remove all casein and gluten products from the child's diet. At first they reported that the problems got worse as frequently there has been overdosing on milk and flour products. After three days it is typical that a transformation takes place. A non-communicating 5-year-old began speaking in coherent sentences, others began to play constructively and in interaction with siblings, and their behaviour came within the normal range.

According to these parents their children still remained on the autistic spectrum but with a less extreme condition, much more like a child with AS, and were able to learn in school and find suitable careers.

Dietary treatment feedback from the National Association for Gifted Children/Potential Plus

Reports received from parents who have tried the diet with their children are typically inconclusive. For example, one boy in the family was diagnosed with autism and another older gifted sibling was diagnosed with dyslexia. The diet was tried with the autistic boy and the other one participated incidentally because it was simpler for all the family to follow the diet.

The result was that the autistic boy's behaviour did calm down and become more manageable but the dyslexic boy became a model pupil and his literacy skills improved as a result. His behaviour had also been extreme and difficult (AS) but the family had hardly noticed because of their concerns with the management of the younger boy. The diet is always worth trying because if there are no positive effects within a week then it can be discontinued and checked off the 'to try' list.

The AS-friendly school

Curriculum

- Visual timetables with pictures and symbols to support the routines.
- Diaries and computer schedules when pupils can read, to show the routines and especially any changes that are due during the day.
- A timer to show the passing of time and to regulate the completion of work. Teach what 'finished' means.
- Plan for independent work and give the pupil folders – 'Work to complete' and 'Work completed' – to aid organisation and prediction.
- 'Visual organisers' to help structure subject contents and procedures.
- Give directions or limited choices as free choice can induce anxiety.
- Arrange so that class activities as far as possible can be taught in small steps or that a worksheet, computer program or LSA can act as a step organiser.
- Avoid the use of abstract ideas or tasks such as 'imagine' or 'invent' unless specific strategies are taught to handle these.

- Give help in ensuring that skills learnt in one context can be generalised to new situations.
- Introduce new ideas or procedures gradually, always checking for understanding.
- Each aspect of the 'hidden curriculum' needs to be taught.
- Avoid using metaphors, fables and figures of speech in the teaching process, e.g. 'My feet are killing me', 'It is raining cats and dogs'. If they are essential or appear in books they need to be explained.

Social

- Teach the specific rules of turn-taking, social distance and gambits for opening and maintaining a conversation.
- Learn calming techniques and strategies such as agreed gestures, signs and calming voice and statements.
- Address the child individually by name at all times to focus attention before any communication.
- Make clear with a firm 'No' and gesture or sign what is unacceptable.
- Give enhanced supervision during practical and physical activity.
- Arrange a 'buddy' system and 'circle of friends' to support and protect the pupil.
- Avoid sarcasm – the hidden meaning will not be understood.
- Protect from teasing and bullying – the school must have a policy on bullying.
- Do not take apparently rude or aggressive behaviour personally.

Environment

- Ensure that the learning environment is quiet and orderly – too much noise can create anxiety or lead to disruptive outbursts.
- Make sure the classroom is not cramped or overcrowded.
- Use sound-damping carpet and wall coverings where possible.
- Have a study carrel to use as a retreat, or a quiet corner with beanbags for younger children and a 'time out' room.
- Ensure the pupil has a personal workspace and a place to keep belongings.
- Organise regular breaks for relaxation in a play area for young children or perhaps using 'Brain Gym' for older pupils.
- Avoid white walls, stripy clothes, whiteboards and fluorescent or bright lights. Black mats in front of doors may be perceived as black holes.
- Avoid moving the furniture about unless the pupil has been prepared.

School–home and staff liaison

- Ensure there is good school–home liaison as parents have key information and experience to share and can support the school.
- Ensure there is in-service development on AS for all staff including administration staff, cleaners and dinner helpers, etc. so that they can understand and avoid confrontation and asocial comments.

Not every item is called for in every situation or raised in every case.

These techniques are freely available to all teachers in regular classrooms. In AS there are usually few problems in gaining a range of GCSEs that require factual knowledge but it is the social difficulties that cause greatest concern and that means that most will need some form of care or support in adult life.

Their extreme need for absolute regularity and routine in which the slightest change requires them to be very carefully prepared is also of major concern for it means that the simplest interaction in a shop or in employment can be unpredictable and disturbing to them and cause an overreaction. In addition many are prone to sensory overload in busy classrooms and need help to manage this.

Conclusions

It may take longer to integrate pupils with AS into regular classrooms than other children but improving self-regulation and management skills will assist this and maintain them there. It must start from the earliest moment at home and continue throughout education. Improving social and communication skills reduces the need for deviant communications and anxiety. These interventions need to be cumulative, developed in appropriate contexts and transfer of the training needs to be ensured through direct instruction, modelling, coaching and extended practice.

As can be seen in most of the cases outlined in this chapter the interventions are occurring too late and need instead to be part of a lifelong learning plan. As knowledge advances we can hope that this will be shared and parents and teachers can develop the necessary skills to help children with AS find their place in society. Improving and extending parent partnerships with schools is essential to this process.

Every school needs one person trained to mentor pupils with AS so that colleagues can learn from them how to deal with the unwanted behaviours and can focus upon developing social and life skills adapting their teaching to take account of literal pragmatic needs. After all, most pupils pass through a concrete stage of thinking between 7 and 11 and some never achieve abstract mental operations. So it will benefit a wider range of pupils than just the individual with AS. Girls with AS are particularly likely to be overlooked and are vulnerable to underfunctioning and exploitation because of their naïve behaviours, leading to a need for lifelong care and protection.

5 Identifying and supporting children with Attention Deficit Hyperactivity Disorder

Introduction

Interest in this condition was first aroused in the United States as a result of the 1918–1919 encephalitis epidemic. Many children who had recovered from the acute phase later showed catastrophic changes in personality: they became hyperactive, distractible, irritable, unruly, destructive and antisocial. It was then discovered that similar problems occurred in children who had suffered brain damage as a result of head injury, e.g. received a severe glancing blow to the head, or suffered anoxia shortly before, after or during birth.

Originally the condition was without a specific label and was included in the Strauss Syndrome. Parents had referred their children for diagnosis and teachers reported that the child could not remain seated and was always moving about the classroom. There was a severe motility problem and overreaction to stimuli (Strauss and Lehtingen, 1947). These were the reasons that it was originally thought to be a 'brain damage syndrome'. Later it was found that most children diagnosed as hyperactive did not have a history suggesting brain damage but it arose from some unknown difficulty with brain function.

To calm the children down they were given sedatives but Bradley (1937) discovered a paradox in their effects. He found that sedatives increased the hyperactivity but stimulants and amphetamines improved the child's behaviour. It was in this period that Ritalin was first synthesised and became the 'treatment of choice'. It is still the most common stimulant in use for Attention Deficit Hyperactivity Disorder (ADHD). About four million children in the US have a diagnosis of ADHD and three-quarters of them were on stimulant medication (Rafalovich, 2005). In comparison in the Nordic countries Zoega *et al.* (cited in Hjorne and Saljo, 2014: 237) found that medication rates varied: 12.46 per 1,000 in Iceland; 4.73 in Norway; 2.5 in Sweden; 2.41 in Denmark; and 1.23. in Finland.

It was not until 1957 that Laufer *et al.* described the syndrome as a 'hyperkinetic impulse disorder'. Only in 1966 did it become included as Minimal Brain Dysfunction, an overriding diagnosis that included hyperkinesis and several other disorders (Clements, 1966) and was agreed by the US Public Health Services.

In the 1970s it was not uncommon to refer a child with hyperactivity for psychiatric or psychological diagnosis only to find there was 'nothing wrong' with him or her. It was also noted that with a few teachers the child behaved perfectly well, without hyperactivity. It was suggested that the cause of this change in behaviour was because fear-inducing situations caused the release of noradrenaline (norepinephrime in the US) in the brain that calmed down or inhibited the hyperactive-impulsive behaviour. Thus discreet classroom observation was also recommended to see the child in a typical setting.

The earliest record of the syndrome is possibly to be found around 2,500 years ago in the writing of Hippocrates (Hippocrates and Adams, 1946). He was a physician who described a condition in some of his patients who had 'quickened responses to sensory information, but also less tenaciousness because the soul moves on quickly to the next impression'. Hippocrates suggested that this condition was due to an overbalance of 'fire over water' and his remedy was to advise them to eat barley rather than wheat bread, fish rather than meat, to drink water rather than wine and to take physical exercise. The proposed origin might seem a bit peculiar today but the diagnosis and similar remedies are often suggested even now.

Heinrich Hoffmann (1809–1894) of Frankfurt was the doctor at a 'lunatic' asylum and also practised in the city and often had to visit children. In 1844 he was looking for a picture book for his 3-year-old son but could find none that showed the hazards of life in an amusing way that would not frighten him. Hoffmann was already a storyteller and illustrator and soon filled a notebook. It was published in 1844 and translated into English in 1848. Hoffmann's poem 'The Story of Fidgety Philip' was the first detailed description of hyperactivity. It can be found in *The Oxford Book of Children's Verse* edited by Iona and Peter Opie (1975, London: Book Club Associates, pp. 208–9).

The general characteristics of ADHD

ADHD is a cluster of difficulties that appear to have some defined neurodevelopmental origins and give rise to behavioural control problems and learning difficulties.

The American Psychiatric Association (APA, 1994) officially identified three types of disorder in ADHD:

1. ADHD – Predominantly Combined type
2. ADHD – Predominantly Inattentive group (six of nine symptoms of inattention must be present
3. ADHD – Predominantly Hyperactive – Impulsive type (six of nine symptoms of impulsivity must be present

When the symptoms are without the hyperactivity, the condition used to be referred to as Attention Deficit Disorder (ADD), but now all conditions are termed ADHD. Two of the symptom patterns have to be present (APA, 2006).

In education in the UK, ADHD is included in the group of Specific Learning Difficulties (SpLD) as a nonverbal learning difficulty. It indicates that there is a specific area of deficit or delay in the presence of normal intellectual ability. 'Normal' can include the whole range of abilities from slow learners through to the gifted and talented.

ADHD is now one of the most common syndromes of childhood. It accounted for 30–40 per cent of all referrals to child guidance clinics (Barkley, 1998) and there has been a 40 per cent increase in referrals in the last decade (Greenfield, 2007).

It is a disorder that is seen in early infancy and it continues into childhood, through to adolescence and into adulthood. It is more common in boys than girls in a ratio of 3:1. The core symptoms of ADHD are disturbances of motor activity, impulsiveness, and a developmentally inappropriate level of attention. Children with ADHD frequently experience difficulties sitting still and paying attention in class. They experience problems with social interaction within the family, peer rejection, and academic failure and underachievement.

Incidence

The incidence varies from one country to another and between surveys. Stewart for example in 1970 estimated that 4 per cent of suburban school-age children in the US suffered from the problem to some degree with a ratio of 9 boys to 1 girl. Rutter (1985) estimated 1–2 per cent of the population in the UK had such problems.

Barkley (1998) showed that epidemiological studies found that 3–7 per cent of children in the US were diagnosed with ADHD. Boys with the disorder outnumbered girls in the ratio of 6:1 in clinic referrals and in community-based samples by 3:1 (Selkowitz, 2004). Currently in the US, 7 per cent of children aged 6–11 have the diagnosis, with a prevalence of 4 million school children, whereas in the UK 1–2 per cent have the diagnosis with 2–3 boys to one girl. The narrower UK definition leads to the lower incidence (Cooper and Ideus, 1999).

The larger number of boys referred is a result of their overrepresentation in the hyperactive-impulsive group. In the inattentive group there are equal numbers of boys and girls. Whether the larger number of boys referred with hyperactivity is due to nature and the lower numbers of girls to nurture is not yet determined.

The differences in incidences reflect a higher referral rate in the US and a greater willingness to include behaviour problems as disorders in the diagnosis, rather than a difference between children in different nations. It may also reflect a 'Zeitgeist', or 'spirit of the age', when a new term enters the vocabulary and every overactive child is in danger of being labelled hyperactive.

Case example –Jordan, just 6 years

Jordan is rarely at his desk working. When he is, he works standing up. He is constantly lolling about or rolling on the mat. When told to sit up straight, the next instant he will be lying down again. He cannot keep quiet in any discussion and constantly blurts out answers.

He will continue a conversation with a friend even when the teacher is directly asking him to stop. He has an extremely short attention span and seems unable to give his attention long enough to grasp something. Thus he has found it very difficult to learn sound–symbol correspondence and a sight vocabulary. As yet he cannot read unknown words or use phonic word attack skills.

He is often the ringleader in scuffles with his friends. He can, however, sustain an imaginary game for an extraordinarily long time when playing with his toy figures. At home his parents report that he is difficult to manage. He responds well for short periods to rewards and stickers for good effort, but saying 'If you don't behave, I will _____ [e.g. send a note home]' does not work.

Comorbidity

In 40–60 per cent of cases with ADHD there is another existing co-occurring disability, according to Barkley (1998). In 40 cases referred for Conduct Disorders with a primary diagnosis of ADHD, Walsh *et al.* (2014) found that 70 per cent had comorbidity with ASD and/or dyslexia. Three-quarters of the group had language impairment and one-third had reading comprehension and reading accuracy deficient scores. The ratio of boys to girls was 3:1. They had tested 40 children between the ages of 9 and 12 attending a Children and Adolescent Mental Health Services (CAMHS) clinic who were all diagnosed with ADHD. Two-thirds were on medication therapy (Ritalin). Three-quarters of the group had previously undiagnosed language difficulties and 70 per cent of these had both receptive and expressive difficulties. The IQs were generally in the above-average range, with just a few with mild learning difficulties.

Other comorbidities

ADHD shows 50–70 per cent comorbidity with handwriting coordination difficulties. One third of pupils, mainly boys, with ADHD also have Oppositional Defiant Disorder (ODD) and 20–40 per cent with ADHD develop Conduct Disorders: bullying, fire-raising, cruelty to animals, stealing, persistent lying, destruction of property, violating the rights of others. One-third with ADHD had anxiety disorders (Root and Resnick, 2003) and a small proportion of those with ADHD also have Tourette's syndrome. They also found that ADHD associated with harsh parenting could lead to Oppositional Defiant Disorder (ODD) and Conduct Disorder. Heritability was identified in 50 per cent with ADHD.

Genetic links and ADHD

It was found that there are 13 genes linked to attention deficits (Ziegler-Dendy, 2000), and three are of particular interest. They are the dopamine detector genes: DRD2, DRD4 and DAT1. These genes control the level of dopamine in the neurons and it was found that people with ADHD have 70 per cent higher levels of dopamine transporter in the synapses. The receptors and transporters do not work properly and this results in a low level of excitation of the neurons by the dopamine. It is this dopamine imbalance that is addressed by Ritalin.

Neurological links to ADHD

MRI scans have found that three sections of the brain in ADHD cases are smaller than in controls and the areas are in the cerebellum, the caudate nucleus, and the corpus callosum. The problem with such studies is that we cannot judge whether the brain differences are a consequence of years of having ADHD or are the cause of it, especially because the scans usually take place in adolescence or adulthood.

The three areas identified were not damaged but just smaller with less white matter (nerve fibres). These areas affect alertness, executive functions, the ability to change or switch from one task to another and the ability to assist the transfer of information between neurons.

In the families of children with ADHD it seems that fathers also have had a history of attentional problems and clinicians such as Stewart (1970) found that mothers did not. The fathers as adults showed irritability, overactivity and aggression.

Misdiagnosis

It is not uncommon for very bright children on entry to school to be absorbed by the newness of it all for a week or two and then to become bored by the routine and the sameness and slowness of everything. They begin to leak a nervous energy that has no intellectual outlet and teachers try to over-correct and suppress it. These children are soon mislabelled as hyperactive and recommended for medication.

If the problems arise episodically then an allergy reaction might be suspected. If they arise only at school then poor teaching, fear of learning failure, or frustration and boredom in a more able child could be the origin.

Many children in emotional distress or with conduct problems are also restless and overactive, as are children with all sorts of psychiatric problems. Hyperactivity

Case example – Sammy, 5 years

Sammy was a well-grown, sturdy, bright boy who had been driving motor boats and sailing dinghies since he was 3. He helped his father at the boatyard and sat with the men at break times. His early life was boats and engines and activity, and school came as a great shock to his system. He had never had to sit down or listen for long periods. He treated adults as familiar mates and did as he wished, whatever the teacher might want him to do.

His parents had been summoned on several occasions to take him home when he had confrontations with staff or had been too rough and over-excitable with other children. He worked off some of his energies by monopolising one of the tricycles and cycling round and round the play-ground and in and out of the classroom. In the Spring term in desperation the parents were sent for and told Sammy was thought to be hyperactive and that the school recommended he should be referred for assessment and be given medication (Ritalin) to help calm him down.

His distressed parents sought a second opinion and were told that given his case history he was a normal little boy, not hyperactive. He needed more time to adjust to the less active life of school and on no account should he be given medication. His teachers needed to manage his behaviours more effectively rather than blame him for his overactivity. The parents could help him by explaining what school was all about and what he needed to do there. They could be less indulgent, reserving the motor boating and other yard activities as treats following a quiet day at school. Sammy gradually settled down and by the end of Reception was a well-integrated pupil.

is a much less common condition in which the extreme overactivity is usually very marked.

The specific characteristics of ADHD

The key features of ADHD are severity, pervasiveness and morbidity, early onset and serious disorders of attention and concentration that do not clear up. Attention deficit is due to a lack of attentional set. Attentional set is the ability to maintain a still body posture and fixed gaze upon an object of interest, then maintain that attention without being easily distracted by peripheral events. Babies in the cradle can normally fix on an object and follow it.

In ADHD the disorder is pervasive, manifested across all lessons and both at home and school. It does not respond to the ordinary management techniques such as reasoning, ignoring aversive behaviour, and punishment. Even computer games may not keep the attention.

There are three main symptoms:

* *Inattention* – in behavioural, ocular and postural set.
* *Hyperactivity* – extreme and incessant mobility and restlessness.
* *Impulsivity* – shouting and calling out, cannot take turns.

The pupil finds it difficult to undertake two tasks at the same time – multitasking such as talking whilst walking along a line or balance bar.

Overactivity does not always continue into adolescence and may be replaced at puberty by underactivity, inertia and lack of motivation.

In each case of ADHD APA (1994) Guidelines (adapted from Barkley, 1998: 63) advise:

* The symptoms must be present for at least six months, to a degree that is maladaptive and inconsistent with the developmental level.
* Some symptoms must have been present before the age of 7.
* Symptoms must be present in two or more settings, e.g. school, home, work.
* There must be clear evidence of clinically significant impairment in social, academic or occupational functioning.
* The symptoms do not occur exclusively during the course of another condition.

*Six or more of the following symptoms of **inattention** must have been present for at least six months to a degree that is maladaptive and inconsistent with the developmental level.*

A) EITHER: Often –

a) Fails to give close attention to details or makes careless mistakes in school work, work or other activities
b) Has difficulty sustaining attention in tasks or play activities
c) Does not seem to listen when spoken to directly
d) Fails to follow through on instructions and fails to finish schoolwork, chores, or duties in the workplace (not due to oppositional behaviour or failure to understand)
e) Has difficulty organising tasks and activities
f) Avoids, or dislikes, or is reluctant to engage in tasks that require sustained mental effort (such as schoolwork and homework)
g) Loses things for tasks and activities (e.g. toys, school assignments, pencils, books or tools)
h) Easily distracted by extraneous stimuli
i) Forgetful in daily activities

*Six or more of the following symptoms of **hyperactivity/impulsivity** must have been present for at least six months to a degree that is maladaptive and inconsistent with the developmental level.*

OR: Often –

a)   Fidgets with hands or seats or squirms in seat
b)   Leaves seat in classroom or in other situations in which remaining in seat is expected
c)   Runs about or climbs excessively in situations in which it is inappropriate (in adolescents or adults, may be subjective feelings of restlessness)
d)   Has difficulty playing or engaging in leisure activities quietly
e)   'On the go' or acts as if 'driven by a motor'
f)   Talks excessively
g)   Blurts out answers before questions have been completed
h)   Has difficulty waiting for turn
i)   Interrupts or intrudes on others (e.g. butts into conversations or games)

The danger with descriptions of such symptoms and use of words such as 'often' and 'seem' is that they are individually interpreted and different people attach different values to them. In addition the symptoms in their less extreme forms can individually apply to many children at some time.

In practical terms Stewart (1970) found that children in his sample were given to fighting with other children, lying and destructiveness. One in four had stolen and one in ten had engaged in vandalism, cruelty, truancy and fire setting. Discipline problems resulted, but the discipline problem was secondary to the problem of hyperactivity. He also found that the onset of hyperactivity occurred:

- at a very early age
- half the mothers noticed unusual behaviour before 2 years
- no history of birth difficulties
- no significant difference in socio-economic backgrounds of parents compared with controls.

The children had a history of feeding problems, disturbed sleep patterns and generally poor health in the first year of life. Many were handicapped by delayed development of speech and poor coordination.

Case example – Matthew, 6 years, 9 months

At school Matthew is frequently in trouble and stressed. He is often surprised that he is in trouble and cannot understand why.

He has a reading age of 6 years, 6 months and a spelling age of 7 years, 1 month but scores in the top 10 per cent on Raven's Coloured Progressive Matrices. On the Dyslexia Screening Test – J, it suggests he is at a strong risk of dyslexia. He does work hard and will apply himself with support in the classroom.

Matthew is often frustrated at school when he cannot do something and is liable to clown around to conceal his difficulties. He knows he can do well at making others laugh and be the best at playing jokes, so he persists in getting their admiration in these negative ways.

He is very impulsive and does not seem to learn from correction. He does the same thing moments after being told not to. He is very competitive and will try things in PE that others will think twice about because he wants to win. He is frequently in trouble for making insulting remarks to others, particularly the girls who seem to him to be able to do everything he finds difficult.

He is a child who has an inability to stop and reflect prior to acting. At home his parents report that he is a calm and happy boy who rarely gets into trouble. In school a cognitive strategy 'think before acting' is having some good effects.

Although he is at risk from dyslexia no action has been taken because he is functioning near grade level. This is a bad practice; he needs remedial help because with his high ability indicated by Ravens we can see significant under-functioning in the literacy area.

ADHD – Impulsivity

This aspect of the condition is often given less attention because it is not so concerning to teachers as it is not so disruptive. There is uninhibited activity and meddlesomeness, plus trial and error learning, and inconsequential behaviour, so that the consequences of any action are not considered. Quiet withdrawal is not a feature.

Distinguishing between high energy levels of gifted students that cannot be coped with by mass schooling contexts and ADHD, as a disorder, is important. It is best seen in sudden and total concentration on a task of special interest or a computer game that a pupil with ADHD cannot maintain.

However, we tend not to see the positive side of ADHD. Jaksa (1999) reported adult cases that manage and use it to advantage such as Phil who insisted that it made him a more exciting speaker, comedian and motivator. He claimed it was a gift, although he admitted that at school, teachers took early retirement when they found he was going to be in their class. Perhaps it is the abnormal environment of classrooms full of confined children that prevents ADHD being used to advantage.

Not only do parents complain, teachers also report that the child cannot remain seated and is always moving about the room. At meal times food is scattered about as well as crockery. The problem is always evident by the time the child goes to school – usually manifested by 3–4 years.

At school their restlessness, noisiness, disobedience, distractibility, habit of rarely finishing any work and the tendency to talk out of turn causes the child to be labelled as a 'discipline problem'. Most of these children have educational difficulties – they never sit still long enough to learn much. Many have developmental delays reported in their case histories. The motor behaviour and lack of concentration is often accompanied by serious social difficulties – difficulties in getting along with other children because of the aggressive, disruptive behaviour.

Stott (1966) gave the term 'Inconsequence' when classifying 'maladjusted' impulsive behaviour in his British Social Adjustment Guide (BSAG). He defined it as a 'Syndrome of Restlessness' – behaviour that was inimical to consistently pursued goals.

The children had an *inability to inhibit responses to stimuli at the primitive physical level.* They did not give themselves time to carry through to completion the mental work that is normally performed upon sensory information preparatory to actual behaviour. For example, they were unable to effect the cognitive rehearsal of the consequences of a proposed course of action.

Case example – Poppy, 16 years

Poppy had difficulties throughout her school years but was gifted in Art in which she gained an A* at GCSE. She had to be withdrawn from most other subjects because of her poor behaviour and lack of attention and concentration. This never applied to making artwork when she could focus for hours on end.

Her behaviour in both primary and secondary school was challenging. She would arrive late without the necessary equipment, often leaving her materials strewn across the desk at the end of lessons. She would sing and doodle on her work and that of other pupils much to the exasperation of all concerned. During revision study periods for the GCSEs she was found running noisily round the school singing and dancing.

She was frequently defiant of authority and the teachers did not know how to manage her without creating a further loss in her already low self-esteem. She had never had a diagnosis of her special need and left school after taking GCSEs.

In 1934, Tolman suggested such individuals do not test their hypotheses about the outcomes of their actions by reference to 'cognitive maps'. Instead they test them by trial and error in the situation. They do not run a mental model of the probable course of events ahead of reality. Kagan (1966) said that their problem-solving strategies had a 'shot gun' character; they give off a fusillade of answers in the hope that one will be correct. They do not evaluate differential validity as do reflectives.

The reflective child, by a process of social learning, finds it does not pay to push people around or behave exhibitionistically. S/he learns to restrain haptic curiosity, respect property rights and restrain primitive attack responses. Whether we call it Impulsivity or Inconsequential, the characteristics are the same and it may be wondered how any such person may have gifts or talents – and yet they do. Too frequently they only find themselves and their talents after they leave school.

Case example – Johnnie

Johnnie was a science teacher. He was an ex Royal Air Force man with a gift for electronics. He said he was a late developer and arrived in teaching at 40. At school he was disruptive and attended as little as possible and left as soon as he could to work on a building site. His son had just been diagnosed with ADHD and he saw himself in him although his own disability had never been diagnosed. In order to cope with his own hyperactivity as an adult he spent evenings and weekends whenever possible back on building sites as a demolition worker. He even made more money at it than teaching.

He whizzed about his classrooms, chatting rapidly and working with the pupils and seemed constantly on the move. He never entered the staffroom unless obliged to for a meeting. Usually he found an excuse to be off somewhere doing something else. He was irascible and easily provoked to anger. The pupils were wary of him but liked him.

Medical interventions in ADHD

There are intense disputes and disagreements about whether the diagnosis is to be regarded as a 'disease caused by biomedical factors' (Visser and Jehan, 2009: 127) or what we see are problems caused by social and environmental conditions and/or inefficient organisations unable to cope with children with different needs (Graham, 2008). A diagnosis of ADHD has increased greatly in the last two decades and with it the likelihood of medication rather than other treatments or interventions.

Medication such as Ritalin is often given for a temporary period whilst behaviour management and other programmes are implemented. It may not always calm down the behaviour but can improve concentration temporarily so that pupils can catch up with schoolwork. It can also depress the gifted child's potential.

Ritalin therapy

Amphetamines release the transmitter noradrenaline from nerve endings. Nor A assists in restoring the dopamine balance, calming down areas of the brain in the frontal lobes.

In the UK the advice is that the drug should be used very carefully and only given to help the child settle back into school in case s/he develops drug dependence. The effect of the drug is temporary and four-hour, six to eight-hour or slow-acting doses can be obtained. After this the psychiatrist seeks to alter the environment and teach the use of behaviour therapy techniques to parents and teachers.

Not all children diagnosed as having ADHD respond to amphetamines, reflecting the several different origins of the difficulty. If a short period of drug therapy does not work and remarkable effects are not produced, it should be terminated and another form of therapy considered.

The National Institute for Clinical Excellence (NICE, 2008) reviewed the research evidence on ADHD and took representations from experts in the field, and it issued its new guidelines in September 2008. Parental training and psychological intervention were at the heart of these. The guidelines stated:

- Drug treatment was not recommended for pre-school children with suspected ADHD.
- It was also not recommended for older children with moderate ADHD.
- It was recommended as the first-line intervention for children, young people and adults with severe ADHD.
- Dietary fatty acids were not recommended.
- General Practitioners should not initiate drug treatments for ADHD; they could continue prescribing and monitoring such treatment once it had been established by an expert.

In moderate cases the parents of children and adolescents should be offered a group training programme based on the principles of Bandura's Social Learning Theory (1977). There should also be the option of individual psychological therapy.

In severe cases the drug treatment should always be part of a care package that included psychological and educational components. Adults who did not want the drug treatment should have access to psychological help.

NICE also called for multidisciplinary specialist ADHD teams and/or clinics to be established. It recommended that teachers with necessary training should provide behavioural interventions in the classroom.

Cooper (2008), whilst welcoming the new guidelines, said that it was a pity that the educational interventions were restricted to behavioural management. He favoured a more educationally informed approach that would emphasise the ways in which teachers might exploit the cognitive features of ADHD for pedagogical purposes. This involved reframing aspects of ADHD as differences in cognitive style rather than deficits. He also regarded this aspect as an important focus for future research.

In the follow-up to the largest treatment study so far on children with ADHD (Swanson, 2001), it was found that those who had taken Ritalin for three years had a decrease in the rate of growth in both height and weight. There was also no indication that in the long run the medication was better than nothing!

Dietary considerations in ADHD

During the 1970s and 1980s it became popular to suggest that diet and food allergies were a contributory factor in ADHD. Foods containing preservatives and tartrazine found in many processed foods such as soft drinks, crisps, sausages and so on, were identified as the problems. Teachers frequently advised parents to remove these from children's diets and remarkable improvements in behaviour were seen in many of these difficult children.

Case example – Sarah

Sarah was a student in teacher training. She knew she had a chocolate allergy but she needed a drink before her bar stint and found the machine was out of everything except a chocolate drink. Thinking about the jokes made about the drinks not containing or tasting of real tea or coffee and that a long drink was very different from bars of chocolate she drank it.

Within minutes she went into a full hyperactive state, whirling about, pouring and spilling drinks and not charging for them. She had to be taken home and did not 'come down' for many hours.

Chocolate, peanuts, crisps and many soft drinks were individually found to elicit hyperactive episodes in some vulnerable children. Schools today have found that when the school shop sells only fruit and spring water at lunchtime the behaviour of pupils in the afternoons can be greatly improved.

Psychological interventions in ADHD

Working-memory training

ADHD has been identified as an Attention Deficit Disorder and therefore the working-memory system will be involved in some way in the problems. The characteristics that have already been noted are:

- the lack of attentional set – difficulties in maintaining postural readiness, control of eye movements and a focus on targets
- the short span of attention when it is directed to any item
- the high distractibility of attention once given
- random switching of attention
- fleeting short-term memory
- lack of inhibition of responses.

Children with ADHD have greater difficulties in switching attention, updating working memory, planning behaviour and generating sequences. Without the ability to control attention, cognitive development is hindered. Working memory is a temporary storage system for information. It was originally referred to as STM or short-term memory. It provides a temporary storage system and manipulation for the complex tasks of language comprehension, learning and reasoning (Baddeley, 1985, 2007).

Baddeley proposed that working memory is made up of five major elements:

- *The central executive* focuses, divides and switches attention. It links working memory to long-term memory. MRI scans show it is located in the frontal lobes.
- *The phonological loop* deals with verbal memory. It stores information to do with numbers, words and sentences. The storage capacity is limited to '7 plus or minus 2' items (Miller, 1956).
- *The visuo-spatial sketchpad* stores our visual information: images, pictures and locations. There are three areas of storage for object-based information, spatial location information and kinaesthetic information. The storage components are in the right hemisphere occipital lobe for visual information and the right parietal lobe for the spatial component. The memory capacity appears to be four items and there appear to be gender differences in the visuo-spatial sketchpad – men are better at spatial manipulation and mental rotation of objects and use a more holistic strategy than women. Women appear to use a more piecemeal analytical and slower approach to visual information, innate or learned we do not yet know.
- *The episodic buffer* appears to offer a cognitive workspace. It has limited capacity but integrates information into coherent episodes from the other parts of the memory including LTM and puts these into long-term storage in meaningful units. The areas of the brain involved thus far are the frontal lobes and the hippocampus.
- *Long-term memory* capacity appears to be limitless. It is thought to be subdivided into episodic memory, autobiographical memory, procedural memory and semantic memory.

The capacity of working memory increases as we develop and grows through infancy and childhood from about three items at age 5 years to five or six at 10 years, and plateaus at 14 or 15 at the adult level.

Many 'gifted' individuals even at 6 years have a capacity of 10 or 11 items on a digit span test, making most schoolwork easy to do and repetition unnecessary. When required to think and reason they may do less well. Alloway (2009) has for example shown that measures of working-memory capacity are excellent predictors of academic success. This demonstrates the lack of cognitive challenge in the school curriculum and its didactic nature.

Research by Klingberg (2009) suggested that in ADHD there are deficits in working memory and these are located in the visuo-spatial sketchpad not with verbal memory and the phonological loop. The deficiencies appear to be in the frontal lobe processes. It was also suggested that a core deficit in ADHD is lack of cortical inhibition and this may affect the visuo-spatial sketchpad more than verbal memory. In addition it may be that there is overload in the frontal lobe areas in ADHD that causes a bottleneck. This could be because the children do not have sufficient brain connections to sort out and isolate the various activities needed for effective working-memory skills.

Klingberg showed that working-memory capacity is increased by various forms of training. In childhood memory capacity grows with increasing myelination (increase in the fatty sheath round the nerve fibres so the electrical messages do not leak out) and he claims that functional MRI scans have linked myelination of connections between parietal and frontal lobe areas with the development of working memory. Myelination is complete between the ages of 18–30 years.

He reported an earlier double blind research study in four clinical centres with colleagues in which children with ADHD had undergone 'brain training' over a five-week period. The subjects were all off medication. The training was computerised and continuously adapted to the level of the child. The child used the program for 25 days at home for periods of about 40 minutes. The results revealed that the training had similar beneficial effects as if they had been on stimulants.

The stimulant drugs in ADHD have been found to enhance visuo-spatial working memory. The training appears to release more of the brain's own dopamine and noradrenaline. The training also increased the children's scores on Raven's Progressive Matrices, indicating the close involvement of working memory in reasoning.

According to Klingberg (2009), previous working-memory training studies did not work because they had acted upon rehearsal processes rather than activities to improve the cognitive pathways. His program based on a video games approach is called RoboMemo, available from Cogmed.

Alloway (2009) reported a small study with eight 7-year-old children with learning difficulties using a similar program called Jungle Memory. She compared their progress with seven matched pupils on the regular IEP system receiving the support of the school. The children on the Jungle Memory program's spelling improved by 10 standard score points over the others. Rote-training methods are frequently used in primary schools to learn spellings and so some of the working memory skills were relevant.

In a later study by Alloway with 8–11-year-old dyslexics using RoboMemo the same transfer to literacy skills was not seen (McGhee, 2010), confirming that their difficulties were in the phonological loop. However, large improvements were seen in the visuo-spatial scores – the right brain function. The behaviour of the pupils improved over the year and they became able to work as a group; however, whether this was a result of the programme could not be determined as there were many other factors to take into account, including being organised and attending school early for the sessions, playing them regularly and keeping on attending to the game.

Applied Behavioural Analysis (ABA)

Behaviour modification techniques

Behaviour modification techniques are widely used in the management of the behaviour difficulties observed in ADHD and, as already indicated in Chapter 4, in ASD. They are positive interventions designed to keep the child in place and on task.

The tasks themselves need to be carefully structured in short steps so that they can be completed and praise given. There may then need to be legitimate opportunities to get up and move about. Brain Gym might be used here.

Firm and consistent disciplining needs to be applied and operated at both school and home. A 'time out' chair or corner can help support the good behaviour and the child learns to take him or herself to it and sit quietly and recover self-control for 30 seconds – even 'time out' needs to be short to sustain it.

Cognitive behaviour therapy (CBT)

There are six central components in CBT (McCarty and Weisz, 2007): the psycho-educational framework, self-monitoring, cognitive restructuring, behavioural activation, social and communication skills, training in problem-solving skills.

The cognitive therapist helps the client identify and systematically challenge irrational thoughts and feelings related to poor self-esteem and self-worth. CBT focuses on the importance of self-concept.

The applications of this theory can be seen in social skills training, such as assertiveness training, anger management and self-control. The strategies begin with training in becoming aware of self and mood and then the effect that the behaviours may be having on others. It places emphasis on language, self-instruction and the internal representation of difficulties. It is frequently used to treat depression which is common in adolescence particularly amongst girls. Relaxation therapy is usually added to CBT in such cases. Depression in adolescence is associated with a range of serious psychological problems including increased rates of suicide.

Social learning theory

Bandura (1977) stressed the importance of social learning and the principles of imitation and vicarious learning in human learning. In an earlier series of experiments these principles were illustrated using a Bobo doll. The doll was child-sized and stood in a corner. A child observer was shown a video of another child entering the toy room and going over to the doll and 'beating it up'. The observer child was then left to play in the toy room unsupervised and recorded. The result was that very soon the child went over to the Bobo doll and beat it up with the same flailing arm movements used by the other child. This especially occurred when the beater child was reinforced with praise and smiles by the experimenter.

When children were put in the room with the doll without the aggressive video they often ignored it or played with it in a non-aggressive manner.

Bandura found that humans were particularly prone to imitate aggressive behaviour or misbehaviour that they had seen rather than quiet and more calming behaviours. Piaget (1952) had witnessed something similar when his 2-year-old son who was in his playpen had witnessed another child have a temper tantrum. The 2-year-old, left to play quietly, suddenly started to mimic the screaming tantrum he had just seen. As abruptly as he had started he stopped, seeming satisfied with his performance. This showed that 'one-trial learning' could and did occur.

Bandura elaborated on the principles and practices of his social learning theory, showing that large amounts of the human repertoire are learned in social contexts especially during early rearing. The power of models to reinforce was also a prominent concept. The more powerful the person to be imitated, the more likely it was that they would be imitated. The more rewarding their offering either as a primary or a secondary reinforcer, the more they would be imitated. This led to targeting parent rearing techniques and their use of reinforcements to improve the behaviour of disturbed children.

Children needing attention will seek it where they can and the gang may be the most powerful source of reinforcement. The bully may be seen as the most powerful in a class. The media was also found to be more powerful in creating imitative behaviours than had previously been recognised. Social learning theory shows that we can learn from TV, video and film as easily as we can from our own social contexts. Vicarious learning had less effect on pro-social behaviours. Learning from books and stories was also considered powerful and these are frequently used in therapy sessions (Sunderland, 2014).

An uncontrolled pupil with ADHD can vicariously have a deleterious effect on other pupils' behaviour and so the school must unite to help teachers deal with both problems.

Behaviour Contract

This was one of the first areas that schools moved into. The problem behaviour is discussed with the pupil and the teacher may say, e.g. 'If you spent more time sitting at your desk your work would improve. Remember the rule is – "Sit at your desk. Then I will help you."' When the pupil sits at the desk for any reason the teacher immediately attends or praises and acknowledges the fact.

In secondary schools persistently disruptive pupils are frequently put on report and carry around a card or paper that the teachers must sign if no disruptive behaviour occurred. The contract is discussed and 'good' behaviour defined; the weekly results are examined with the pupil and often the parents. Exclusion may follow if the contract is broken. If it is kept for several weeks it is discontinued. In the keeping it gives a chance for teacher attitudes to the pupil to become more positive and support the procedure.

One of the reasons why Behaviour Contract has been found to work is because during the daily report stage there is an opportunity for a pupil to receive interest and attention from an adult. If the adult is concerned and fair then the relationship develops so that the pupil wants to try to behave for the adult and may begin to see his or her behaviour from the perspective of others. The improved behaviour when it occurs gives an opportunity for learning to take place and it is important to target this particularly during the report stage.

Social Services often draw up a semi-legal document with adolescents beyond control of their parents that causes all the participants to negotiate the issues and define their roles and actions. These are written into the contract and held to be binding; the document is signed by each participant.

Case example – Joe, a sporting talent

Joe is the middle son of three. He is 13-years-old and currently in Year 9. His academic performance is weak and he underachieves across the board except in sport. He has recently joined the under 15s rugby team at a well-known club.

In class his behaviour record is poor and he is frequently in conflict with both peers and staff and he has been suspended three times since Year 7. A number of staff have refused to teach him. His mother is in absolute despair about his lack of success at school and her inability to control him at home. Staff in the school regard him as a 'bad lot' and the sooner he is permanently excluded the better. Joe has difficulties sustaining attention, often does not seem to listen when spoken to directly, does not follow through on instructions and fails to complete schoolwork or chores, and he often interrupts or intrudes on others' games or conversations.

When he was observed in a lesson there was conflict from the outset. He refused to complete tasks and exhibited threatening and antisocial behaviour to the teacher and had to be withdrawn from the room, giving her a barrage of abuse. However, he does have a nicer side and has been kind to younger children.

At home he has a large amount of unstructured time and his mother is very quick to defend him even when he is plainly wrong. The teachers at the school seem to lack any understanding of his problems and expect him to misbehave and when he does they punish him so that it all becomes a self-fulfilling prophecy.

Although we have no further information on Joe's case he is a candidate for ADHD without the hyperactivity. Although good at rugby he may well have associated handwriting difficulties that would result in underachievement and cause him to avoid and evade written work as noted in his profile. This aspect needs serious investigation. Consistent school failure can predispose pupils to become alienated and aggressive as in Joe's case.

Educational interventions in ADHD

Two interesting pieces of research are that green play settings are as good as medication for children with ADHD (Taylor *et al.*, 2001) and that children with attention deficits concentrate better after a walk in the park (Taylor and Kuo, 2009).

A composed, slow-moving child shows slow, controlled eye movements and steady ocular and attentional fixations. A hyperactive child tends to show very rapid movements, fleeting fixations and mercurial attention. The qualities of the hyperactive child's behaviours are that they are inappropriate, non-directed, irrelevant in nature, and the child is initially unable to control them. Action and response are haphazard and disorganised. Thus calming techniques and careful organisation and routines are essential. Quiet order in classrooms helps reduce distractions for the inattentive learner.

Gifted and talented pupils are cognitively strong and it is this attribute that can be used to help address their needs and enable them to gain cognitive control over their difficulties.

General educational provision

More attentive behaviour in classes can be promoted by:

- keeping the pupil as close to the teacher as possible;
- seating alone or with a calm, quiet peer;
- a calm, orderly environment with a low work noise;
- sound-damping carpet;
- a fairly complete structuring of the child's school day and activities;
- limiting academic tasks to very small steps. Reducing the number of distractions during any one task, this also increases the child's experience of success;
- avoiding overstimulation and excess fatigue;
- repetition of instructions by teacher and then by child to try to make sure they have received adequate attention;
- avoid negative nagging – so 'catch them being good' (CBG);
- rewards for desirable behaviour need to be emphasised, starting with something small – positive behaviour management.

Reduction of seat leaving

Teacher wears counter on forearm and presses it every time J leaves his seat. *J left seat four times in three minutes.* The class is told that every time J manages to leave his seat no more than twice in three minutes a light will show on his desk. They will then get a reward. It concentrates on his desirable behaviour but not quite in the English tradition of education in which secondary reinforcers are usually used such as attention, praise, smiles, stars, etc.

Other techniques

- set class/group task;
- reset specific aspect for J to complete, then he may come to you;
- inattention – ask him to repeat his instructions;
- hand on shoulder/non-verbal cues;
- great praise and encouragement when completes or complies;
- reduction of auditory distraction by use of tape-recorded lessons and headphones;
- quiet background music helps some children;
- a particular child may be allowed to go and kick a football, bang a drum, or play bat and ball for a few minutes when the need is felt;
- as they are less distractible in visual mode, always provide visual stimulation and structure for the learner: videos, computer-assisted learning, etc.

Social learning and cognitive controls

I messages

This is a technique to help a pupil learn to deal with the problem behaviour (Bowers and Wells, 1988). The pupils are given a problem to discuss in small groups of three which include the child with ADHD.

> A pupil is in trouble from a teacher and after a telling off says to his friends, 'He never listens to me'. What can the friends suggest? Discuss the difference if he says, 'I have a problem. I feel he never listens to me'.

> Step 1: Establish the facts.
> Step 2: Establish the feelings.
> Step 3: What would you like to happen?
> Step 4: What could we do?

Pupils with ADHD find lessons in which they can contribute and work with peers in pairs or small groups help them to manage their own behaviour better. Giving them examples of behaviour that may also be relevant to them to resolve can also prove helpful in gaining cognitive control. Peers also provide important feedback and control in these small problem-solving settings.

Cutting the loop

Barkley (1997) suggested that when teachers told a child with ADHD to 'Be quiet' they were too quick to repeat the instruction getting louder each time.

The attention deficit meant that the instruction was not attended to or processed before the teacher was repeating it, increasing the tension. Instead it was important to name the child, give the instruction and pause, make eye contact only then repeating the instruction quietly if there had been no response, or making a calming gesture.

Circle time

During circle time problem behaviours can be addressed with the whole class or group and simple strategies or protocols can be developed (Chapter 6 provides more detail). See also http://www.circle-time.co.uk

Cues, signs and cognitive self-control

The teacher can agree with the pupil a particular sign or hand signal that means 'Stop' and whatever the pupil is doing he or she must stop and wait, count to three, and answer the teacher's question or sit down, whatever is appropriate. This 'good' behaviour then needs to be reinforced.

Cognitive strategy training: Pause – Think – Act strategy

Because of the impulsivity associated with this condition with and without the hyperactivity it is important to train the pupil in a Pause – Think – Act strategy. That is to learn to follow this little strategy before calling out, jumping up, shouting at other pupils and so on, up to crossing the road rather than running out into it without looking. A visual cueing system can also help encourage this.

The essence of these cognitive approaches is that they gradually shift from increasing the child's awareness of what has been done in past situations to awareness of the behaviour as it occurs, and finally to awareness of situations in which an explosive, impulsive or hyperactive event might build and occur. They learn to avoid them or to stop at an early stage in the process.

Learning to switch off the process

Learning to switch off the process may be the ultimate goal, with switching to a more desirable behaviour a goal on the way. The teacher will quickly learn the predisposing clues and situations that provoke the ADHD and learn to cue the pupil to it, so that working together they can stop it.

Cutting down distractibility

In addition to a time out area it may be necessary to introduce a study carrel, a small workstation that has side panels to cut visual distractions and headphones through which music or instructions can be played. It may also help to record the pupil reading his or her own reading books and other texts so that they can be listened to as the text is followed, or read along with.

Control of multitasking

Those with ADHD find it almost impossible to do two tasks at the same time. They cannot do a jigsaw and converse at the same time, write and spell at the same time as thinking about a story line, or keep a ball under control whilst following or giving instructions. As can be seen, a teacher's strategies need to take account of these factors. Making up a story and writing it down need to be separated until the child can spell and write fluently from automatic store.

Switching smoothly from one task to another is often impossible in ADHD and each time there can be a complete loss of direction and confusion. Changes during lessons are also switches and can precipitate problem behaviour, as can tasks that go on for too long.

Task analysis

Many tasks that children have to do in schools can be broken down into a series or hierarchy of shorter tasks leading to the final outcome; pupils with ADHD benefit from this. Steps that can be closely monitored by the pupil and the teacher, with each success reinforced, can improve the pupil's self-esteem and cognitive control.

Brain Gym and relaxation therapy

Brain Gym activities are brief exercises that younger pupils enjoy and are frequently used as 'warm up' activities or release of energy after long periods of concentration. They follow a strict little routine and can be used to release the energy in ADHD or distract from a build up of tension leading to an explosive outburst.

A routine might be 'Left hand in air, left hand on right knee, both hands on shoulders, arms out wide, arms by sides, stand still' (see Chapter 2).

Some schools have introduced yoga as part of calming and relaxation therapy.

HANDLE

HANDLE stands for Holistic Approaches to Neurodevelopment and Learning Efficiency. Bluestone (2001, cited in Kokot, 2003) suggested that no one lacked attention as is implicit in the typical ADHD diagnosis. Instead she contended that everyone is attending to something. Individuals who show difficulties in sustaining attention may be blocking certain types of information and seeking others. They may have difficulty shifting attention or using it flexibly. She therefore renamed the condition of ADHD: Attentional Priority Disorder (APD).

She identified the disorder as arising in the neurological subsystems, in particular the vestibular system. The symptoms identified in APD were input signs such as:

- hypersensitivity in at least one modality such as touch, vision or hearing;
- weakness in the vestibular system which supports and regulates the functions of listening, eye function, balance, sense of self in space and muscle tone;

and output signs such as:

- insufficient integration between the two sides of the body and brain;
- immature reflex integration and irregularity in differentiation of movement/ response.

Details of the HANDLE technique and ADHD casework can be found in Kokot (2003).

Self-Instructional Training (SIT)

A range of cognitive training examples fall under this heading or sometimes it is referred to as *Self-Regulated Learning*. The purpose is to enable the children to regulate their own behaviour through self-direction or teaching oneself. The strategies start by getting the child to slow down and delay acting inappropriately.

- Impulsive children need to stop and think before blurting out an answer or writing an answer to a question.
- An aggressive child needs to learn to stop and think before lashing out.

Talking to self out loud may be a good starting point: 'Now what am I asked to do here'.

In Wallace's problem-solving TASC wheel (Thinking Actively in a Social Context) (Wallace, 2000, 2009) children work round the wheel and use the questions as a scaffold to give them help in structuring their approaches to problem solving. It reduces the trial and error approaches and impulsive responses and scaffolds the learning.

Other classroom support resources

Observer support

It can be very helpful if another colleague can come to the classroom for a session or two to observe the child and record what provokes the behaviour and the general level of ADHD. This should be part of a psychologist's assessment if this has been called for.

Equally important is for someone else to take the class so that the regular teacher can have the opportunity to stand back and unobtrusively observe the child's behaviour. This discreet observation can make intervention procedures better focused and more effective.

Video feedback and counselling

It can be agreed with parents and older pupils to use video feedback to provide a focus for discussion on how to improve behaviour and gain self-control. A pupil seldom has any idea how absurd, extreme or inappropriate the behaviours are.

Watching oneself on TV is also absorbing and will focus the attention long enough to have some impact and enable a discussion to take place.

Learning and Behaviour Support Assistants

It is essential that any LSA who is assigned to helping manage the pupil with ADHD should have specific training in a range of management interventions and not be expected to learn on the job with a teacher who may also have had little training. Both need training and together they need to observe the pupil as suggested and arrange to try specific strategies for set periods of time. Not all will work but some will and specific combinations may work with one individual and not another.

Parental support

It is essential that the parents are fully involved in the decisions that are to be made about their child and can if possible support the strategies employed in the classroom at home. They need to be part of the therapeutic team. Obviously there will be some parents who are less cooperative than others but an open and welcoming school and an active Parents Association can bring many in, especially those whose own school experiences were less than pleasant.

Resources

There is a wide range of resources and gadgets available to support the learning and good behaviour of pupils with symptoms of ADHD. Some of these are:

- Attention tracker – teachers or the children can set the control to a fixed interval such as 3 minutes and then the counter will count up or down at a rate of 10, 20 or 30 seconds to the target giving warning lights red, yellow and green to mark progress.
- Sand timers – plastic timers large and small, and audible timers.
- Wiggle cushions, wobble shells, balance balls and balance seats.
- Calming resources – dressing-up clothes, toys to hug and reassure for young children.
- Concentration bits for fidgets – things to fiddle with and bend.
- Privacy partitions – e.g. a mini carrel (see http://www.specialdirect.com).

Handwriting, DCD and ADHD

Difficulties at school are very common in children with ADHD and often lead to the initial referral for psychological assessment. Impairments in their handwriting seem to be very common as 70 per cent of children with ADHD appear to have motor coordination problems and this will hamper writing tasks and quickly lead to fatigue.

Their impairments in handwriting are poor handwriting quality, legibility, grammar, spelling and written expression. Because handwriting is one of the fundamental skills required of school-age children, pupils with ADHD will be at a significant disadvantage and likely to underachieve because of this alone. Therefore to address this one area of the problem may help the pupil significantly.

It was noticed by Tucha *et al.* (2008) that when pupils with ADHD were on methylphenidate their attention and behaviour improved, but what surprised them was that the handwriting did not. In a series of controlled studies Tucha and her colleagues discovered that when on medication the pupils were very conscious that they must try hard to improve their writing and the attention they gave to it slowed them down but was ineffective.

After several simple training sessions on automaticity and fluency, with encouragement to 'write faster' and teaching an efficient running style, the quality and quantity of their written work improved. Follow-up one and two months later showed that the improvements had been maintained.

Using word processors can help with the legibility problems but may not be the best answer for all pupils. Fluency training (see Chapter 2) needs to be given a chance as in examinations it is often difficult to be permitted to use word processors without a very specific diagnosis of motor coordination difficulties or slow speed. The quality of children's composition on computers is not always as high as in handwritten work (Oliver *et al.*, 2009).

Case example – Steven, 12 years

Steven is in Year 7. His parents teach at the school and he is the youngest of three siblings. He is an able pupil but finds concentration and behaviour difficult to control. He is an excellent skateboarder, rock climber and musician on guitar, saxophone and drums. He is bilingual, fluent in English and German.

He fidgets continually, frequently leaves his seat when he should not, runs about and climbs excessively in inappropriate situations, has difficulties playing quietly, blurts out answers, has difficulty taking turns and butts into conversations or games. He often loses things and is reluctant to participate in tasks that require mental effort. When observed he was unable to sit still, was constantly blurting out and avoiding written work. He continually acted the clown and his peers found him funny. His behaviour in various situations was silly and immature. He appeared to have specific difficulties with written work but his high ability enabled him to function at the level of peers.

His parents are not worried about his behaviour and generally laugh off teachers' concerns; they are convinced he will grow out of it because he is not failing academically. For them it is a niggling behavioural matter. For colleagues it is not, as he disrupts the learning of other pupils. He is over-familiar with teachers and calls them by their first names; this is encouraged by the parents bringing him to staff social functions.

Attitudes to ADHD that influence practice

At one extreme is the view that ADHD is a *postmodern social construction*, resulting from a modern technological system and media-driven society. This is a system unsympathetic to the social and psychological well-being of humans, in which media sound bites stand for a reality which is surreal and dissociated from reality. Television lives in which families never sit down to talk and eat together but 'graze', shout and 'zap' through TV programmes concentrating for very short periods are thought by some to induce ADHD behaviour in susceptible individuals.

At the other extreme, ADHD is regarded as a *pathological condition* that has to be medicated. In reality it is possible that both extremes can evince ADHD.

Just as specialists' beliefs act upon their use of medications to treat children, Couture *et al.* (2003) argued that teachers' beliefs about ADHD determined their practices in the classroom. She and her team attempted to measure this with the ADHD Orientation Scale (ADHD-OS) with the following results. Ninety-three per cent of 21 British teachers in initial teacher education had received no information or training on ADHD, whereas 60 per cent of 21 teachers in Quebec had received some training.

- *Moral and ethical attitudes.* These teachers saw the behaviours in ADHD as bad or a moral deficit and believed they were intentional. Chosen interventions were likely to be punitive.
- *Allopathic medical.* They saw ADHD as a biological problem with no conscious control from which secondary psychological problems would result. They would recommend medication combined with therapy and firm discipline.
- *Socio-cultural.* ADHD was seen as a social construct and that related difficulties were not localised within the individual. Interventions were directed towards environmental factors and the family, not to the individual.
- *Alternative medical.* They believed that ADHD was due to toxic environmental influences such as deficient diets or allergies, or to biological causes not proven by traditional medicine. The teacher preferred interventions arising from various alternative trends.
- *Cognitive style – political.* Society was seen as controlling and marginalising some people by making pathological those behaviours that were actually legitimate responses to the intolerable. Society was seen as undervaluing creativity, nonconformity and a concrete style of learning. The teacher would seek to modify society's expectations rather than change the individual. The approach would be to seek to understand and to adapt to the individual's characteristics rather than ask him or her to conform to a mould.

Although Couture's sample is small, previous data on which it is based and experience do indicate that there is more than 'face validity' in these categories and the teachers' responses. Appropriate training is needed to demonstrate effective interventions and move these attitudes to promote more positive interventions and outcomes.

Wider perspectives

Systemic therapy

This has been the move of the unit of analysis from the child to the family and the child within it. The family systems view helps reduce the pathologising of the child who is exhibiting the problem behaviours. It is often inferred in this system that the child is the 'symptom carrier' for the family problems. The therapist's role is to work with the family not just the individual child.

Schools that practise family-friendly policies can also contribute to family therapy by including parents in the discussions and planned interventions can be shared and reinforced at home.

Social constructivism

In terms of Cognitive Behaviour Therapy, the systemic move is seen in the development of Social Constructivism and then to Social Constructionism and the use of narratives. In this approach attention is drawn to the ways in which humans make sense of their experiences through narrative. Our concept of self is greatly influenced by the stories that others have of us.

Disturbed children are helped to construct alternative and less distressing stories to account for their experiences and views of themselves. In the case of pupils with ADHD they quickly learn the story that they are school failures and badly behaved. The cognitive therapy and the strategies are designed to help them develop a story that has success in it and control over their behaviour.

Social competence

Social competence is construed as age-appropriate social and communication skills, and enjoyment of classes and a liking for school. The factors are:

- establishing and maintaining a range of positive social behaviours;
- refraining from harming others;
- contributing collaboratively to peer group and school;
- engaging in behaviours that enhance and protect health;
- avoiding behaviours that have serious negative consequences for self and others.

Conclusions

In real terms teachers may only occasionally expect to meet a pupil with ADHD. The most severe cases will already have been referred for support and medication.

Others will have symptoms that can usually be managed if teachers have had appropriate training.

In all cases it is essential that any handwriting and dyslexic difficulties are identified and addressed because failures and frustrations in these areas will provoke unnecessary outbursts.

The school environment, the teacher and the routines need to be calm and orderly. There need to be quiet areas and a time out place for calming and recovery when needed.

Teachers will need behaviour management training as well as training in specific attention and impulsivity control procedures. The curriculum will need review and development to include active participation, task analysis, small group problem solving and energy release opportunities and strategies.

The aim is that with understanding of their condition and appropriate support, pupils can gain cognitive control over their attention and impulsivity and learn to channel their energies in positive ways and become self-regulated learners.

6 Identifying and supporting children with Social, Emotional and Behavioural Difficulties

Introduction

Emotional and behavioural difficulties mostly arise in social contexts and have social consequences for those involved and the wider society. An overview of the Social, Emotional and Behavioural Difficulties (SEBD) research and practice area reveals three strands of concern. These are emotional, behavioural and communication difficulties. The latter involves both language and social skills.

We know from the research of Freeman (1991) and Niehart *et al.* (2002) that gifted children are no more likely than others to develop emotional problems, although specific difficulties arise for some of them from dyssynchronicities and perfectionism.

The DCFS (2008a, para 49) changed the term from Social, Emotional and Behavioural Difficulties (SEBD) to Behavioural, Emotional and Social Difficulties (BESD) to focus attention on behaviour in schools and defined it as follows:

> It is a learning difficulty where children and young people demonstrate features of emotional and behavioural difficulties such as:
>
> - being withdrawn and isolated
> - disruptive and disturbing
> - being hyperactive and lacking concentration
> - having immature social skills
> - or presenting challenging behaviours arising from other complex special needs.
>
> (para 10)

BESD can include conduct disorders, ADHD, school phobia, depression, Tourette's syndrome. There are higher rates of BESD in socially deprived areas, amongst boys and amongst Black Caribbean and Mixed White and Black Caribbean pupils and travellers. (para 60)

This information and instruction is sent to all English schools but it can result in confusion by lumping different conditions together, by considering behaviour to be the prime target for intervention and, although learning difficulties may result, SEBDs are not in themselves learning difficulties. The definition also locates the problems as 'within child' and yet in the expert field this is not the case.

A medical reading of SEBD is also difficult to sustain because of the confusion that can arise between gifted children and children affected by ADHD. Both these groups are frequently diagnosed with SEBD because they can display identical behaviours and are subject to the same levels of exclusions (Webb *et al.*, 2005).

There are about 8.3 million pupils in English and Welsh schools and government statistics (DfE, 2014) showed that in 2011–2012 permanent exclusions from schools had risen to 0.08 per cent of the school population. More children were excluded from primary schools in England than before: 12,690 were expelled, 230 for persistent disruptive behaviour, 200 for assaults on teachers and 120 for attacking pupils. At secondary schools 4,390 pupils were expelled: 1,050 for physical assault and 1,700 for persistent disruptive behaviour.

After a number of years of decline in exclusions they have risen as schools have been given more control over them. Now boys are three times more likely to be permanently or temporarily excluded than girls. Black Afro-Caribbean, groups with SEN and Gypsy children are eight times more likely to be excluded.

Depression and behavioural difficulties do not follow social divisions or socio-economic categories. SEBD occurs not only in relation to teachers and others in authority but also in relation to peers (Visser and Dubsky, 2009) and the pupils are usually identified with SEBD when they have fallen behind academically. However, it is school success that can change teacher attitudes towards misbehaviour and encourage them to adopt a more flexible approach. Success can also change pupils' behaviour from disaffection and disruption to active participation and motivation.

Case example – John

John was in Year 9 at a secondary school in a socially and economically deprived area outside London. He was of dual heritage and had a history of some racial and sexual abuse. He was on the school's learning support register and on the verge of being statemented for his special needs, mainly his behaviour but also in part for his emotional needs. He was better behaved in practical lessons where there was more flexibilty about talking and movement.

> He is an able but disruptive pupil, excessively loud, constantly calls out in class, interferes and affects others' work – underachieving across the curriculum (Levels 3–4), but is thought capable of levels 5–6 … He is frequently being sent out of class and is at risk of permanent exclusion from the school. (Turner, 2000: 13)

As can be inferred John's problems were deeper than the school's analysis. He needed counselling help and systematic positive support to structure his learning and give him much more attention than he was currently getting. He also needed a mentor.

In this chapter an **ecosystemic approach** is used as the framework for understanding and intervening in cases of SEBD. The school is seen as a system in itself interconnected to other systems and children belong to a set of subsystems. Their behaviour, good or bad, is a product of the interactions between these systems. Problem behaviour occurs when there is a dysfunction between them. Changes in one part of the ecosystem will produce changes elsewhere.

An ecosystemic analysis leads to the view that a complex net of interactions give rise to highly individual patterns of behaviour and needs which means that one intervention will not fix all problems. This can be seen in the case of John. His teachers cannot cope, so the school will exclude him. He has already missed so many lessons that he has lost the plot and is failing despite his recognised ability. He is highly distractible and disruptive but more amenable in practical and more flexible lessons and with teachers who try to understand and help him. The last thing he needs is to be excluded. He needs psychotherapy/counselling and learning support from the teachers actually teaching him.

The survey by Wedge and Prosser (1982) showed that social disadvantage had an enduring effect even on high ability children and its effects worsened at secondary school. Primary schools have already been shown in earlier chapters to adapt more successfully to the needs of children in their care and maintain them in school longer and this is also the case for pupils with SEBD. Children also become more vulnerable in coercive and rigid schooling environments where 'policing' is the disciplinary attitude (Galloway and Goodwin, 1987); this has not changed (Steer, 2009).

In the attitudes of some teachers, social disadvantage places pupils in a low academic expectation group and predisposes them to develop anti-schooling attitudes if they do not already arrive with them. Low expectations lead to low attainments and become a self-fulfilling prophecy.

Social disadvantage also puts pupils at greater risk from an unhelpful curriculum and teaching ethos. Successful pupils from poor and disadvantaging backgrounds learn to live in two cultures, that of the home and that of the school. It helps if they can have models and mentors to mediate this learning. John had not found these in his environment. To help pupils such as John a case profile is needed to show how his problems have been constructed and to clarify what needs to be done to support him and reduce the problem behaviour.

The nature of behavioural difficulties

As already discussed there is a strong resistance in the UK educational field to labelling problem behaviours as medical 'disorders', but it is accepted in the psychiatric field where they deal with extreme cases. The APA *DSM-V* (2006) identified Oppositional Defiant Disorders (ODD) and Conduct Disorders (CD).

CD may be diagnosed when the child seriously misbehaves with aggressive or non-aggressive behaviours towards people, animals or property in essentially repetitive and persistent patterns in which the rights of others and major age-appropriate norms are violated.

ODD is diagnosed when children show a recurrent pattern of negative, defiant, disobedient and hostile behaviour to authority figures. Like those with CD they are disruptive, challenging and troublesome children.

Behaviour difficulties are generally divided into Externalising Behaviours (EB) that are termed *'acting out'*, as in attention-seeking and disruption in class, and Internalising Behaviours (IB) or *'acting in'*, as in the emotional behaviours – becoming anxious, passive, dreamy and withdrawn.

Behaviour difficulties are generally regarded as inappropriate or unwanted behaviours in social settings that cause teachers concern and interrupt the progress of lessons or the progress of individual children's learning. For example, running round the classroom is inappropriate whereas running round the play-ground is not. Talking to a friend is a normal and acceptable behaviour, whereas talking to the friend when the teacher is talking is not.

There is frequently a *continuum of behavioural difficulties* and an individual pupil may move forward and back on such a continuum in different lessons and with different teachers. At different ages and stages problem behaviours may emerge and later disappear. It is the cases where the problem behaviours become persistent and pervade all areas of school life (morbidity) that there is serious cause for concern. Problem behaviours may or may not be present at home and such discrepancies need to be explored.

The problem behaviours range from attention seeking at the mildest level to disruption, aggression and violence at the other extreme. A range of factors may put a child 'at risk' of increasing problem behaviours. See the behavioural 'Richter scale' in Figure 6.1.

Minor attention-seeking behaviours can be exacerbated by other 'at risk' factors. For example if the teacher's social and communication skills are not well-developed this can result in the pupil's response becoming more disruptive. Coercive environments can have a similar effect.

A tendency to be attention seeking may also be exacerbated by other 'at risk' factors such as a new baby in the family, family discord and quarrelling. The extra stresses may prove too much for the pupil to manage and they leak out as an increasing wave of nuisance behaviour inimitable to school work. When this becomes a habit it may finally cause exclusion from school.

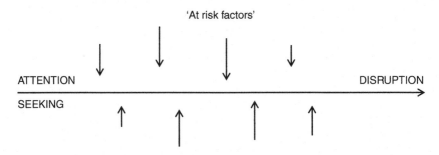

Figure 6.1 The behavioural continuum in classrooms

Disruptive behaviour

Disruptive behaviour is that which interferes with the learning and opportunities of other pupils and imposes undue stress upon the teacher (Elton, 1989). Disruption in class consists of bullying, aggression, verbal and non-verbal abuse to the teacher and other pupils, physical abuse of others or school property (destructiveness) and spoiling other children's work.

Negativism and disaffection, dreaming and worrying, unmotivation, refusal to comply with rules and requests are quieter forms of disruption, and the quietest of all is when pupils exclude themselves from education by daydreaming or truancy. Truancy is absenting oneself from school, from lessons, within lessons, or after registration and remaining on site. Pupils can then become vulnerable to other influences, take to petty theft in small groups, glue sniffing or alcohol abuse, or join gangs and be drawn into criminal activities. On any day in the school year (DCFS, 2014) there were 60,000 unauthorised absences from school.

Attention-seeking behaviours are constant chattering, calling out, silly noises, humming and whistling, chair and desk noises, hand constantly up for attention, crawling around the floor, clowning, verbal abuse, distracting other children, wandering. These too can arise from behavioural or emotional origins, or both.

Any level of problem or challenging behaviour is just the visible tip of a problem of disaffection that is widespread in schools particularly at secondary level and as such it cannot be effectively tackled in isolation from a systematic programme of school improvement. This has to begin with the upgrading and upskilling of all the teachers so that they know how to make the curriculum relevant and motivating for the learner. What also has to be tackled is the different views teachers have about what constitutes a problem and their role in its manifestation.

The main difficulties are that SEBDs are *socially disapproved* behaviours and teachers may have very different attitudes, perceptions and tolerance of them as shown in Chapter 5 on ADHD. These attitudes, such as a moral-punitive attitude, lead to very different interventions, some of which make situations worse.

Classroom disruption by various forms of attention seeking and distractibility is the problem behaviour of most concern to teachers. It can take many different forms depending on the pupil's personality. Underlying many of these problem behaviours seems to be a general inability to relate to peers, the teacher and the task. This may be because of lack of social skills training in the home, or from poor social models in the peer group and the media, because of the perceived irrelevance of the curriculum task and school goals, or because of a learning difficulty.

Delinquency

Delinquent acts such as stealing, truancy, arson, vandalism and substance abuse are 10:1 more common in boys than in girls. However, there is no clear-cut psychological distinction between a delinquent and a non-delinquent youth; the difference is a legal one. The delinquent is a young person who has been caught, not any pupil who has committed such an act. Surveys have revealed that 50–90 per cent of school children had committed indictable offences.

Delinquent acts by girls are in a ratio of 5:1 sexual acts before the legal age of consent. The rationale behind legal sanctions against these girls is questionable; abuse is a more likely diagnosis and they need care and protection. This is in the context where television portrays models engaging in overt sexual activity and in an age where the onset of puberty occurs nearly two years earlier than when such laws were made.

The Gluecks (1968) maintained that they could identify pre-delinquent behaviours in two-year-olds and the prognosis was poor where the onset appeared in early childhood. Teachers, however, are mostly concerned with pre-delinquent or non-delinquent problems, e.g. fighting, disruption, bullying, aggression, defiance, destructiveness, attention seeking and lying.

Other ways of looking at or dealing with these problems need to be considered, particularly in the form of education for parenthood for both boys and girls. In 2008 the incidence of delinquent acts by girls including aggression and violence had markedly increased in the UK and in many other countries (Zhang, 2008). The number of women consigned to prison has doubled in the last decade. However, it is argued that they are treated more harshly by judges than men committing the same crimes.

Girls are involved in the justice system at a younger age than previously and some for more violent offences (Zahn, 2009). Girls, compared with male counterparts, bring unique health and mental health issues with them into the juvenile justice system related to sexual assaults/abuse, trauma, unplanned pregnancies and adolescent motherhood (Lloyd, 2005).

Grooming on-line and in the community and cyberbullying have recently become major concerns. Teachers need training to identify the sometimes subtle changes in behaviour such activities bring. Disaffection and alienation may be bound up with this for both boys and girls and exclusion is the last response that is needed. These issues pose serious problems for intervention programmes. The current exclusion rates are 4:1 boys to girls.

In addition to these problems a number of other factors, including the over-filled national curriculum, the teaching methods encouraged by Ofsted inspections and the effects of high stakes assessment systems (Gregory and Clarke, 2003; Zhang, 2008), all conspire to construct failure and provoke disaffection. However, the behavioural problems are often secondary and may mask, for example, a learning difficulty or an emotional problem.

Perhaps the most difficult problem to deal with is the attitude held by the teacher. Some few teachers hold bizarre, rigid or inappropriate views about social behaviour in classrooms. This can seriously affect their interactions to the detriment of pupils. One such colleague can have a pervasive effect.

What really constitutes a problem?

The 'problem pupil' is distinguishable from the normal child only in degree. The differences are all relative as most normal children manifest adjustment problems and difficulties at some time in their school careers. They are really *pupils with problems* rather than problem pupils. Psychological maladjustment is a result of exaggeration of deficiencies or handicapping combinations of the behaviour problems common to all children.

In 1989 the Elton Report found that it was the constant low level of disruption in classrooms that caused teachers the most problems. These consisted of constant chattering – low-level talking and talking out of turn – and being out of place. In March 2008 the National Union of Teachers repeated an earlier survey with 1,500 teachers and found that low-level disturbance had increased and bullying had decreased. Overt aggression had decreased except in some low-functioning schools. They called for lower class sizes to enable them to cope. The Steer Report (2009) confirmed low-level noise was still the over-riding problem.

Although many pupils will come from difficult circumstances and have learnt to misbehave, the majority of them can become good learners with socially acceptable behaviour. It is the pupils who are emotionally disturbed whose behaviour cannot without therapy and special support come within normal bounds.

We too often locate the problem in the pupils or belonging to them and not in ourselves and our traditional systems and pedagogy. School is an unnatural place for a group of young people to be. At the most active and energetic period of their lives they are herded together in large groups and made to sit still for long periods, listening to a person who may not actually be teaching them anything but simply talking at them about things they see no point in knowing.

The nature of emotional difficulties

Emotion is a stirred-up state of the organism. It is non-specific in direction until environmental cues trigger fight, flight or freeze. If we fight we are angry; if we flee we are fearful. All individuals under emotional stress demonstrate a similar pattern of cues. They differ in their levels of reactiveness to stress. The bodily forces are mobilised for action as a result of some perceived danger.

Stress is the engendering of a higher than normal or useful level of emotion over a long period of time maintained by some perceived unpleasant or fear-inducing situation, as in bullying and abuse. There are three levels in emotion: physiological, behavioural, cognitive or experiential changes – feelings.

There are ten physiological changes in emotion: dilation of pupils of eyes, eyes widen, blinking increases or decreases depending on the reaction; increase in heart rate; pilomotor reflex – goose pimples, hairs on skin stand up; muscle tremor/ tension – may shake, become immobile or weak at the knees and sag; blood composition changes – more glucose released, adrenaline or noradrenaline circulated; galvanic skin response changes in sweat gland activity in the skin; respiration rate changes – sighing or rapid breathing; blood capillary flow changes – leading to blushing or blanching, muscles' supply of blood increased ready for 'fight or flight'; intestinal changes – digestive activities stop, in severe emotion 'decks cleared for action' – involuntary urination and defecation occurs; salivation response – mouth may become dry (c.f. the Biblical story of the Wisdom of Solomon and the Thief).

The behavioural changes in emotion include lunging forward, finger pointed, teeth bared, uttering high-pitched vocal noises in anger, head back, open mouthed, teeth bared, baying, whites of eyes wide and clear, gesticulating in 'threat' prepared to flee (see the faces of protest crowds, for example).

Cognitive or experiential aspects of emotion: In many instances the child feels 'hurt' and frustrated or justified in his/her behaviour, perceiving only a simple relationship between the 'trigger' and the action rather than being aware of the deeper seated emotional distress.

Emotional signs in the classroom:

- Fixed smile showing both sets of teeth bared in anxiety and fear. A cross teacher often says, 'Wipe that smile off your face!', and the child is so frightened he or she cannot.
- Child sitting or standing reading but just noticeably jigging shows undue sign of tension on task and perhaps fear of failure.
- Fixed watchfulness – eyelids retracted showing whites of eyes, fixed gaze, child seems unable to approach or withdraw, white round mouth, possible perspiration on upper lip and mottled red round neck. Common in cases of extreme approach-avoidance conflict in child abuse.
- Regression to thumb sucking when habit had previously been outgrown.
- Regression to temper tantrums and outbursts when these had previously been outgrown, after 3 years plus when they normally are repressed.
- Regression to baby talk and babyishness, even bedwetting, often when a new baby has arrived in the family.
- General attention-seeking behaviour, continuous low-level chattering, or uncontrollable giggling for no apparent reason. (Giggling as a response may also be a normal East Asian cultural response for girls).
- Sometimes enuresis or more severely encopresis, violence, fire setting, hypersexuality, some forms of stealing, each of which need specialist advice or referral, e.g. noting carefully what is stolen, shape of objects etc.

Pupils who 'act in' are more difficult to detect. They may go completely unnoticed in busy classrooms because they are quiet and withdrawn and cause no fuss. Their problems, however, do not go away and unless they receive help they may in later life develop severe emotional problems such as depression and self-harm that cause them to be hospitalised. These pupils need therapy.

In the area of emotion there is also the consideration of 'nervous health' and 'nervous illness'. In the former the child manages to maintain a relatively normal life and social interaction, whereas in nervous illness they cannot. Nervous illnesses include severe anxiety, phobias, depression, obsessive-compulsive disorders (OCD), hysteria, psychosomatic problems and anorexia.

There are also the two psychiatric illnesses: schizophrenia with an onset often at puberty (hebephrenic) but sometimes identifiable around 7 years, and bipolar disorder formerly known as 'manic depression' which was thought to have an onset well after adolescence but much earlier cases are now being detected. For the latter the signs are often very high energy levels and overactivity in adolescence, bordering on hyperactivity.

Case example – Jennifer

Jennifer, a bright girl, always had a propensity to giggle but in secondary school at puberty this developed into a severe, pervasive and continuous problem. She also maintained a continuous stream of low-level disconnected, often inane chatter. Her achievement levels declined and by 15 she was referred to the child mental health services and eventually diagnosed with schizophrenia.

Some people are more emotionally sensitive than others or are set to react in a more anxious manner to small stresses. Others require a considerable amount of sameness and order and become distressed if put under pressure or if there are too many unheralded changes. Those who cope with these problems and function adequately in society are said to be in neurotic health and those who do not can become 'neurotically ill'.

Education itself, if it is safe, supportive, enjoyable and motivating, can be *therapeutic* for such children. School for some may be the only safe place and behaviours such as staying in the classroom or lingering late around the school need to be identified and discreetly investigated.

While 'acting in' may be a function of the personality that the more introverted person is likely to do, certain types of trauma can also cause this, even in extroverts. For example, child abuse and bullying in and out of school can make children fearful and withdrawn. At the extremes, **'fixed watchfulness'** can be observed. The child stays on the outside of groups and activities watching; their eyes are wide, they have a tendency to look glazed and the whites or sclera can be seen above the iris – this is the fear profile.

Some children may seem to be tearful for no apparent reason or always sad. Even very young children in preschool can be depressed and weepy. It is essential to note this and take action, first by discussing the behaviour with the designated person who can observe and give advice. It may be necessary even at this early stage for the school to make contact with social services because there is a possibility of abuse.

An alternative explanation may be that the child is being bullied or ostracised within the school, in the playground or on the way to school. At the extremes such experiences may lead to suicidal thoughts and statements and even to action. It must not be forgotten that some teachers have a tendency to bully and School Phobia may arise not just from a separation anxiety related to the fear of leaving the mother but also of a genuine fear of being at school or journeying to and from it. Gifted children are often bullied or ostracised for being 'boffs' (boffins), or 'little professors' or just for being different.

Sexual abuse may cause children to 'act out' aspects of their experience with other children and adults, showing totally inappropriate behaviour and knowledge for their age.

Case example – Claire

Claire was an able pupil in Year 10 and had been a model pupil and academically successful, destined to do well. Half way through the year a new baby boy was born into the family. Within weeks, Claire became highly distractible and attention seeking. She never stopped talking; nothing could stop her. Over time she grew louder and more aggressive and disruptive. Temporary then permanent exclusion followed. Years later in therapy it transpired that her father had been sexually abusing her since the new baby had been born and she had been 'groomed' leading up to it.

Food fads and missing or refusing food at mealtimes may be the early signs that an anorexic problem could develop if there is a 'trigger'. Food is often the battleground for power conflict in families.

Although some children are naturally quiet and somewhat withdrawn it becomes a concern when it prevents them interacting with peers or the teacher or gaining educational experiences. An extreme case would be of the child who engages in '*selective mutism*'. He or she will not speak to anyone at all except perhaps at home or may only speak to friends and not to the teacher. Sometimes the onset can be observed as an apparently shy and very quietly spoken pupil gradually sinks into silence and seems even fearful of whispering. Reaching out to them through writing can help begin the therapeutic journey, whereas demanding them to speak out will not.

As can be seen, the reasons why a pupil may 'act in' can be very serious. However, it must be remembered that there are some pupils who are genuinely quiet. Others may have decided that school is too difficult or others that it is too easy and not really worth bothering about or engaging with. 'Acting in' can be indicative of more deep-seated problems, more difficult to identify and especially complex to deal with.

The nature of communication difficulties in SEBD

Many pupils lack the necessary social and communication skills to keep themselves out of trouble and this is the third important strand in the study of SEBD. Ten per cent of children in England and Wales have speech and language difficulties (Law *et al.*, 2000) and 71–74 per cent of children with SEBD have some type of communication problem (Benner, 2002); for some reason these are being recognised as behavioural rather than communication issues (Mackie and Law, 2014).

The nature of these difficulties also seems to be more to do with Pragmatic Language Disorder (PLD) rather than Specific Language Impairment (SLI). Law and Stringer (2014) noted it was very possible for difficulties with PLD to be interpreted as Behavioural Difficulties, e.g. causing disruption in group activities and conversations could be due to lack of understanding of turn-taking, failure to respond appropriately, not picking up on non-verbal information through facial expression and tone of voice. A PLD-focused approach is needed, as discussed in Chapter 4.

SEBD in all its forms may be accompanied by a high level of ability but with poor language and communication skills, especially in written communication (Montgomery, 2000, 2009). Gifted children often misbehave as they become bored at the slow progress of lessons or lack of intellectual challenge. They can quickly become labelled as 'disruptives' and excluded. Cole *et al*. (1998) identified at least 10 per cent of their special school SEBD population as more able learners, reluctant to write or share their feelings.

In oral terms we are used to the stereotype of the gifted, loquacious learner who is able to explain the most unlikely topic from an early age and ask questions that teachers have difficulty answering. We easily miss the gifted monosyllabic girl or boy communicating by grunt. They do not use extended language and when asked, for example, to describe what is happening in a series of cartoons showing a boy kicking a football which accidentally breaks a window will say, "'E dunnit dint 'e". He or she has sized up the situation very precisely but lacks the structure and practice needed to communicate this to someone else. The teacher needs to become the mediator helping the pupil learn the language and culture of the school.

The 'Talking Curriculum' described in Chapter 7 is essential for this pupil, as is the teaching of structures, scaffolds and protocols to make explicit what they know and understand. Communication games can begin this process where pupils sit back to back and one tells the other how to draw an apple or an elephant, or pupils tell the teacher how to journey from the classroom to the head's office, make a box and so on. It can be fun but the learning is serious. Science revision with younger pupils can be done through role-play. It is funny, problem-based and the players end by explaining what the experiment was.

Cohen *et al*. (1998) suggested that it was possible that 40 per cent of children with SEBD had undetected communication difficulties. These children were more likely to be referred to the Child Mental Health Services (CAMHS) for more difficult, more delinquent, and more severe behavioural and emotional problems than detected cases. They suggested that the behavioural incidents could be interpreted differently if it was known the children had communication difficulties. Unfortunately specialist provision for SEBD does not always address the communication issues, but we can and must in regular classrooms.

Able children and specific problem behaviours

Able children, like any others, come from a range of backgrounds and may arrive at school already showing emotional and behavioural difficulties. Others integrate happily into school but may eventually come into a situation where the curriculum and the delivery is too mundane or moves too slowly for them and they begin to find other amusements. These may include annoying other children, playing games on a smartphone, playing tricks on the teacher, clowning and so on. Some teachers can cope but others may be more rigid disciplinarians and soon the pupil is excluded from the class. The pattern is good behaviour in many classes but disruption in a few. It is often the only form a child's protest can take and it is the pedagogy and curriculum's cognitive challenge that need improving.

Provocateurs: Other pupils may behave impeccably but deliberately ask difficult questions to put teachers at a disadvantage. They can be very clever at making a teacher look foolish and getting other pupils in trouble for it. Teachers can find this intolerable and leave. Alternatively the pupil may deliberately orchestrate low-level disruption that is very tiring and has the same effect, promoting teacher stress and undermining authority. Mentoring both teacher and pupil is essential in these circumstances.

Perfectionism appears frequently in the gifted education literature but it is a widespread phenomenon across the ability range, perhaps more noticeable in this group. It appears to be a combination of thought and action associated with high standards and expectations about one's own performance. One way gifted students handle this, according to Sisk (2003), is to refuse to try a task if they feel they cannot do it in the manner in which they want to accomplish it.

> Perfectionism can become a stimulus for a lifetime of underachievement ... 50% of the referrals for problem behaviours came from homes and schools in which parents and professionals were unaware of the special needs and strengths of the gifted and talented.
>
> (Sisk, 2003: 134)

Perfectionism is again on the dimension of neurotic health and neurotic illness. The normal healthy perfectionist is successful, well integrated and functioning. The neurotic perfectionist is overly stressed by mistakes and failures. The following problems characterise neurotic perfectionism (Sisk, 2003):

- excessive concerns over mistakes
- high parental criticism
- peer criticism
- excessive emphasis on precision
- excessive need for order and organisation
- doubts about actions.

Internet Gaming Disorder

The *DSM-V* (APA, 2006, updated 2013: 797) identified Internet Gaming Disorder (IGD) as a problem arising from video-gaming and internet-based virtual communication, rather like the problems that arose from the 'one-armed bandits' fruit machines in earlier decades. The intermittent reinforcement they give sets up habituation and it is hard to disconnect.

The identifiers are that in a 12-month period five out of nine of the following are present for the diagnosis:

- forms the dominant activity in daily life
- abstinence causes withdrawal symptoms

- tolerance builds up
- lack of success in controlling participation
- loss of interest in previous hobbies
- continued and excessive gaming rises despite knowledge of the problems
- deceitful use and participation in gaming
- deceitful information on amount of regular use
- jeopardises marriage, career or school attainment.

Adolescents are most at risk of IGD and it jeopardises their school career and their mental and physical health.

Hillman (2014) was concerned about her gifted cases with IQs of 145+ whose parents were referring them for counselling. Characteristically they were spending longer on gaming than on schoolwork to the extent of six or seven hours and two hours or more on texting. They were getting only six or seven hours sleep and this was not enough. They became irascible and overactive, and could not concentrate on schoolwork. Some who joined virtual communities and had been given special roles within it can be drawn into a dark world and become brainwashed. Two girls, one on a gifted and talented programme, tried to murder a third on the programme acting out such roles.

Vulnerability

According to Sisk (2003) there is a common misconception that gifted adolescents, and particularly those in colleges and universities, have fewer personal problems and traumas. In their search for identity they experience diverse pressures and this can be manifested in rebellious behaviour, depression or in some cases suicide to solve it all.

Depression: Troubled students who take their own lives fall under the Anxiety Withdrawal dimensions of disordered behaviour and Perfectionism increases the chance of suicide more than Hopelessness. Some key indicators listed by Appleby and Condonis (1998) were:

- an actual suicide threat or statement indicating a desire to die
- an unsuccessful attempt at taking own life
- signs of mental depression, low energy levels and expressions of hopelessness and worthlessness
- changes in eating or sleeping patterns, more time spent alone or less interest in previous activities
- giving away prized objects.

It is important that peers, educators and counsellors respond immediately and work to change attitudes that make them resistant to gaining help and support. In this process many turn to Dabrowski's (1972) developmental theory of emotional development, which consists of two parts. The first are five overexcitabilities (OEs): psychomotor, sensual, imaginational, intellectual and emotional.

The second are five levels of development. At level 3 individuals are attempting to be true to themselves and uphold their principles whereas at levels 1 and 2 they are not so steadfast. At level 4 they are on their way to self-actualisation and at level 5 they have made it. Interventions involve using moral stories and myths to build emotional development.

Major Depressive Disorder (MDD) (APA, 1994) is often regarded as suppressed anger or even rage at, for example, the death of loved ones, earlier abuse or identity crisis. It is being considered as a factor in the vulnerability of some able youths to conversion, radicalisation and externalised aggression.

Problem pupils or problem schools?

The consequences of SEBD in schools are that the pupil misses a lot of the lessons and opportunities for learning. Lost learning opportunities can lead to underachievement and loss of life chances. These are effects that can last life long if there is no opening to get back into education and training.

Learners who have led undisciplined lives at home will be ill prepared for the needs for self-control and self-management in classrooms. Their behaviour patterns will be likely to predispose them to conflict with the discipline and ethos exerted by the teacher and another dynamic interaction arises as conflict. The personality of the participants in the conflict and their social and communication skills will determine the route that the conflict will take, either to disruption or to control.

Boy and girl 'codes' and cultures will predispose learners to react in certain ways to different types of classroom experiences. For example, it may not be 'cool' for boys to be seen to work or make an effort. Older girls may feel it is unfeminine to appear brainy and succeed in school or STEM (science, technology, engineering and mathematics) subjects. Clever children do not want to be bullied or laughed at because they are 'boffs', so often underperform. In some schools difference of any sort may be picked on and exploited in unpleasant ways and encourage behaviour problems such as bullying. Amusing pupils with SEBD are better tolerated by the system and survive better in it and for longer. The more demanding pupils with SEBD take up too much teacher time and are rejected by peers (Warnock, 2007).

The English high stakes assessment system also has its consequences. If pupils do not achieve high levels in SATs (School Assessment Tasks), at Level 5 or above (4 is the mean) they can feel that they are failures, just as they did under the old Eleven Plus system when children at 11 were given an IQ test and the top 20 per cent went to a grammar school. The rest went to a secondary modern or a technical school and an underclass of losers was created, the 80 per cent who had 'failed' their 11 plus. In East Asian schools, one in three primary school children felt that life was not worth living and fear of failure was dominant (Gregory and Clarke, 2003).

Such assessment systems not only induce feelings of fear and failure in large numbers of pupils who are not failures at all, but also cause the teachers to narrow the curriculum and teach to the tests. They do not give enough time to pupils' learning and so didactics and drill predominate. Pupils from disadvantaged backgrounds cannot thrive in such environments. These systems create disaffection and alienation in large numbers of pupils so that the behaviour problems increase as the pupils see much of what they have to do as irrelevant. Stronger disciplinary regimes are then brought into play, using extrinsic and coercive techniques to suppress unwanted behaviours. Self-regulation and lifelong learning are expunged in such systems (Ryan and Deci, 2000).

When there is an over emphasis upon academic goals and a neglect of personal needs more children seem disposed to fail and become 'problem children' in the schools' eyes (Lawrence *et al.*, 1989; Mongon and Hart, 1989; Rutter *et al.*, 1979). It is also a system that can be regarded as a bullying culture from the government down. Official bullying begins with targets and instructions that are enforced by a rigid inspection system and league tables that promote competition on a wide scale for pupils and resources. Teachers bully and coerce pupils into working hard to meet the targets to enable the school to rise in the league tables. In the classroom, playground and on Facebook and Twitter we see the result: bullying, scapegoating and 'trolling'.

The differences observed cannot be attributed to the catchment areas which the schools serve. The implication is that the number of pupils regarded as having SEN on the basis of their difficult behaviour depends more on the school they happen to be attending than on the pupils themselves or their families (Galloway and Goodwin, 1987).

Mongon and Hart (1989) emphasised the 'role of fear' in schools. Although we are often most concerned by pupils asserting themselves and challenging the teachers' discipline, they drew attention to the fact that despite the kindliest intentions on the part of teachers fear was the central debilitating characteristic of many pupils' school experience. They stated that the effect of the hidden curriculum may be a legitimate criticism of the schooling process which exerts a destruction of dignity that is so massive and pervasive that few subsequently recover from it.

All these factors represent a *coercive* schooling ethos which when faced with difficult or awkward pupils immediately rules them as out of order, blameworthy, problem pupils to be excluded.

The teacher factor – the dynamic driver of the system

Teachers are the prime motivators and managers of all the interactions in classrooms. They are part of the dynamics of the situation and drive it. They design and direct the curriculum, the tasks and the pedagogy. Those pupils whom teachers regard as more successful tend to be given far greater attention than others. The teachers interacted with them more frequently, paid closer attention to their activities, subtly structuring and directing their efforts in ways that were noticeably different from the relationships with pupils less favourably categorised (Good and Brophy, 1986; Sharp and Green, 1975). Spender (1983) found that boys in particular received and demanded more attention and information from teachers than girls. This can contribute to their greater success and opportunities in classrooms. It can also mean they are given higher marks for lower standards of work (Briggs, 1980; Soloff, 1973; Sweedler-Brown, 1992). A decade later these differences could still be observed (Montgomery, 2002).

Self-esteem, self-concept, self-image

Pupils with SEBD underachieve and suffer from a massive lack of self-esteem, as recorded in many researches. The worse their behaviour, the lower their self-esteem and their likely achievement, however bright they really are. Self-esteem is a barometer of school/college life well-being and success, as well as a vulnerable entity to be protected and built by positive experiences if the person is to be successful, well-adjusted and fulfilled.

Self-esteem reflects the evaluation that a person typically makes of him or herself. It conveys an element of approval or disapproval and the extent to which you see yourself as worthwhile, significant and capable of dealing with life. It can undergo constant revision throughout life and is a personal judgement. How we see ourselves is constructed from the information we receive from others, such as in the interactions in the home, school and the environment.

The Steer Report (2009) emphasised that most pupils behave well in school and it is rare to find challenging behaviours. Those that do engage in them do not do so all the time. The Report found that the small minority who engaged in problem behaviours were usually from difficult and disadvantaged family circumstances and their needs were becoming increasingly complex. Their needs were to be distinguished from the general 'irritating low-level nuisance behaviours' identified by the Elton Report (1989) and account should be taken that childhood is a period when mistakes are made and lessons learned.

School leaders did not make sufficient use of the powers that they had, according to this report. They needed to *intervene early* and not permit problem pupils to disturb the learning of others. They needed to make use of 'withdrawal' sooner and more frequently than they did. Every school needed a 'withdrawal room' or rooms to use as a temporary measure to stop class disruption.

The strongest recommendation among many in the report was that *schools be required to have a learning and teaching policy that underpinned the behaviour policy.* Despite English schools being required to have more than 60 different policies, the official bureaucracy omitted this one! It is the most important of all and Ofsted surveys and inspections had consistently shown that the quality of teaching and learning experienced by pupils directly affected their behaviour in schools and classrooms. A system governed by professionals would not have overlooked this.

Successive English governments have issued a multitude of reports, initiatives and notes for guidance on SEBD and Boyle and Bragg (2007) analysed the effects of 14 of them since 1997 on Key Stage 3 results at 375 schools during 2004–2005. They took into account such variables as school size and free school meals entitlements. The research found none of the initiatives had any positive effect on attainment, numeracy and literacy. They labelled initiatives such as the Secondary Strategy (£170 million) and the Excellence in Cities (£1.7 billion) as costly wastes of time.

Brain, behaviour and development of SEBD

The key message is that relationships change brains (Sunderland, 2014). Because childhood is a period of exuberant brain development, early experience has a disproportionate impact on the development of brain systems. In adulthood relationships change the brain; in childhood they organise actual brain systems (Perry, 2002). In order to learn well we need optimal levels of noradrenaline/dopamine and opioids. This enables us to be alert, focused, thinking well, and able to block out distractions. Levels of noradrenaline (norepinephrine) which are too low result in lethargy, depression, dull flatness, boredom and a compromised immune system. Levels which are too high result in irritability, anxiety, agitation, fear and anger.

Recent biochemical studies of attachment. Studies of brain chemicals have shown how important early relationships are for brain development and the kinds of therapy that might be appropriate when things have gone wrong. Some children have so few positive relational experiences that they do not develop the capacity to be socially appropriate, empathic, self-regulating and humane. By the age of 10 years they have only had the number and quality of the social interactions of a 5-year-old (Perry, 2002). Perry suggested that these children need repeated positive and constructive experiences and that school staff should record the numbers to ensure that a child who needs them is not overlooked.

The case of Stephen

Stephen had entered Reception class like a little wild thing and could not sit still for an instant on the mat to listen to a story. But within a month had learnt to do so. Whenever the teacher or LSAs saw a near appropriate behaviour, he would receive positive reinforcement using successive approximations techniques.

Those children destined to be the most troublesome offenders in teenage years were already violent by 3 years old (Tremblay *et al.*, 2005). They had experienced relational stress and relational poverty. The most violent adolescents did not become more violent; they were already very violent at age 6 and were distinguishable at the age of 3 by levels of aggression 10 times higher than the most peaceable 30 per cent of toddlers.

Leaving children in high levels of stress can programme the brain's alarm systems to be hypersensitive and over-aroused and this interrupts learning and concentration and enjoyment of friends and play. It is therefore essential that schools provide safe places for distressed children and use calming techniques to help them. Typically schools use tai chi, drumming, meditation, Massage in Schools and yoga at the beginning of the school day or lessons to help calm the body down.

It is only since advances in cognitive neuroscience such as fMRI that more subtle organisation and differences in brain functioning have been uncovered. Viding *et al.* (2009) found that the amygdala in severely conduct-disordered boys was smaller than in controls with similar results found recently in behaviourally disturbed girls. The amygdala is part of the limbic system in the paleocortex (the old 'reptilian' brain) and is involved in feelings of empathy.

A smaller amygdala is thus thought to be associated with lower or a lack of empathy, predisposing children and adults to behave in callous and unemotional (CU) ways. CU subjects did not respond to punishment and negative consequences but self-interest strategies and rewards were more effective. It is possible that a number of conditions can lead to the smaller amygdala size in different people. It may result from damage, genetic inheritance or *suboptimal family care over months and years.* This could account for the ways in which discordant families create disruptive behaviour in their offspring. Even so, not all children in such a family become conduct disordered so some are more vulnerable and others more resilient.

It is also known that brains, particularly young ones, are extraordinarily plastic and thus a Multisystemic Therapy is recommended (Sunderland, 2014). The cases of child murderers have shown that their conduct can be retrieved in many cases where in secure confinement they find a caring and consistent carer and mentor.

School breakfasts have also improved academic performance, psychological well-being and behaviour. Non-breakfast eaters were found to be 30 per cent more likely to be hyperactive. Pupils who went from rarely eating breakfast had big upswings in academic performance. They became significantly less depressed, anxious and hyperactive (cited in Carper, 2000: 113–14). The introduction of free school meals in English infant years from September 2014 is hoped to have the same effect.

Attachment theory and emotional development

Attachment theory holds that a distinct pattern of attachment is evident in infants by the age of 10 months to 1 year, whether it derives from a secure or an insecure attachment relationship. The outcome of this primary attachment is a sense of self in relation to others – an internal working model.

A secure attachment will result in a person who is likely to approach the world with confidence and when faced with potentially alarming situations will tackle them with confidence or seek help in order to do so. The notion of self develops as a potentially loveable and valuable person.

The infant who has not experienced the secure attachment rearing process and whose needs in this respect have not been adequately met comes to perceive the world as a comfortless and unpredictable place. This infant will respond by shrinking from it or doing battle with it – an insecure working model (Bowlby, 1990).

The key relational needs for secure attachment are attunement, empathic listening, containment, soothing and calming (Sunderland, 2014). Secure attachment relationships create the appropriate balances in brain chemistry in the frontal and other areas. Where there have been attachment failures, appropriate educational and social and communication experiences can retrieve the situation, according to these new researches.

Such experiences should have been provided within the family but schools may need to provide for them in cases where they have been absent. A trained Reception class LSA can help support such children and ease them into education. This is also where Nurture Groups in both primary and secondary schools have been able to help.

Common causes of interruptions to learning include (Sunderland, 2014):

- a family culture of commands and criticisms
- parents who do not know how to do relational play
- too few experiences of parent as co-adventurer
- a family culture of questions not comments.

Examples:

- 'Look I will show you how to do it correctly/properly' (parent takes over the paintbrush).
- 'No, not like that! See you are getting paint everywhere. Do it like this'.
- Wrist gripping, disapproving taps; frowns, glaring eyes; talking over child's talk – not listening.

Even though these are not abusive interactions they apparently still have very serious deleterious consequences for the child's biochemical balances and learning.

Early Years education has a distinct role in counteracting this style of parenting by providing an educative framework that acts as a counterculture and corrects the effects of these experiences. Even secondary schools need to make such provision as problems emerge. First they need to consider how their systems may have provoked the problem and if necessary change them. Successful schools in disadvantaged environments achieve this. Tatum (1984) stated, 'I would argue that schools … need to change so that they become less rejecting of certain categories of pupils' (p. 95). Thirty years later this is still the case.

The pupils' voice

Something that is vitally important in a discussion of need are the views of the young people themselves. In a study by Wise and Upton (1998) 36 pupils aged 12–16 (31 boys and 5 girls), all attending special school for EBD in the south of

England having been excluded from mainstream, were interviewed about their perceptions of schools. They said that:

- schools were too large, impersonal and institutionalised;
- classes were too large and teacher/pupil ratios too high;
- 'bad' teaching, involving inconsistency, unfairness, lack of control, aggressive and authoritarian methods of discipline, lack of academic and/or personal support in meeting individual needs, impersonal relationships;
- irrelevant curriculum or too challenging;
- social difficulties such as bullying, coupled with inadequate support and understanding from schools and teachers when dealing with this issue. (p. 10)

These findings replicate those of Kerry (1983) with gifted learners and Pomerantz and Pomerantz (2004) with gifted underachievers and many other similar surveys that include the pupil voice. For example, McManus (1989) found:

> Many studies find that pupils of all ages and dispositions to be in general agreement about how teachers should behave. Teachers must keep order, explain things clearly, have interesting lessons … teachers who had not interested them and had picked on them unfairly deserve to be treated with disrespect.
> (p. 112)

Size of school was also found to be a relevant factor. In 2005 there were only five schools in England containing more than 2,000 children; in 2008 there were 21. Research has shown (DCFS, 2007) that pupil attainment increases up to a school size of about 1,200 students and then tails off. The US experience is that smaller schools have had a positive effect on pupil attendance and behaviour but, as yet, no gain in exam performance (Stevenson, 2006).

Checklist for identification of SEBD in classrooms

- sudden deterioration in standard of schoolwork
- restlessness and inability to concentrate in class – poor work
- irritability and sulkiness
- aggressiveness often with little provocation
- acts of delinquency, particularly stealing articles of little value to give away, despite punishment
- attention-seeking behaviour, e.g. repeated clowning as a means of attracting attention
- emergence of a speech defect
- excessive daydreaming
- a tendency to rapidly changing moods
- failure to keep or make friends, e.g. over-shy or inhibited
- oversensitivity when criticised or corrected

- withdrawn, e.g. isolated in class, lives in world of his/her own; difficult to make contact with
- continuous stream of chatter and an inability to stop, or uncontrollable giggling
- explosive outbursts at the least provocation
- negativism and refusal to work or make any effort
- setting light to other pupils' work on shelves or in cupboards
- scribbling over other children's work.

Many of these difficulties may stem from inconsistent rearing patterns at home and an aversion to school or from more deep-seated emotional origins. These origins may not be easily discovered and thus, as well as effective teaching and learning geared to the pupil's need, the education on offer needs to be 'therapeutic' including opportunities for affective and social skills training and resilience building.

Helping the most challenging pupils

Challenging behaviour is that which is beyond the attention-seeking mild end of the continuum. It is disruptive of other children's learning and the teacher may find it very difficult even impossible to manage without help. For children who have consistently displayed challenging behaviour Harris (1995) identified the following strategies that were found to be most effective:

- forming a positive relationship with one adult
- amending the rewards and sanctions system for this pupil
- matching learning tasks to strengths of pupils
- focusing on teaching language and communication
- helping the child to anticipate sequences of events and activities
- allowing the child to opt out of specific activities
- conveying adult expectations clearly and providing instant feedback
- providing a written protocol for all staff, describing how to respond to specific behaviours.

Again we can see the evidence for good teaching and learning strategies helping improve even the worst behaviour in schools. Giving the child some autonomy and developing social and personal skills as well as basic skills also support better behaviour.

General strategies for dealing with SEBD

Applied Behavioural Analysis

Applied Behavioural Analysis (ABA) is of necessity positive and supportive, builds self-esteem, re-teaches basic skills where necessary and improves academic achievement. The main principles were discussed in Chapters 4 and 5 and included positive reinforcement, time out, modelling, behaviour contract and CBT (Chapter 5). Rogers (2007) has been a major exponent of positive behaviour management in classrooms.

Increasing emotional literacy

Goleman (1995) identified emotional literacy as a necessary component but one that was lacking in many school curricula. It has been found to help in diminishing SEBD. Emotional literacy involves the ability to manage yourself and your emotions and to understand how other people are thinking and feeling.

Teaching for emotional literacy tries to get the pupils to change from feeling and taking action (fight or flight) to FEELING – THINKING – ACTION. The idea is to get them to employ coping strategies and reduce the angry outbursts (Stop-Think-then Do). The strategies involve use of stories, circle time, problem-based learning, mediation, conflict resolution, peer mentoring and buddy systems.

Circle time

This is a popular method for promoting emotional literacy. It originated with the Quakers in the US to assist in crowd control and was introduced by them in the UK in the 1980s. Bowers and Wells (1988) with Rawlings (1996) helped reduce behaviour problems in local schools using the techniques.

If teachers can learn the warning signs of emotion they can stop triggering the outbursts. This involves work in small groups and pairs as well as class activities. Talking, listening and empathising with others, with little or no written work involved, enables pupils of all levels to feel involved and engaged. It promotes better relationships, improves social skills and increases positive behaviour and self-esteem, as reported by schools and teachers engaged in the different projects (Curry and Bromfield, 1994).

Circle time can be used to:

- identify children who have SEN
- promote sharing feelings and experience
- help develop self-esteem and achievement
- influence curriculum content and school policy.

The pupils sit round in a circle and first there is a 'warm-up' activity, e.g.

- complete a sentence or tag line in turn round the group
- pass an object and only those holding the object may speak (throw a sock bundle)
- mirror me
- listening to one minute's 'silence'.

There is then the central theme, followed by a finishing-off activity. A central theme might be 'listening skills' and the pupils engage in 'celebrity interviews'.

They sit facing each other, feet or knees just touching, and one pupil tells the other pupil about themselves for two or three minutes (depending on age). The group then return to the circle and the listeners report to the rest of the group what they have learnt about their partner. This is a useful beginning for a class activity when they do not know each other very well. They reverse roles and do the task again. At the end, the facilitator draws out from the group their experiences during the task and their reflections on it and how they might improve their listening skills.

Another theme may be bullying and a problem-solving activity using a story can be the central topic for discussion. The facilitator can then draw out personal experiences and the group can work on suggestions for avoiding and preventing bullying. Part of a series of sessions may be to get them to see the bullying from the victim's point of view and vice versa.

The social skills of taking turns, listening, being sensitive and supportive are all targeted in the various sessions. Circle time works best and has the most impact when the teacher is the facilitator. Throughout the sessions it is very important to celebrate success.

Circles of support

Although weekly circle time has been used within schools for many years to resolve issues, it has also evolved and developed. The DfES (2005) published *Social and Emotional Aspects of Learning* (SEAL) and within that programme was small-group work called 'Silver Set' that had similar aims and methods.

Research into circle time has been undertaken by Campaign for Learning (Mosley, 2008) and has shown that attainments in literacy and numeracy were lifted, boys' scores had been improved, more resilience was created and some inappropriate behaviours had been modified.

Circles of support was developed from circle time and is designed to provide more intensive work for children who cannot access or completely benefit from mainstream approaches. They involve four or more children with greater need and some without, but not more than ten children in a group. Each group needs two facilitators and a quiet room in which to work with a formal slot in the timetable in which to operate.

> In many cases these children need to regain or reinforce their sense of self-worth; a feeling of control over their behaviour and action; a positive new image; a guarantee of some success within school. (Mosley, 2008: 20)

The programmes develop emotional literacy and social skills and offer some therapeutic time within school. Schools should introduce a whole-school system to support communication before introducing circles of support.

Conflict management and mediation

Following the work of The Kingston Workshop Group (Bowers and Wells, 1988), the members ran conflict management workshops for victims of bullying who had called in on a local helpline. These sessions were run for a number of months every Saturday morning to enable the victims to talk about what had happened to them and to teach them ways of avoiding conflict by negotiating themselves out of potentially difficult and hostile situations, and by enabling them to learn and practise interpersonal and conflict management skills.

Problem management was the tip of the iceberg and not all problems were resolved. However, practising together the skills involved helped considerably. Through practising these skills and developing a framework for problem management to which everyone has access, a problem can be explored with a constructive solution more likely to be the outcome. In other words, the problem is separated from the people.

Peer mediation

'Mediators not Gladiators' – reducing playtime conflicts that often spill over into the classroom can be effectively achieved by training pupils to become playtime mediators.

Mediation is when a neutral third party intervenes in a dispute, not to decide on a course of action which is binding (arbitration), but who will, through a formal process, guide the people in dispute to a solution that is identified and agreed by themselves. Mediation is *not*:

- finding out who is right or wrong
- apportioning blame
- deciding what ought to be done.

Mediation does not start with a preconceived outcome, other than to discover the way forward from the present situation, which is most likely to bring about reconciliation, solution or an acceptable accommodation of the problem. The benefits of mediation are improved communication and the schools involved reported improved behaviour, e.g.

- a decrease in the number of playtime conflicts
- the development of critical thinking, listening, self-confidence and self-responsibility
- increased awareness of other pupils' problems. (Rawlings, 1989)

In addition, pupils who had been trained in the mediation process used their skills at home and with other adults. The process allowed the disputants to:

- define their own problem
- identify and express their feelings and needs
- hear the needs and feelings of the other person
- visualise their own solutions
- create options

- negotiate and agree a course of action
- write and sign an agreement
- evaluate progress and re-negotiate if necessary.

Nurture groups

Nurture groups were devised and set up in the London area in the 1970s by Marjorie Boxall (2002), an educational psychologist working with the local inspectorates. The Nurture Group (NG) was devised to help integrate preschool children with severe social, emotional and behavioural problems into mainstream Reception classes. At its zenith there were over 30 NGs in operation. The experiment continued for more than ten years but then was discontinued when 'secondary school teachers took over the inspectorate and could not see the value of them' (Bennathan, personal communication, 1998).

It was fortunate that detailed records had been kept and Bennathan and Boxall were able to track the original NG children into secondary school and beyond. They found that compared with similar children with SEBD their NG children had been able to maintain their places in mainstream and had not been excluded for SEBD. The patterns for the two groups were significantly different and thought worthy of further trials and investigations (Bennathan and Boxall, 2000; O'Connor and Colwell, 2002).

The NG is an educational bridge into full-time education in mainstream school. The purpose is to meet unmet developmental or early learning needs so that the children are prepared for schooling. The Group room therefore contains some elements of the home environment such as soft furnishings, kitchen and dining facilities. The preferred group size is 10–12 children, with two adults always present.

In the classical NG situation the pupils remain on the mainstream roll. They attend registration in the morning and attend the mainstream activities for at least one afternoon a week to maintain contact with peers. This attendance at regular classes is increased during the phased reintegration period.

The purpose of the NG is not to usurp the parental role but to provide educational attachment. The two adults model positive, proactive social interactive behaviours and cooperation.

The daily routine of the NG is explicit, uniform and predictable, unlike many of the children's own backgrounds. There are periods of individual interaction and periods of group instruction. There are periods of literacy, numeracy, free play and structured physical activity. The children take break with the other children in the school but there is a traditional mid-morning breakfast with staff and the N. Groupers – a formal dining period usually with toast and jam, in which social interaction takes place. Using the Boxall Profile, a Developmental Inventory, developmental and social needs are assessed and worked on.

In the 1990s permanent exclusions rose by 400 per cent and these were mainly from primary schools. This quickened the interest in NGs because the evaluation data had just become available. New NGs were set up, not only in primary but also in secondary schools, and some of the classical conditions were altered. In addition a number of other researchers set out to evaluate their effects. For example, Reynolds *et al.* (2009) studied 179 pupils aged 5–7 years with SEBD. Half the children were in NGs in 16 different schools and half were not in NGs. They found that the pupils in NGs had made significant improvements in self-esteem, self-image, emotional maturity and attainment in literacy compared to the rest.

They examined the records for 546 children with a mean age of 6 years, 5 months in 34 different schools that were in high deprivation areas with low academic attainment. The most significant gains were found in Terms 1 and 2 in SEBD. The gains over Terms 3 and 4 continued in educational tasks. NGs that had been established for more than two years were significantly more effective as the effectiveness of NG staff improved over time. They concluded that NGs contributed significantly to the nurturing school by using social constructivist pedagogy.

Iszatt and Waslewska (1997) examined the cases of 308 children in NGs during 1984–1998 and found that 87 per cent were able to return to mainstream within a year. In 1993, 83 per cent of the group was still in mainstream. Secondary schools had similar successes with NGs.

Resilience building

Pupils' behaviour has for a considerable time been viewed through the lens of deficit, adversity and disadvantage. Recently a more positive initiative is to try to identify how some pupils triumph over such adversity and achieve well in school and later life. This is the 'resilience perspective' of competence and success despite adversity and disadvantage.

By adversity is meant severe and prolonged disadvantage such as poverty, membership of an ethnic minority or individual/family traumatic experiences. Early studies showed that what shielded and hardened children changed focus to what were protective factors. The following were identified:

1. Caring and supportive relationships between pupils and teachers and amongst pupils
2. An accessible, meaningful and engaging curriculum
3. Active participation in the classroom

These factors not only benefitted already motivated children (Solomon *et al.*, 2000) but also operated in adverse circumstances to help disadvantaged children (Masten and Coatsworth, 1998).

The conclusions from resilience research showed that resilience building can be done by the common contextual processes that apply to all pupils irrespective of individual or group characteristics.

> These schools are proactive, inclusive and health-promoting social systems, promoting well-being, learning and achievement of all, rather than trying to prevent failure and dysfunction amongst students considered at risk.
>
> (Cefai, 2004: 151)

Resilience is regarded as a dynamic process changing over time and situations. In school it is viewed as contextual and relational, dependent on processes taking place in school and classroom contexts. It is a holistic view of development and competence.

Within this ecological context (Bronfenbrenner, 1989) schools assume a very important role in the lives of children. According to Watkins and Wentzel (2002), focusing on the 'grammar school' model of schooling that concentrates on teaching performance rather than on students' learning hinders pupils' development as creative, caring and responsible learners. It makes it impossible for a substantial number of pupils to succeed and be 'resilient'.

Resilience is construed as both socio-emotional competence and educational engagement. Social competence is construed as social and communication skills as age appropriate, and enjoyment of classes and a liking for school – the antithesis of disaffection and alienation. Social competence factors include:

- establishing and maintaining a range of positive social behaviours
- refraining from harming others and avoiding harming behaviours
- contributing collaboratively to peer group and school
- engaging in behaviours that enhance and protect health.

Mindfulness and Cognitive Behaviour Therapy (MCBT)

Mindfulness (Dweck, 2006) has become popular recently even with politicians but Hillman (2014) recommends it for children with behaviour difficulties in particular. She uses it with her gifted caseload to open up conversations about their problems and makes it part of her cognitive behavioural interventions with significant success. The slow breathing and counting and pausing as a starting exercise helps the child to centre in him or herself and is a calming strategy widely applicable to pupils with ASD, ADHD and SEBD.

Developing social and self-management skills

It is not untypical that children with behavioural difficulties often have problems interacting satisfactorily with both peers and teachers, although this is not always the case. Poor social skills may well be the reason for them being seen as a challenge to teachers and to good order. But there are necessary conditions for positive social interaction and the development of friendships, such as the opportunity to be with other children frequently enough; continuity – being involved with the same group over time; support – being helped and encouraged to make contact with other children, such as visiting and staying at a friend's.

However, children with difficulties do not always model the age-appropriate social models around them or they may have immature development in these areas. Other children may reject or provoke them because of this difference. Identifying these difficulties in classrooms can be undertaken by discreet observation and mapping friendship patterns using checklists and rating scales.

Intervention strategies to help develop social interaction skills

- collaborative group work involving real group activity and problem solving
- think – pair – share strategies in all curriculum areas (see Chapter 7)
- use of circle time activities
- topic work – using it to make friends, team building
- planned programmes of work in personal, social and health education (PSHE) to include conflict management and anger management
- role-play and trust building work in drama, dance and physical education (PE)
- team-building work in games, PE and other curriculum and extra curriculum activities as appropriate
- adequate and appropriate teacher and adult models, showing respect to children
- character analysis in relation to social skills in English and History
- deliberate intervention, modelling and direct teaching as appropriate
- cognitive intervention, modelling through use of videos or TV where appropriate
- discussion and information time to create understanding of differences
- social and therapeutic stories giving models of successful strategies
- peer mentoring and buddy systems
- setting up a nurture group
- pre-teaching to the problem pupil a special skill or information which the group needs
- developing mediation skills and buddy systems
- assertiveness training to harness aggression and help children understand that they have rights to express their feelings
- using imaginative story reading as a basis for learning about social skills.

Maintaining positive interactions with others

These are particular behaviours that help us initiate and maintain positive interactions with others and then how to close or terminate these when desired in appropriate ways.

- eye contact
- smiling, showing interest
- social space
- greeting and meeting
- quality of voice
- engaging in age-appropriate conversation
- play with others
- gaining attention and asking for help
- personal hygiene
- accepting criticism
- dealing with aggression and anger in others
- dealing with one's own anger and frustration
- inhibiting irritating behaviours, e.g. interrupting, not listening, etc.

In some instances specific social skills may need to be taught and the following procedure is generally used in social skills programmes.

Social skills training model

1. *Define the skill* to be taught, describe and discuss it. Illustrate it if possible with a video or simulations using puppets.
2. *Model the skill* Break it down into components or steps, then demonstrate these or get a pupil to do this.
3. *Imitation and Rehearsal* The pupil tries out the skill.
4. *Feedback* is given on the performance in a supportive manner, e.g. coaching is required and video recording can help.
5. *Application* Provide opportunities for the skill to be used and generalised to the school setting.
6. *Intermittent reinforcement* Watch for the pupil applying the skill on his or her own initiative and provide praise and reward.

As social skills improve the pupil receives natural reinforcement from peers, rewarding the progress with more and more positive interaction.

Self-regulation in the learning situation

If a pupil is intrinsically motivated by something s/he will want to study for its own sake and complete the task in hand whether the teacher is present or not. The fact that pupils, especially those with behaviour problems, spend a lot of time off-task shows that they are not fully 'brain engaged' and motivated by the task.

Behaviour management as already described can help settle the pupil to the task. Pupils may also need help in organising themselves – self-management skills. For example, they may need help with organising materials, knowing how and when to seek help from the teacher or from peers, knowing what to do when work is completed, checking work, maintaining attention and concentration without constant supervision.

Behaviour management also includes how to follow the established class and school routines for collecting apparatus, changing lessons, bringing PE equipment, walking not running in the corridors, talking quietly not loudly, and so on. In addition it includes the management and control of one's emotions and behaviour and links can be made here with mindfulness and the emotional literacy techniques already described.

Restorative justice

Restorative justice has developed from traditions in a number of different communities that include the New Zealand Maori people, North American First Nation groups and Christian faith groups. It is a process by which all the parties with a stake in a particular offence come together and collectively resolve how to deal with its aftermath and the implications for the future.

Individuals harmed by a particular act are vital to the process and addressing their needs is central. Engagement of all those involved in an offence include the person who committed the offence and their supporters, and the person who was harmed and their supporters. These people must work together to ensure the needs of the harmed individual have been met. Full participation and consensus are required to heal what has been broken, seek full and direct accountability, reunite what has been divided and strengthen the community to prevent further harms.

The circle seating structure is often used in restorative justice conferences. It represents the equality of all participants and encourages group interaction. In First Nation cultures it describes how everything is connected together and events that happened in the past continue to affect the present in a person's life. It also represents the natural order of creation.

In practice restorative justice is used in persistent cases of bullying, theft and exclusions from school when other interventions have failed. It demands a considerable investment of time as one session is seldom effective. It also requires the services of a trained and skilled mediator.

Assertive Discipline

Assertive Discipline (AD) was developed by Lee and Marlene Canter in the US in the 1970s (Canter and Canter, 2002). It is a method of disciplining based on behaviour modification. It consists of a highly structured system of rewards and punishments. Rewards may be stars, merit marks, play time, and even tangible rewards such as prizes and gifts earned by the collection of tokens or merit points. Gifts are less popular in the UK than in the US.

The punishments or consequences are at no more than five levels of increasing severity. AD makes explicit what children are expected to do and what will happen if they disobey the rules. Rules are kept to a minimum and the emphasis is on rewards and praise. At the beginning of the school year the rules and sanctions are explained and the pupils are left to choose if they will obey.

- Every time the teacher gives an instruction two children are praised for following it before one is corrected for not doing so.
- Notes are sent home to parents telling them when their child has worked very well, as well as when they have not.
- The rewards and sanctions vary to be age-range appropriate.

When pupils break a rule (such as 'no running in the classroom') there are levels of sanctions, e.g.

- On the first occasion the pupil's name is written on the board or in a special notebook. Three namings lead to a level-two sanction.
- Isolation within the class for a short period.
- Then loss of part of playtime.

- Then sending to the deputy head or head or isolation in a different classroom for 30 minutes.
- Report to parents and parent interview.

Different sanctions have to be worked out for different rules as well as different age groups. There are also a few pupils who will not or cannot respond to such techniques and special rules and strategies need to be developed.

One Manchester junior school whose pupils were extraordinarily difficult and disruptive, some of whom had tried to burn their school down, was introduced to AD. After one training day the teachers were able to use it. The rules were:

- follow the rules the first time they are given
- hands up for attention
- keep hands and feet to yourself
- finish work within the given time
- call everyone by their given name.

If the children reached the end of the discipline line in one day, teachers visited the parents. In the first week the deputy head visited four families each day. They discussed sanctions to reinforce the messages of the school, e.g. no television that evening or early bed, never physical punishment. In week two only one visit a day was needed and by the third week only one child was causing problems. When previously difficult children got through a whole day without breaking a rule their parents were immediately telephoned to celebrate the success (Makins, 1991).

This account is typical of reports from many schools using AD and similar systems. What it shows is the powerful effects of a positive, consistent and fair system of reinforcement used in a reasonable way by all the school staff working together and in cooperation with parents.

Teachers said of it:

'The whole atmosphere of the school has changed for the better.'
'We were always being drawn into arguments with the children, now there is none you never have to raise your voice.'
'They are doing so much more work, achieving so much more.'

The teachers reported they could see the difference AD made within a day.

AD practices are difficult for some teachers to maintain. They often need termly reintroductions and revisions. By Year 8/9 pupils are more mature and appreciate more negotiable adult approaches. Nevertheless in October 2014 BBC Radio 4 reported the system in effective operation in a secondary school.

Self-development relaxation project

This is designed as a journey of self-discovery (Powell *et al.*, 2008) using massage, yoga and relaxation techniques. It is set in a framework of self-efficacy as the central mediating mechanism in human agency (Bandura, 1977). It requires mastery experiences, role modelling, persuasion and reinterpretations of physiological and affective states. The pupils were trained in relaxation techniques such as hand massage and deep breathing in a safe environment for example.

All 53 children in the intervention group showed improvement in self-confidence, social confidence, communication and contribution in class compared to controls. Teachers reported that they also used their new skills during the school day.

Managing an effective teaching and learning environment

Well-organised teachers and lessons can help pupils considerably but there will be some who need explicit teaching of the routines and their reinforcement.

- If the teacher requires, for example, pupils to stop talking and put hands up to answer the question, then pupils must stop talking before anyone is allowed to answer the question. If this is not feasible the teacher must only choose someone to answer who has a hand up and not accept called-out answers. The rule can be reinforced by saying, 'Dale, you have your hand up, tell us your answer'.

- LSAs may offer too much support and guidance rather than requiring the pupil, for example, to read the worksheet for themselves several times. The pupil may read it but not be able immediately to follow the instructions. Instead of the LSA reading it to the pupil and prompting step by step the pupil should be asked to read instructions aloud sentence by sentence and implement them step by step.

- Teachers can help the development of self-regulatory skills by being explicit about classroom rules and routines, writing them up on posters or on the whiteboard. Such rules need to be discussed and agreed with the pupils first so that they understand why they should not run about and shout.

- When a piece of writing has been finished, it should not be accepted until it has been proofread. The work should be given a date, heading (and name if not writing in books).

- Completed and corrected work can be signed and put in the teacher's tray and the pupil proceeds to the next task. Thus the teacher must have a set of activities for 'next tasks', e.g. silent reading, computer application, problem-solving task, preparation for next piece of work and so on.

- It is also important for the teacher to introduce 'rest periods' when the pupils can legitimately sit back from their labours and listen to a reading or further ideas. Alternatively a 'pair and share' talking interlude about an aspect of the work can give tension release and reduce the emotional need to engage in conversational self-expression.

Overcoming learned helplessness

Many pupils with learning and behaviour difficulties have had so many negative school experiences that they feel that their efforts have little impact on their progress. They think what happens to them is unrelated to their own actions and are thus said to have an external locus of control. In its extreme form it is seen as 'learned helplessness' where the learner anticipates failure in any new situation and uses avoidance and evasion strategies to avoid loss of self-esteem through failure.

They need to experience success and to relearn that persistence and careful analysis can enable them to overcome failure, as evidenced in the Cognitive Process Strategies for Spelling (CPSS) examples given in Chapter 3. This will help them increase 'internality'. Working in pairs can help provide a behavioural and cognitive scaffold to enable aspects of the work to be completed successfully within the Zone of Proximal Development (Vygotsky, 1978), which is the area between what the pupil can do unaided and what can be done with structured guidance. Pupils can provide the scaffold or some teaching within this area by pairing their knowledge and discussing what to do. The teacher with a class of 30 cannot be on hand to do this re-teaching every time it is required. Different working pairs offer the widest experience.

In addition to this, achievements in self-control and self-regulation should be noted by the teacher and supported through recognition and quiet praise. There will always of course be lapses but over time they will be less frequent and in the end will only reappear under duress and direct fear of failure.

Effective classroom management

In a typical classroom one teacher is in a closed space with 25–30 pupils who may have spent several years together each weekday. The teacher must organise the task and the intended product through the actions of the 'workforce'. The plant consists of moveable furniture and objects. The teacher must control the behaviour of the workforce, keep it in place and motivate it to stay on task, despite no wages to distribute, as well as control and organise the plant. Room, plant, task, individual and 'herd' management are all involved (Montgomery, 1989).

This is a complex managerial setting in which teachers can make over 200 decisions an hour 'on the hoof'. It can be extremely stressful, especially in the first six weeks of term when the teacher works to gain and maintain control and keep the work progressing. Until members of the public try to teach such a group they have little idea of what is involved. It is a high stress occupation even without the external stresses imposed by the flood of initiatives, curriculum changes, league tables and inspections.

When any large group such as a class comes together it can act very differently from a small group. Student teachers who can work effectively with groups of up to eight pupils or with individuals may be quickly out-manoeuvred by a class, even of 5-year-olds. The problem is the 'herd instinct' and the anonymity that a large group offers. The constant deliberate low-level chatter is a sign of this and it wears teachers down. The strategic approach can deal with this.

The strategic approach to class control

There are five strategies involved (Montgomery, 2002):

1. Catch them being good (CBG)
2. Management, Monitoring and Maintenancing (3Ms)
3. Positive Cognitive Intervention (PCI)
4. Tactical Lesson Planning (TLP)
5. Assessment for Learning (AfL)

These strategies have to be used in concert to gain and maintain class control. The 3Ms and CBG are the easiest to acquire and the first essentials. The other three are the ways in which control once established can be maintained. They were derived from observation and appraisal of over 1,250 full lessons across age groups and schools.

The most successful teachers operate with all these strategies in a complex way that often defies analysis by researchers who put success down to 'charisma' or the 'X factor' (Lawrence *et al.*, 1989; Scott MacDonald, 1971). When the strategies were taught to failing teachers on the verge of dismissal they were converted into satisfactory and often 'good' teachers. One became the school's 'star' performer (Montgomery, 2002).

1. Catch them being good (CBG)

The teacher deliberately and systematically rewards, comments favourably, attends to, supports, praises, smiles, stands near or positively reinforces whenever s/he sees desirable behaviour. This may be prosocial behaviour or work on task. Lots of teachers praise correct responses to their questions but frequently fail to support on-task behaviours and this is essential teacher work to gain and maintain control.

2. Management, Monitoring and Maintenancing (3Ms) Cutting out lower level noise and disruption.

Phase 1 – Management
The teacher makes an *attention-gaining noise* such as 'Right!', 'OK, class 3', 'Good morning, everybody', 'Uhummm!', or bangs the door or desk, or claps hands. Some teachers simply wait quietly until the noise subsides as the pupils 'notice' s/he is present.

Next the teacher gives a *short verbal instruction* such as, 'Everybody sit down', 'Get out your books', 'Come and sit on the mat', 'Sit down and listen' and so on. At this point 20 of the pupils will do as requested and ten do not. The teacher repeats the instruction in a stronger voice but not a shout and a few more comply.

The effective teacher now pauses, looks round, spots those who are not doing as requested and *quietly names* them and individually instructs them to stop what they are doing and listen. This is usually quite sufficient if a *checkback look* is given to bring the whole class to attention. The checkback rule is that it must be done within 3–5 seconds of the individual instruction.

The mistake that ineffective teachers make is to repeat the 'short verbal' more than two or three times and begin to shout 'Be quiet' and 'Sit down', as a general instruction to all pupils. The raising of the teacher's voice and the general command to those who are already behaving as requested begins to engender hostility and amusement.

Some who were attending now begin to chat causing the instruction to be repeated louder still, thus contributing to the general noise level. This transmits the information that the teacher is not quite in control and can surreptitiously be disobeyed by an even larger group. Thus in a short period of time the class has become out of control.

The teacher at this point usually becomes very exasperated and red in the face and shouts the class into submission. These 'shock tactics' become less and less effective the more they are used and within three days the voice has been lost and time off sick has to be taken.

It takes time and effort to reconstruct this teacher behaviour to make it effective, allowing the opportunity to teach something. Many give up the struggle and 'teach' over the noise so that the level of attention and achievement of all pupils is low. If this is a school-wide problem then it is likely to fall into 'special measures' and all the staff need help.

The effective teacher, having gained the pupils' attention and silence, will immediately launch into the introduction to the session or begin reading the story. During the teacher talk or story it is necessary for a range of *attention-gaining and maintaining tactics* to be employed, e.g.

- pausing in exposition to look at pupil talking until s/he stops
- walking to pupil and gently removing tapping pencil or object
- asking the talking or inattentive pupil a question
- quiet naming then continuing the narrative
- repeating the phrase just given slightly more emphatically
- inserting 'and Goldilocks said to the three bears!' in the middle of the story looking hard at the miscreant
- sometimes a 'stink look' will be effective.

Telling the pupil off or nagging only spoils the concentration of the others. Younger children may respond well to finger on lips or a quiet 'Ssssh' or an agreed hand signal and calming gesture. If a large amount of these controls need to be exerted then the nature of the material and the length of the input needs cutting short.

As soon as the introductory session is completed it is essential to give the pupils something they can immediately do (see below) – not more teacher talk.

Phase 2 – Monitoring

An activity change from listening or question and answer to getting out workbooks and writing will inevitably permit a release of energy and noise and behaviour problems can arise.

This is where the brief monitoring phase needs to be operated. Having set the work the teacher stands tall and looks all round the class to see that the pupils are doing as requested. The teacher needs to move quickly round the groups/areas, starting with the noisiest and settling them down quietly and quickly moving on.

If the teacher gets bogged down with one request then the rest of the class can take advantage of this and go off-task. The teacher must say, 'Make a start and I will come back to help you'. 'Settle down now Shiv', 'Well done Karen, you've made a good start', 'Lisa, don't shout please'. All these quiet instructions to named individuals will help them all settle and create a *ripple effect* – target one noisy pupil in a group and the others nearby settle down too.

The whole monitoring phase should not take longer than 30 seconds to a minute. When all heads are down working, quiet naming or a calming gesture can settle the last one or two and the maintenance phase begins. If the space is tight monitoring can be achieved from a vantage point in the room and each group surveyed in turn. Some CBG and quiet instructions can be given from there.

Phase 3 – Maintenancing

This is when the pupils are all engaged on the task(s) given and they need to keep at it for a set period. It is important to return to those promised help but not to stay too long with head down buried in their work. Enough help needs to be given to begin and the teacher must return later to see how they are getting on. During the help the teacher must look up at intervals and check the class for potential disruption, noting loud voices and making calming gestures.

3. Positive Cognitive Intervention (PCI)

Maintenancing is where the teacher systematically goes to each pupil in turn and looks at the work and says something positive and constructive about it. Every pupil should expect a constructive comment on his or her work in every session.

This is a very powerful motivator and controller of behaviour. Pupils get to know the teacher is coming and busy themselves. They know they are going to get help if they need it, even though they may be reluctant to ask for it. They know that the teacher is interested enough in their work to comment on it and care about what they do. This makes the work and the teacher important in the pupils' eyes and they will care about it and want to do it well.

At intervals in the Maintenancing phase, as a squeak or a loud voice is heard over the general quiet murmur of work noise, the teacher needs to revert to Monitoring mode for 30 seconds. This is best achieved by eye contact, calming gesture and quiet naming, rather like conducting an orchestra.

Developmental PCI (formative AfL)

This is when the teacher takes every opportunity to explain exactly what has made this or that piece of work or behaviour good. A high level of cognitive intervention should be given wherever appropriate; it is not just for pupils with special needs. PCI need not be lengthy, often 10 seconds of input will suffice to encourage the pupil. It is part of Assessment for Learning.

CBG and PCI should not be withdrawn as soon as the pupil is on target. Each has to be maintained on an intermittent but strong level. This complex of high positive support was seen in the classrooms of very successful teachers who created a high level of learner participation and learning success.

The functions of PCI are that it:

- enhances self-image and respect
- helps overcome learning difficulty
- helps motivate and involve through 'engaging the brain' with the task
- provides strategies for academic and skill development
- provides personal interaction moments with the teacher in an academic context.

Teachers who had difficulties with class control found PCI one of the more difficult strategies to acquire and operate. They needed to learn CBG and 3Ms and get them working before they could focus on PCI.

Teachers who 'taught from the front' and did not do the maintenancing often seemed fearful to work amongst the learners. Learners inferred, 'He does not care about this work he has set, so why should we?' The teacher can and must be a powerful source of motivation and inspiration. This is hard work day after day.

When teachers who were asked about the relevance of tasks said it was 'because SATs demanded'; they lost the intrinsic motivation of their pupils to do the task for its own sake. They needed to seek to make it relevant and show this in their lesson design.

4. *Tactical Lesson Planning* (TLP)

Teachers in the past were trained to plan their lessons under the following general headings: lesson objectives, introduction, method, contents, apparatus, evaluation. More recently trainers have been telling students to use the following plan: lesson objectives, starter activity/warm up or ice breaker, Q/A to check understanding, main part of lesson, plenary and set homework (after Rosenshine, 2010). Both are teacher centred and focus upon content-based didactics.

Such plans design in difficulties for teachers with class control problems by allowing a long section on one activity in the middle of the lesson that the pupils may not be able to sustain. The Tactical Lesson Plan seeks to avoid this. It focuses not upon the teacher but on the learners and what they should be doing at any point. It allows sections that are going well to be extended and those that are not to be curtailed and replaced with an alternative activity. The lesson content remains the same but the activity on it changes, e.g.

a) *Central objective*: The teacher states concisely or makes clear what the lesson is about and its main purpose.

b) *Introduction*: (3–5 minutes) This occupies the first few minutes when the teacher reviews or revises previous or related work, finds out what they know about the topic (Q/A), or starts straight in with Phase 1.

c) *Phase 1*: (about 5–10 minutes depending on age and concentration span) The teacher presents the first part of the lesson content including where possible any visual/auditory stimulus, or *concrete* examples. This is probably mainly teacher-talk (with pupils LISTENING) or perhaps story reading or story telling with young pupils (LISTENING).

d) *Phase 2*: (about 10–15 minutes depending on task) This must present an *activity change* for the pupils so that from listening in Phase 1 they turn to writing, drawing, practical work or to some different activity, e.g. pupils writing answers to questions on worksheets with reference to Phase 1 (WRITING).

e) *Phase 3*: (about 3 minutes depending on task requirements) If the pupils begin to become a bit restless then it is time for an activity change and this could be to hear some of the answers they have written, or for them to share some ideas with each other (SPEAKING or LISTENING).

f) *Phase 4*: (about 5 minutes) Return to Phase 2 and finish off task (WRITING).

g) *Conclusion/plenary*: This should be short where the teacher restates the goals and asks individual pupils to give their responses to key points about what has been learned, etc. (Q/A). Homework can then be set if required, or given earlier. Pack things and dismiss quietly.

If the lesson is long, a double period, it may be necessary to introduce a number of activity changes. It is important to ensure that there is a genuine activity for the pupils. The cue to the need for an activity change is increasing restlessness and an inability to settle them down again easily and the need for monitoring becomes too frequent.

Problems arise when the content is unstimulating or difficult or when there is too much writing and not enough legitimised talk or action. As many pupils with Dual or Multiple Exceptionality (DME) and underachievers in general have writing problems, the request for a lot of writing can provoke restlessness and disruption. The act of writing may quickly become painful and tiring and so they do as little of it as possible. Tasks spin out to fill the time rather than being completed efficiently and quickly, as pupils know that all they get is more writing. This is where small intervals of Brain Gym, video clips and role-play are used to release energy and tension.

5. Assessment for Learning (AfL)

AfL is when the pupil is given feedback on a performance so that it is affirmed or improved. The feedback not only gives information on the quality and standard of the work – a *summative* assessment such as a grade – but is also *formative* so that the pupil learns how to improve that performance.

The formative assessment is a valuable and personal tutorial or teaching medium that may be a written comment couched in positive and constructive terms or it may be verbal as in PCI as the teacher moves round the class. It is especially helpful when the assessment is based on a set of criteria that are shared with the pupils or that are evolved as a practical part of the task with the class.

Pupils particularly appreciate helpful notes even when they check the grade or mark first. The comments should show how and why a particular grade was given. Young pupils may need visual symbols to support AfL, such as a traffic light system or smiley faces.

The main principles behind AfL are:

- sharing learning outcomes
- sharing success criteria
- effective questioning
- self-evaluation
- feedback.

Room management

Room management is an important factor in controlling unwanted behaviours. The four Gs are frequently cited:

'Get 'em in; Get on with it; Get on with them, and Get 'em out'.

Getting them into the room

Easier said than done. Getting them into the room can be a crucial strategy in behaviour management. If the class cannot enter the room in reasonable order and relatively quietly then steps need to be taken, e.g.

- Close the classroom door and wait by it; ask the pupils to line up outside; wait until they are all quiet; name quietly any who are pushing or talking. With young groups, teachers say 'Show me who's ready'.
- When the line is quiet ask the class to enter quietly in good order, sit down and get out books.
- Enter last and go to the front and survey them all. If they have not complied with the request quietly and satisfactorily, with regret say that it must all be done again until they can behave in a mature way. State that this procedure will continue until they show that they can do it properly as reasonable people.

Time spent in this procedure is not wasted. It demonstrates that the teacher is in quiet and calm control, treats the pupils with respect and expects the same in return.

Getting them out in good order

At the end of the lesson getting them out in good order is also important. They will want to escape and may bang desk lids and try to rush out as soon as possible if the teacher is not in control. The following is a simple and helpful routine:

- Say something like, 'Put your books away and then sit quietly'. The teacher stands by the door.
- Dismiss them one by one, but only those sitting quietly.
- As the rest leave even the less amenable will grow quiet and stop talking.
- Ask them to put the chairs in close to the desks. It is essential to leave time to end the lesson well especially in the initial training period.
- If the pupils are relatively well ordered, dismissal can take place by tables or rows or even areas.

Finally when they can move in and out of a classroom in a reasonable way the routines can be dropped and only reintroduced perhaps after some upset in a previous lesson.

The room itself

The room itself is also worthy of careful consideration for the way it is set out can contribute to the smooth running of a task.

- A room that is too small for the number of pupils will increase control problems whereas a well spaced-out room can help keep things calm.
- Space for the teacher to walk to all pupils to help them in PCI is essential.
- Tables versus rows: pupils sitting singly in rows stay more on task than when seated at tables in groups and pairs.
- Furniture that is moveable and adaptable to suit different teaching strategies can help underpin teaching.
- The double horseshoe is recommended in plenary and class discussions. Every pupil can see the teacher and everybody else, but it takes time to organise inside a lesson.
- Circle time needs a flexible space and the chairs to be set in a circle or horseshoe.
- The teacher needs places to stand, not only at the front but also at the back and sides of a room in order to see all the pupils.
- The 'cone zone' is the area of viewing usually directed to the teacher's right side where most of the pupils get attention. Surveying the whole room is essential to classroom management and ensures pupils in all areas get equal amounts of attention.
- Having a tidy, well set out room makes the session feel businesslike and ready for important work.
- Equally, leaving a room tidy and well ordered is a small routine that pupils easily learn and shows respect for those who follow.

- Having no more than three or four classroom rules on a poster on the wall can help as a reminder and be pointed to when verbal intervention is not required.
- Classroom rules should be evolved with the pupils and agreed by all so that they understand the reasons for not running, etc.
- With younger pupils an agreed hand signal is often helpful, e.g. if the teacher puts up her or his hand all the pupils should stop what they are doing, be silent and follow suit until all are silent and attentive. Any pupil likewise can request silence in the same way.
- Fluorescent lights have been shown to have a flicker rate that can provoke restless and more attention-seeking behaviour in a range of pupils. They increase headaches and impair concentration. Interactive whiteboards also increase the problem by reflecting light into the pupils' eyes. Apparently 90 per cent of classrooms are too bright. Natural light is preferable and makes a distinct difference in behaviour.
- Sound-damping carpet is a very useful asset in reducing the furniture and ambient noise.

Although some of these factors are not within the individual teacher's control, over time school management can be persuaded to change to more suitable room equipment.

Conclusions

Three key aspects to SEBD have been identified: the behavioural, the emotional and communication difficulties. The emotional and behavioural difficulties have causes and consequences that can be addressed by schools becoming part of the therapeutic community. Teachers, however, need to be supported and trained in the appropriate techniques.

The communication difficulties observed in a large number of cases have hitherto been missed and thus appropriate interventions have not taken place. These children are most likely to have pragmatic language difficulties and been excluded from school. Early identification and intervention would have helped maintain them in school and changed the attitudes towards them. Teachers and schools can also make significant contributions to easing these children's lives.

A facility with language can also help circumvent social and behavioural problems and a child's language development and comprehension can be improved in the early years by a high frequency of informative rather than supervisory or controlling language, by high rates of answering the child's questions, high rates of active rather than passive play, high numbers of adults to whom the child is exposed and high numbers of outings per week.

It is important that adults expand the child's utterances and there is extensive reinforcement and feedback of them, not just in the truth of utterances. There now appears to be a negative correlation of language development with TV watching, use of iPads and touch screens, evident in some children arriving at nursery school and play groups. Some children are arriving at school with severe language delays because parents have not considered it worthwhile to respond or talk to them until they can speak (Sunderland, 2014).

The school and the pupil are part of the ecosystem that can create and maintain problem behaviours. Teachers may need help in *reframing* the way they consider behaviours to see them and the pupils in a different light that makes them easier to deal with. Equally the school can become the therapeutic lead in constructing an ecosystemic response; key strategies for achieving this have been outlined in this chapter. The overall aim is to develop pupils as resilient, self-regulated and lifelong learners.

In a summary of research on what built resilience and success in children, Cefai (2007) detailed: a sense of belonging and connectedness in classrooms, inclusion, positive beliefs and expectations, and recognition. Chapter 7 explains how teaching and learning can contribute to children's well-being and their academic achievement.

7   How to create the DME-friendly school through inclusive teaching and learning

Introduction

Teaching method in England and Wales derived from two different traditions. Primary education, particularly Early Years education (nursery or kindergarten for children aged 4/5 to 8), emerged from a focus on the individual child and development to his or her full potential based upon the precepts of Pestalozzi, Froebel, Montessori and Rachel McMillan. It was child-centred.

It operated on the basis of the way children learn naturally in the home. Emitted behaviours and children's interests were responded to by the teacher and expanded and enriched in appropriate developmental terms. Toys, games, experiences and topics that interest and excite young children were brought into the classroom to promote learning and the extension of experience. Alternatively at times the children were taken out of the classroom to enjoy them. Basic skills in reading, writing and number were introduced and developed in this context.

Secondary education methods and the curriculum derived from a watered-down version of university education in which the focus was and still is the transmission of subject knowledge. It is a subject-centred education in which it is assumed that the pupils have all acquired the necessary basic skills. For many decades it was not considered necessary for secondary teachers to have teacher training, instead a subject degree from a university was all that was required. A one-year emergency training system introduced in 1945–1951 for returning military personnel demonstrated that programmes of training were needed in this sector but they did not become compulsory until the 1970s. Now this regulation is being relaxed as different routes into teaching are being developed, including school-based training.

The Junior stage of education from 8 to 11/12 years operated a mixture of these traditions depending on the experience and leadership of the headteacher. At various periods Middle schools were introduced then closed. They educated children from 7/8 to 13/14 years.

Running alongside state education has been a private education system that includes the famous 'public' schools such as Eton, Harrow, Rugby and Roedean. Seven per cent of pupils attend private schools and 43 per cent of their graduates hold the top jobs in the fields of education, politics, the Church, medicine and the law. It demonstrates the advantage that wealth can confer, rather than being an indication of academic excellence or high ability. Only 40 of the 80,000 children in England eligible for free school meals secured places at Oxford or Cambridge universities in 2013.

In the twenty-first century I should like to record that we have now moved forward and operate a 'learner-centred' education. It is true in theory but not so much in practice; not all schools or all teachers have moved in this direction.

The reason for this in part is that the profession of education unlike others is not run by experts in that profession but by administrators who have seldom taught a child or a class. They advise politicians and run the system. Together they have imposed the subject-centred approach through the Education Reform Act 1988 and subsequent legislation, even on primary schools. Over the last 25 years we have seen all sorts of initiatives being introduced to improve the quality of that education and then fading as their effect is usually negligible except to increase the rules, regulations and paperwork for teachers.

In 2010 a move was made to improve schooling by handing back responsibility and autonomy to the teachers within some broad guidelines. However, we can predict that as the teachers have been trained in a government-specified teacher education system since 1989 and will be inspected to government criteria there is little prospect of change, as independent thought and creative action do not fit this model.

It also raises questions about teacher expertise. Teachers located in a single school who move infrequently to others have little chance to develop notions of what make the best methods. They believed they were 'differentiating' or offering problem-solving and challenging opportunities but most observed were not (Montgomery, 2002). The ORACLE project (Galton *et al.*, 1980) similarly found that only 0.8 per cent of teacher time was spent in cognitively challenging questioning.

My own theories about teaching and learning were extended and enriched only by becoming a teacher educator and working alongside many students and teachers across the age ranges. It also took at least three to five years to develop some mastery of what was needed to develop appropriate professional skills and programmes. There were and still are no training programmes for teacher educators on meta-teaching and the higher order knowledge and skills to teach it.

The first attempt to express an overview of this teaching theory was in 'Education comes of age' and 'Teaching thinking skills in the school curriculum', which detailed a model of modern teaching (Montgomery, 1981b, 1983). The main points were that teaching method had moved from a nineteenth-century theory that rote learning of subjects was the way for people to become educated. They rote-learned the catechism, the Bible, poetry, prose, basic skills and so on and were thus imbued with moral standards and knowledge of various kinds thought necessary.

In the twentieth century our understanding of learning needs and what was useful in society for children to learn had moved on to a content-based transmission model. Education theory had moved from a pre-operational mode to a concrete operational one, rather like Piaget's (1952) theory of children's intellectual development.

In the 1980s we looked forward to moving into the Piagetian phase of 'abstract operations' in which the central objectives in teaching and learning were: 'To enable children to think efficiently and to communicate those thoughts succinctly whatever the subject being taught' (Montgomery, 1981b: 5).

These were to be the objectives in every subject or skill area and from preschool onwards. My teacher education programmes were designed to transmit these ideas and practices. It was not, however, until the programmes themselves were transformed to illustrate this at the teachers' level that behaviours changed. The result was that in the final exam year the programme results in the Learning Difficulties course rose from 1 or 2 per cent gaining first-degree standards to 23.6 per cent (N=72) (Montgomery, 1993). Unfortunately during the same period the government agency took over responsibility for teacher education and set back progress for over two decades.

Since 1993 the methods and techniques have been developed as five Distance Learning MA programmes (SEN; SpLD/Dyslexia; Gifted Education; Management Education; SEBD). Teachers worldwide have followed them and confirmed the validity of the strategies and contents summarised in this chapter, and they can be found as study guides at http://www.ldrp.org.uk

The situation worldwide according to Skilbeck (1989), Rogers and Span (1993) and Wallace and Eriksson (2006) is that education is still stuck in concrete operational mode. They found that 90 per cent of education worldwide was didactic. In other words most teachers engage in a lecture style, teacher-led mode, 'content ramming'. Those that do this compare themselves favourably with primary educators whom they perceive as 'child minding'.

Wallace and Eriksson (2006), summarising the main points from a galaxy of contributors worldwide, concluded that although educationalists were full of hope and optimism there was:

- a universal stubborn adherence to a content curriculum
- a dominant culture that sought to preserve itself
- bureaucracies resistant to change
- nineteenth-century education systems based upon authority, didactics and authoritarianism.

(p. 361)

High stakes assessment-driven systems researched by Gregory and Clarke (2003) in England and East Asian schools were shown to generate an elite of winners and an *underclass of losers*. Singapore, one of the top in the academic stakes, was found to produce teenagers who 'exhibit a narrow mindedness, tend to be smug and egocentric, and see the paper chase as the means to a good life … they make good employees, but few can think out of the box, much less lead' (cited in Heng and Tam, 2006: 172). These societies are becoming aware of the problems and are trying to move to a more learner-centred approach, using concrete apparatus and methods once again to teach early maths for example.

What follows is a *learner-centred approach*. It can be adopted on a gradual basis as experience grows and successful feedback is experienced. It must be emphasised that 'good teachers' have always used such techniques.

Inclusion in education

The UK ratified international human rights treaties dating from 1969 that placed the government under an obligation to provide education free from discrimination. In 1978 The Warnock Committee (Warnock, 1978) produced a report that identified 20 per cent of the school population as having some form of special need but recommended that wherever possible these children should be integrated in mainstream education and not be segregated in special schools or units.

Three types of integration were identified involving different levels of participation in mainstream education. *Locational* integration – where the special pupils were educated in a close location such as a special unit on the mainstream campus. *Social* integration – where the pupils joined each other for play activities in and out of the classrooms and perhaps did art work and movement activities together. *Functional* integration – where it was made possible for pupils with special needs to take part in mainstream classroom lessons. This often required 'learning support' from a learning support assistant (LSA), or in the case of physical disability with a welfare assistant.

A mixture of these different levels of support was often organised, so that for example a pupil with profound hearing impairment might join the mainstream class for registration, go to the special unit for the rest of the morning and return to class in the afternoon.

In subsequent years one of the key criticisms raised about integration was that it still fostered segregation but within the ordinary classroom as LSAs helped or special work was given to the pupil to meet the curriculum needs. It simply served to isolate or segregate them within the mainstream class and remained a discriminatory system.

The UK, along with many other nations, signed up to the Salamanca Statement (1994) in which inclusion was a major theme. Inclusion in education involves:

- valuing all students and staff equally;
- increasing the participation of students in, and reducing their exclusion from, the cultures, curricula and communities of local schools;
- restructuring the cultures, policies and practices in schools so that they respond to the diversity of students in the locality;
- reducing barriers to learning and participation for all students, not only those with impairments or those who are categorised as 'having special educational needs';
- learning from attempts to overcome barriers to the access and participation of particular students to make changes for the benefit of students more widely;
- viewing the difference between students as resources to support learning, rather than as problems to be overcome;
- acknowledging the right of students to an education in their locality;

- improving schools for staff as well as for students;
- emphasising the role of schools in building community and developing values, as well as in increasing achievement;
- fostering mutually sustaining relationships between schools and communities;
- recognising that inclusion in education is one aspect of inclusion in society.

(Based on CSIE, 2015)

Inclusion thus has a wide agenda for schools and has to be an ongoing developmental process. It is a long way from the integration agenda of the 1980s, although it was presaged there in a less sophisticated fashion. For a considerable period the Integration – Inclusion debate ensued as teachers and educators worked through the differences between what was seen as current 'good' practice and what the implications of inclusion really were. In summary:

Integration involves helping the pupils adapt to the school's needs and curriculum.

Inclusion means adapting the school and the curriculum to meet the needs of the individual child.

The inclusion agenda also touches gifted education and can create an inclusion paradox. It might be thought that comprehensive schooling would resolve integration and inclusion issues, until the systems and practices are analysed more carefully. Structural methods (see Figure 7.1) all involve segregating gifted and talented pupils in some measure. However, some forms of inclusion and mixed ability teaching may be denying the talented from achieving high learning outcomes, thus discriminating against them.

For this reason the concept of 'differentiation' was introduced to show it was possible for more challenging work to be offered to the more able within the same classroom. It was a system teacher educators recommended in the 1970s

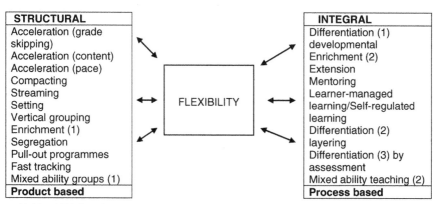

STRUCTURAL		INTEGRAL
Acceleration (grade skipping)		Differentiation (1) developmental
Acceleration (content)		Enrichment (2)
Acceleration (pace)		Extension
Compacting		Mentoring
Streaming		Learner-managed
Setting	←→ FLEXIBILITY ←→	learning/Self-regulated learning
Vertical grouping		
Enrichment (1)		Differentiation (2) layering
Segregation		
Pull-out programmes		Differentiation (3) by assessment
Fast tracking		
Mixed ability groups (1)		Mixed ability teaching (2)
Product based		**Process based**

(1), (2) and (3) indicate that these are not the same forms of enrichment or differentiation, although they are referred to by the same names.

Figure 7.1 A model of methods of provision in gifted education

to cope with the range of individual needs in classrooms! However, most methods of differentiation can also create discriminatory forms of segregation within classrooms even in integral gifted education provision (see Figure 7.1). The main reason for this is because of the didactic style of teaching that is used.

The structural methods

The structural methods of provision in gifted education all involve accelerating the learner through curriculum contents in various ways and operate against inclusion. Even some enrichment materials (indicated by (1) in Figure 7.1) merely teach what the learner could expect to learn in another phase of education, for example primary pupils might be given sections of the secondary school or even university curriculum in the periods allocated to 'enrichment'. Most structural approaches tend to be traditional product or content-based approaches, whereas integral approaches have to be concerned with process, in particular cognitive processes, but are still content dense.

Streaming means dividing cohorts into classes by ability (A, B, C streams). Setting involves dividing pupils into ability sets by subject particularly in English, maths and science. A pupil could be in an A set for English and a C set for maths or vice versa. Vertical grouping is practised mostly in small rural schools where there are only one or two teachers and a few pupils. Children aged from 5–8 or even 11 years may all be taught together and so the most able 5-year-olds can join in the work of the older pupils and it does not seem to disadvantage any of them in SATs results. Because it was seen as a successful method some larger primary schools practised it with 5–7-year-olds to avoid the lock step of the age cohort until their autonomy was removed.

Most English primary schools operate in mixed ability age-related cohorts, but the 'Red Table' soon learns that it is the bright group and does the difficult work. On rare occasions individuals may be grade-skipped (accelerated), usually by one year.

At secondary level a system of grammar schools (gymnasia) operates alongside 'comprehensive' schools in some areas of England. Inside the comprehensives streaming or setting may operate. In comprehensive school A in central London teachers insisted that they must set for maths but there was no need to do so in science. Four miles down the road comprehensive school B's teachers insisted they must set for science but not for maths. Both schools were high in the league tables for success in GCSEs!

A seminar of expert mathematicians (Gardner, 2000) concluded acceleration in maths was unnecessary. Pupils were best taught in mixed ability sessions using extension and enrichment strategies. The Mathematical Society (2010) concluded that acceleration in mathematics left gaps in pupils' knowledge and undermined their potential. Acceleration is, however, widely used in gifted education and along with compacting is found to be the most effective of the methods (Rogers and Span, 1993). It has to be remembered though that this is in the context of didactics or traditional content-led teaching methods.

Reception learning – traditional didactics

Ausubel (1968) believed that beginning learners learn more effectively by 'reception'. In this method the teacher presents the whole content of what has to be learned in its final form. It places a great emphasis on the teacher's skill in structuring the content to be learned. The learning is meaningful if it allows reproduction with understanding at a future date.

The term 'advance organisers' was coined by Ausubel to describe the short outline of the whole material introduced before the lesson begins, now wrapped up as 'lesson objectives' or targets. As will be seen, reception learning does not meet the effective learning criteria although its ideas and the principles have been incorporated into the lesson plans required by English government edicts. It is a highly structured form of didactics.

Reception learning and didactic teaching methods are likely to lead to superficial or 'surface learning'. This means that the material needs frequent revision to make it available for use. Also it will have a low degree of transfer to new and different situations and remains relatively inert. The question it raises is that if we have to keep revising knowledge can it have been effectively taught and learned in the first place?

The integral methods

A different theory of knowledge and instruction informs integral methods. Poorthuis *et al.* (1990) argued that enrichment materials 'for the gifted' should meet the following criteria:

- They should be beneficial to the development and use of higher order thinking abilities.
- They ought to provide the possibility to explore continually new knowledge and new information.
- They should learn and encourage students to select and use sources of information.
- The content should aim at a complex, enriching and in-depth study of important ideas, problems and subjects, and at integrating knowledge between and within subject areas.
- They should offer the opportunity increasingly to engage in autonomous learning activities.

Experience in teaching gifted and slower learners in mixed ability settings led to the conclusions that all children benefit from an education engaging interest and offering cognitive challenge (Montgomery, 1990). The differences between the structural product-based approach to education at all levels and the integral cognitive process approach are illustrated in Table 7.1, which draws on ideas expressed in the same period.

The integral methods are based in the critical theory style described by Paul and constructivist approaches (Piaget, 1952). Critical thinking is the art of thinking

Table 7.1 (adapted from Paul, 1990)

Didactic Theory	Critical Theory
The fundamental needs of students	
To be taught more or less *what* to think not how to think; are given details, definitions, explanations, rules, guidelines and reasons to learn.	To be taught *how* not what to think; that it is important to focus on significant content but accompanied by live issues that stimulate students to gather, analyse and assess content
The nature of knowledge	
Knowledge is independent of thinking that generates, organises and applies it. Students are said to know when they can repeat what has been covered. Students are given the finished products of someone else's thought.	All knowledge of content is generated, organised, applied and analysed, synthesised and assessed by thinking; that gaining knowledge is unintelligible without such thought. Students are given opportunities to puzzle their way through to knowledge and explore its justification as part of the process of learning.
Model of the educated person	
Educated, literate people are fundamentally repositories of content analogous to an encyclopaedia or a data bank, directly comparing situations in the world with facts in storage. This is a true believer. Texts, assessments, lectures and discussions are content dense and detail-orientated.	An educated literate person is fundamentally a repository of strategies, principles, concepts and insights embedded in processes of thought. Much of what is known is constructed as needed, not prefabricated. This is a seeker and a questioner rather than a true believer. Teachers model insightful consideration of questions and problems, and facilitate fruitful enquiry.

about your thinking so as to make it more precise, accurate and relevant, consistent and fair.

Flavell (1979) termed it metacognition. He argued that thinking about how we are thinking and learning whilst we are doing so contributes in a major way to intelligence. Thus if we can promote metacognitive activities, especially in those who would not normally use them, we could be likely to be promoting and enhancing people's intelligence or at least their intelligent action.

According to Paul, most education worldwide was still geared to inducing monological thinking that is single track and context-defined because of the overuse of didactic methods. Critical thinking, in contrast, is:

- The art of identifying and reversing bias, prejudice and one-sidedness of thought.
- The art of self-directed, in depth, rational thinking.
- Thinking which rationally certifies what we know and makes clear where we are ignorant.

(Paul, 1990: 32)

Integral provision is a 'way of life' in classrooms approach. Mixed ability classes learn together and work together on the same curriculum tasks and the key concept in this style of working is 'developmental differentiation'.

Some benefits of mixed ability teaching

Hallam's research (2002) on mixed ability teaching found that it can:

- provide a means of offering equal opportunities;
- address the negative social consequences of structured ability grouping by encouraging cooperative behaviour and social integration;
- provide role models for less able pupils;
- promote good relations between pupils;
- enhance pupil/teacher interactions;
- reduce some of the competition engendered by structured grouping;
- allow pupils to work at their own pace;
- provide a sense of continuity for primary pupils when they transfer to secondary school;
- force teachers to acknowledge that the pupils in their class are not a homogeneous group;
- encourage teachers to identify pupil needs and match learning tasks to them.

(p. 89)

Hallam also warned that to engage in successful mixed ability, and we can add inclusive, teaching the teachers needed to be highly skilled and appropriately trained and have at their disposal a wide range of differentiated resources to match to their pupils' needs.

It can be seen that with so many advantages for all pupils inclusive teaching based upon mixed ability methods is what we need to aspire to for as much of school time as possible.

The nature of differentiation

Differentiation is a process whereby planning and delivering the curriculum takes account of individual differences and matches what is taught and how it is taught to individual learning styles and needs. It seeks to provide opportunities for *all* children to participate and make progress in the curriculum by building on their past achievements, presenting challenges for further achievement and providing opportunities for success.

Three models of integral curriculum differentiation

- By inputs: The setting of different tasks at different levels of difficulty suitable for different levels of achievement.
- By outputs: The setting of common tasks that can be responded to in a positive way by all students but assessed differently.
- Developmental: 'The setting of common tasks to which all students can contribute their own inputs and so progress from surface to deep learning and thus be enabled to achieve more advanced learning outcomes.' It is the basis of *inclusive* teaching.

(Montgomery, 1996: 86)

Of the first two models perhaps the best that can be said is that they offer more than the formal or didactic methods of teaching to the middle, but there are inbuilt disadvantages. In differentiation by inputs teachers provide some core work in which all pupils participate but after that they provide simpler conceptual and practice work for the slower learners and more complex problem-solving extension work for the able groups.

The pupils doing the easier work began to feel lower in ability and value (Montgomery, 1990). The rest of the class quickly recognised this. It can in the long run prove academically handicapping as these pupils come to expect that they can never achieve a high standard in any sphere of activity and cease to try, so that they compound their difficulties and begin to fall further behind. It is a form of segregated provision within the classroom.

The able pupils in this system began to feel special for they were doing the 'clever' work. They can develop inflated opinions of themselves and their abilities and begin to look down on the other children, even poke fun at them. All of these attitudes are destructive and wasteful so that none of the groups are motivated to develop their abilities and talents to the full. Only those with great strength of character or individualism can survive these social pressures and develop freely and these are few. A second and major problem is that it is the teacher who has to select who will do the advanced or less advanced work and thus too much hangs upon the teacher's diagnostic skills.

The second method of differentiation is where all pupils participate in the same task but different assignments are set or the children may do the same tasks at which they progressively fail. Sometimes the assessment criteria have different levels against which the work is marked and some pupils are entered for lower level qualification. Again the pupils soon become aware that different standards are being applied and inclusion fails.

These forms of differentiation are no more than a within-class selective education system with all the potential for social and political division that were witnessed in the grammar school system.

The method that avoids these problems has been termed **'developmental differentiation'** because it takes account of developmental levels in the individual and creates inclusive learning experiences for all the pupils. However, it is not always simple to effect. Some enrichment materials provide it and some do not. Early good examples developed in the 1980s were The Motorway Project, Townscapes and The Village of Edenfield led by Johanna Raffan (Adams *et al.*, 1993) and some of the Essex Project materials initiated by Belle Wallace, founder of the TASC project, and used currently in 10,000 schools worldwide.

Approaches to inclusive teaching and learning

Developmental differentiation

Developmental differentiation takes account of the range of individual differences and assumes that even in so-called homogeneous groups the range of differences in thinking abilities, language and literary skills, social, emotional and perceptual development will vary considerably, as does the experience and learning history that each child brings to the task.

The first and foremost strategy is to select a curriculum task and content to be learned and invent a problem or question (problem finding) that will motivate and interest the pupils to want to solve it. The human brain is set to engage in this form of scientific investigative activity (Kelly, 1955) unless it is ill.

Framing inclusive teaching problems

Tasks can be adapted to suit different age groups:

- *Design problem solving and technology* – Using one broadsheet newspaper and half a metre of sticky tape, in pairs design a house big enough to sit in. Afterwards draw a set of instructions to show your process. Can another group follow them?
- *Physical education* – Using four different parts of the body move from one side of the room to the other and over one piece of apparatus. Then with a partner use four parts between you to get back again.
- *History* – You are a building company in an area in Medieval England. A local merchant would like a new house built on the main street to be consistent with her wealth and status. In groups of three examine the pictures and records of the period and the ways in which the people lived then and design her house. Research and compare the costs of the building materials then and now. Display the results; each group gives a short presentation on their design.
- *English* – Groups of three or five pupils are set to produce a holiday brochure for their town or suburb. They start with an analysis of the style, content and format of typical holiday brochures. The groups should delegate different tasks/roles to the members of their 'consortium'. The brief includes developing costed, all-inclusive 'packages', bringing people to the area for a range of seasonal breaks based upon actual prices 'at the time of going to press'. The sessions end with a presentation by the groups of their package.
- *Science* – In the context of the study of solvents and solutions pairs of pupils are given an envelope whose contents (sand and salt) they must investigate. It is clearly a mixture, but of what? Could it be harmful? They have to design apparatus that could be used to separate the mixture and then use it to see if it will work. This is followed by a 20-minute plenary for debriefing. After this a lot of pupils like to return in a lunch hour just to work through the experiment again and correct their method, especially if the problem of how to get clean sand and salt is left open.

Pairs work and group collaboration means that pupils work with each other towards the framing and design of problems and strategies as well as in their resolution or solution. Each contributes some part to the whole in cooperative learning.

The second approach to designing inclusive teaching and learning experiences and developmental differentiation is to address the teaching and learning strategies. These were termed cognitive process strategies (CPS) or pedagogies (Montgomery, 1996).

Cognitive process pedagogies and the Cognitive Curriculum

Over a period of two decades, in order to achieve developmental differentiation and inclusive teaching goals, it has been necessary to develop teaching methods and materials to illustrate the theory in practice. Thus the 'notion of a cognitive curriculum' was developed that all teachers could incorporate into their everyday lessons whatever subject they were teaching and whatever level of education. Teachers did not have to learn vast quantities of new information; they merely had to change their teaching methods. Easier said than done! Most resistant to change were the teachers' habitual methods and styles of teaching.

The Cognitive Curriculum

The Cognitive Curriculum consists of:

- challenging questioning to provoke thought and reasoning; it involves more open questions;
- cognitive process study and research skills in all subjects;
- teaching thinking skills and encouraging investigative learning in all subjects;
- reflective teaching and learning;
- real world problem-based learning;
- developing creativity;
- games and simulations;
- experiential learning;
- language experience methods;
- self-regulated learning in topic and project work.

Some detailed examples of many of the above may be found in Montgomery, 1996, 2000, 2009. Free electronic downloads of examples may be requested at http://www.ldrp.org.uk

> Although it may seem self-evident, focusing on thinking skills in the classroom is important because it supports active cognitive processing which makes for better learning. Thus, pupils are equipped to search out meaning and impose structure; to deal systemically, yet flexibly, with novel problems and situations; to adopt a critical attitude to information and argument, and to communicate effectively. ... Standards can only be raised when attention is directed not only on what is to be learned but on how children learn and how teachers intervene to achieve this...
>
> (McGuinness, 1999: 5)

Accompanying the Cognitive Curriculum needs to be a Talking Curriculum to establish the importance of increasing pupils' social and communication skills that are especially important to overcome UAch in disadvantaged groups.

CPS and the Talking Curriculum

- TPS: Think – Pair – Share
- circle time
- group problem solving
- reciprocal teaching between teacher and pupil
- 'thinkback' (Lockhead, 2001) – peer story approach of thinking during problem solving
- role-play
- demonstrations
- debates
- book clubs
- presentations, teach-ins
- exhibitions
- collaborative learning.

The essence of CPS is to increase intrinsic motivation of learners to want to learn and to enable them to participate actively in their own learning. Through the Talking Curriculum they contribute and share what they know, learn to work collaboratively and record using a variety of different formats. In this process the teacher provides a positive and supportive framework and *formative* as well as *summative* feedback (AfL) on the learning.

The Recording Curriculum

Using CPS involves all the learning codes and many different modes of input and output other than writing. These can include mind maps, diagramming, cartooning, PowerPoints, drawing, painting, construction, role-play, videos, film, exhibitions and so on.

Self-regulated learning (SRL)

In gifted education SRL has become an important area of research and development. Wang and Lindvall (1984) showed that self-monitoring and self-regulatory activities not only contributed to improved acquisition of subjects but also to improved generalisation and transfer of knowledge and skills. They also gave students a sense of personal agency, a feeling of being in control of their own learning. Over the years many different titles have evolved for SRL: Experiential, Self-directed, Independent, Action, Reflective, Open, Independent, Self-organised, Self-managed, Learner-managed, Autonomous Learning and Independent Research Strategies.

Self-regulatory activities were defined by Brown *et al.* (1983) as including planning, predicting outcomes and scheduling time and resources. Monitoring included testing, revising and rescheduling; evaluating outcomes using criteria developed by the individual and also those that were externally defined. These are the executive intellectual functions (Gagne, 1973).

SRL is involved and most enjoyed by students in HE when they undertake their own research projects and project work is recommended by Renzulli and Reis (2008) as the highest level in their School-wide Enrichment Model. However, gifted achievers and underachievers do not necessarily develop self-regulatory skills in didactic systems. They need some training (Fischer, 2014; Renzulli and Reis, 2008).

Self-regulated learners according to Niehart (2011) do well at school but may not be in the top 10 per cent. They handle stress well, are persistent, self-directed, self-regulated, self-motivated, tend to be risk takers and good self-advocates. This means that in the UK SRLs may not make the G and T registers to gain access to 'enriched' provision.

Fischer's (2014) research on SRL with pupils of different abilities taught them information-processing strategies – study skills (SQ3R!); metacognitive strategies – reflection and discussion of learning; and achievement motivation strategies – reinforcement and feedback. The results were that all learners of different abilities profited to the same degree. He showed that SRL should be taught in combination with a concrete skill – text understanding in his research. In the SRL group 47 per cent improvement was found in text understanding There were no differences between pupils with high or low scores on Raven's Matrices.

However, pupils with 'goal avoidance orientation' or learned helplessness – 43 per cent – did not improve their scores. Motivation was the key to their improvement. The reason could be that SQ3R (Survey, Question, Read, Rehearse, Review) is a tedious didactic method of text comprehension and especially avoided by creative individuals (Bond and Tinker, 1967).

Not all pupils need to be taught to become self-regulated. It appears that some arrive at school with skills in this area, for example children who learn to read self-taught at the age of 3 or 4 or in rare cases even younger (Leites, 1971). Montgomery (2014) found that 10.7 per cent of 4/5-year-olds (N=112) arrived in school already able to write decipherable communications. Although a few may have been taught in preschool, it is unlikely that all were.

Front-loaded learning and SRL/Learner Managed Learning

In a Study Skills and Effective Learning project with teacher education students, front-loaded learning strategies linked to SRL increased the number of 'firsts' in the degree programme from 1–2 per cent to 23.61 per cent (Montgomery, 1993) when CPS were employed. Work was designed as problems to be solved, e.g. Identify the five main points in this piece of text/ chapter/article; Complete a flow chart of the main points in _____; Classify these _____; Explain why this makes a good reading test using the criteria _____ etc. The strategies focused on deep understanding of textual, visual and other material. The result was that students needed to spend little time on revision for the exam; they 'just knew' it.

Deep and surface learning

Marton and Säljo (1984) identified HE students who engaged in either deep or surface learning and found that in order to secure deep learning the learner must be an active participant not just in childhood but throughout life. They reported that students with a deep approach achieved better results than surface learners.

Gibbs (1990) defined the characteristics of surface learning as follows:

- a heavy workload
- relatively high class-contact hours
- an excessive amount of course material
- lack of opportunity to pursue subjects in depth
- lack of choice over subjects
- lack of choice over methods of study
- threatening and anxiety-provoking assessment system.

All these surface characteristics are implicit in high stakes education systems.

Fostering a deep-learning approach rests on the obverse of surface approaches:

- relatively low class-contact hours
- intrinsic interest in the subject
- freedom in learning in content and method or scope for intellectual independence
- experience perceived as 'good' teaching.

Gifted pupils may have such good memories they never need to engage in deep textual analysis. They seldom fail so may not learn how to cope with failure and use it to learn.

Learning styles and strategies

What we observe in schools is a tendency for the learning mode or style to be through the spoken and written word and different attempts have been made to extend these, including through notions of learning style. These other modes of learning and responding are particularly important for pupils who have literacy difficulties.

In a review and meta-analysis of research on cognitive and learning styles Riding and Rayner (1998) found that we do not really have multiple cognitive styles but a preference for or bias towards the ways in which we deal with situations. These apparently all boil down to an orthogonal model (see Figure 7.2).

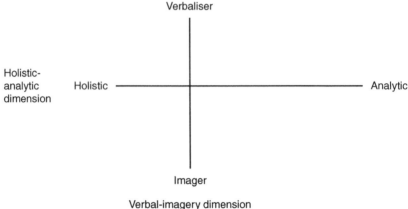

Figure 7.2 Riding and Rayner's (1998: 9) orthogonal model of learning styles

Most of us adapt our styles to the situation but have a preference for using an analytic or holistic approach to, for example, problem solving. Some like to tackle problems in an ordered, analytical and sequential manner, following instructions and protocols when assembling flat pack furniture or model aeroplanes. Others like to take a more holistic approach – shake the pieces out of the box, look at the picture and start the construction and only read the instructions when their strategy runs into difficulties.

Similarly we have preferences for verbal versus pictorial material and methods. As can be imagined, those who have difficulties with reading and writing are going to be obliged to practise holistic and imager (iconic) styles and show a preference for them.

Learning style is held to be the composite of:

- Cognition – People perceive and gain knowledge differently.
- Conceptualisation – People think and form ideas differently.
- Affect – People feel and form values differently.
- Behaviour – People act differently.

Styles are said to serve as relatively stable indicators of how a learner perceives, interacts with and responds to the learning environment. Thus in schools we can find children's learning being damaged by labels on their desks saying, 'I am an Active Learner' or 'I am a Visual Learner' and teachers giving them only tasks and experiences to reinforce these prejudices (Coffield, 2005).

One of the most popular models widely applied in management training courses is based upon the work of Honey and Mumford (1986). They claimed to have identified four 'learning styles' corresponding roughly to four stages in the learning process defined by Kolb (1984) (see Figure 7.3).

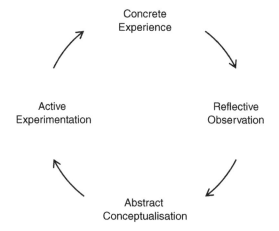

Figure 7.3 Kolb's (1984) experiential learning cycle

Honey and Mumford (1986) developed their Learning Styles Questionnaire (LSQ) to access four learning styles equating with the four stages in the cycle:

a)   Concrete Experience – Activists involve themselves fully and without bias in new experiences.
b)   Reflective Observation – Reflectors like to stand back and ponder experiences and observe them from many different perspectives.
c)   Abstract Conceptualisation – Theorists adapt and integrate observations into complex but logically sound theories.
d)   Active Experimentation – Pragmatists are keen on trying out ideas, theories and techniques to see if they work in practice.

The management 'coach' does not have to be highly knowledgeable or skilled to help a learner adopt a more balanced style. It is done by helping the learner review, explore the 'models', create an action plan and implement it. There is, however, a lack of evidence to support such styles because the questionnaires do not appear to be sufficiently sensitive.

The cycle can be entered at any point but must be followed in sequence. Kolb recognised that not all individuals are equally well equipped to handle each stage of the cycle. He argued that learning occurred not in the doing but in the reflection and conceptualisation that takes place during and after the event.

However, if learning takes place the learner does not return to the same point each time but at each turn progresses further. It changes the processes and the understanding in an additive way. This learning process can be described as a Cognitive Process Learning Spiral (Montgomery, 1994) (see Figure 7.4).

The model indicates that learners can progress from surface to deep learning by a variety of experiential learning methods mediated by the teacher and

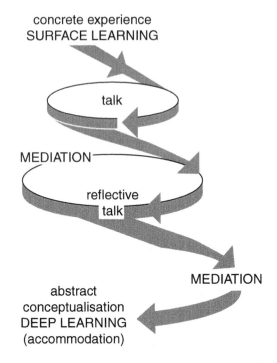

Figure 7.4 The Cognitive-Process Learning Spiral (Montgomery, 1994)

encouraged by reflective talk – metacognition. Metacognition is regarded as a highly important contribution to higher order learning that contributes to the development of self-regulatory and self-management skills, as well as a sense of personal agency.

Multiple intelligences (MI)

Gardner's (1993) notion of multiple intelligences (MI) caught the imagination of teachers and many MI schools were established round the world. He did originally say multiple intelligences or 'talents' and my preference would be for 'talents' as the evidence for eight separate intelligences does not exist. But it did encourage teachers to broaden their concept of high ability and the scope of their teaching and learning strategies to take account of the different talents. Thus a pupil who excels in science may not excel in maths or English, but will gain recognition and affirmation for success and achievement in science. The interest and motivation thus generated is then used and developed in other areas. They are not expected to be good at everything.

Cognitive codes

Bruner (1968) first discussed symbolic (verbal), iconic (imagery) and enactive (motor) codes by which we learn to process and use information. This was used as a developmental model in which the baby first encodes in the enactive mode and then the iconic and finally the symbolic mode.

Munro (1996) developed this notion into a wide range of codes that are patterned upon the curriculum subjects similar to Gardner's multiple 'intelligences'. The ideas manipulated during learning need to be coded or represented in the 'sites', in forms that allow learners to think about them. Whenever we think about an idea we need to link it with other ideas, using what we already know. Our existing knowledge gives us these ways of thinking or 'thinking codes'. The codes represent what we already know about how ideas can be related or linked. Ideas can be coded or represented in different sites. Piagetian theorists would call them concept schemas and scripts that are built into hierarchies of knowledge and skill.

Wills implemented these ideas in a curriculum development project for the gifted at Ruyton Girls' School in Victoria, Australia. Through topic work all modes and sites were interlinked (Wills and Munro, 2009), motivating and enhancing the knowledge and skills of the learners. The codes were: verbal/linguistic; scientific/mathematical; episodic/spatial or visual-imagery; body/kinaesthetic; rhythmic; affective/mood representation; interpersonal representation.

The ideas are manipulated within each code: either a) analysed into parts that are then linked up, or b) integrated with other ideas, with each idea being treated as a whole. Although most learners use these strategies, some use one excessively and need to be helped to broaden their approach. Formal teaching often assumes that students learn best by being presented with small parts of an idea at a time arranged sequentially. This is not always the case. Often it is helpful to show how the parts relate to the whole or even show the whole first.

Presenting key ideas in a variety of ways allows pupils to learn in 'learner-friendly' contexts that take account of preferred ways of learning. Individual learning characteristics are acknowledged and accepted. It also encourages the valuing of others (Munro, 1996).

Accelerated learning (AL)

The original concept emerged from the work of Philip Adey and Michael Shayer during the 1980s on science education in schools (Shayer and Adey, 2002). They ran projects in which one lesson per fortnight was reserved for talking with the pupils about what had been learnt and how it had been learnt. The idea was to develop language and metacognitive skills in science. It was found that in Cognitive Acceleration through Science Education (CASE) projects not only did the pupils learn more than controls but they retained it better and understood it more. The effects were not, however, limited to science: they spread to better results for the CASE pupils in English and maths GCSEs.

The principle underlying AL is that the methods develop the thinking ability of the pupils. This includes knowledge acquisition, concept change and the development of processing power. AL encourages the concept of Lifelong Learners. There are three main principles:

Cognitive conflict involves stimulating thinking and motivation to learn by offering cognitive or intellectual challenges of moderate difficulty. This is accompanied by support in the form of leading questions, invitations to discuss problems and ideas, looking at them from different angles and so on. This work could be in the form of class discussion, group or pairs work.

In order to promote discussion the learning environment is supportive so that pupils are not discouraged from putting forward their ideas. The teachers model fairness, consistency and a problem-solving approach.

Social construction of knowledge and understanding the work is based on Vygotskian (1978) principles – understanding develops during social communication and then becomes internalised by individuals, this is promoted by the discussion and 'group think'.

Bridging involves developing new thought processes in which a range of associated ideas are taught and solutions generated which apply to new contexts.

AL in popular use is said to be structured on 'learning cycles':

- At the beginning of the task the pupils are introduced to the 'big picture'.
- The learning outcomes are then described; sometimes these are written on cards.
- The learning input follows and may involve visual, auditory and kinaesthetic activities. The student is then asked, 'What are the most important things for you?'
- Take five key words and sing them to a tune.
- Next the pupils demonstrate what they have learned to the rest of the class.
- They review together what they have done and learnt and finally it is all linked back to the 'big picture'.

As can be seen many influences such as Brain Gym, collaborative learning, reflection, active learning and cognitive challenge have all been bound into AL. The research on its more general effectiveness is still awaited but pupils and staff enjoy the collaborative enterprise and it should have some long-term gains in promotion of language skills.

Philosophy for children

In the late 1960s during the student unrest, Matthew Lipman at Columbia University became concerned about the low level of thinking skills that students brought to the university. He decided that this needed to be tackled at the earliest level in schools.

In his programme, Lipman (1991) listed 30 thinking skills and first on the list was formulating concepts precisely. His objective was to improve thinking in every way of learning. In addition children would be offered a specific course in the study of thinking to help increase their metacognitive awareness. The aim was for all the children to become more thoughtful and reflective. He decided that this was best done through stories and so he wrote a short story *Harry Stottlemeier's Discovery* (Aristotle in disguise). Harry does not listen in class and misses out on parts of the information and is laughed at by peers, so he tries to fathom things out for himself by argument.

The programme is successful when there is thoughtful and animated discussion often on subjects not traditionally thought possible with young children. Teachers learn to promote the discussion by Socratic questioning and the pupils have to develop the discipline of listening to each other. The teachers develop rules with the pupils such as:

* listen carefully and follow the story line or argument
* ask if something is not clear
* think of one or two relevant things to say
* make suggestions to carry the argument further
* say things in a positive way so that others do not get upset
* take turns
* share ideas.

Each session begins with reading and rereading half to three pages of a story. There is now a comprehensive programme of materials published by The Institute of Philosophy for Children. Many children's texts already provide good material for such discussions and English teachers are usually adept at using them. The Lipman programme has been very effectively used in many UK schools with the support of training from, for example, www.sapere.org.uk

Pupils, both gifted and the rest, using Lipman's programme were very enthusiastic about it and the teachers found it was having a noticeably good effect on their logical abilities and behaviour in class (Montgomery, 2009).

Discovery learning

This term was used by Jerome Bruner in the early 1960s to describe the activities which he thought were essential to make teaching and learning realistic and constructive for pupils. Discovery learning is an inquiry training that enables pupils to gain a fundamental understanding of the underlying principles of the subject they are studying.

In this process they also learn the concepts and relationships. When pupils worked in these ways he found that they grew in intellectual potency, were intrinsically motivated, had mastery of principles that enabled them to apply their learning, and showed gains in memory as a result of the organisation of their knowledge (Bruner, 1968). Taba (1962) identified four steps in discovery learning, which can also be used as a teaching-learning protocol:

- the problem creates bafflement
- the learner(s) explore the problem
- the learners are prompted to generalise and use prior knowledge to understand a new problem or pattern
- there need to be opportunities to apply the principles learned to new situations.

Bruner illustrated his ideas in 'Man: A Course of Study' (1968: Chapter 4).

Discovery learning, however, is frequently misunderstood and regarded as a method in which children are taught nothing but have to discover knowledge for themselves and 'reinvent the wheel' on every occasion.

The Schoolwide Enrichment Model

In a period when giftedness was defined by IQ and the only question was what level of IQ defined it, 1 per cent as in the Terman studies or 3–5 per cent in other studies, Renzulli (1977) initially proposed the three-ring concept of giftedness and that there were two types of giftedness: 'schoolhouse giftedness' and 'creative productive giftedness'. The latter was the more valuable to society. Creative productivity depended upon the task commitment and motivation of the individual and it also came and went, whereas schoolhouse giftedness was relatively stable. Creative producers also tended to be domain specific and very few.

Renzulli *et al.* (1981) devised the 'Revolving Door Model' of identification in which pupils could opt in and out of the provision and it was not dependent on IQ. After the US equity-in-education moves in the early 1980s and the Marland Report (1972), Renzulli with Reis (1985) developed the inclusive Schoolwide Enrichment Model.

At that time 'acceleration' and 'enrichment' were the two pedagogical models in operation in gifted education with enrichment projects being random and piecemeal. Renzulli argued that enrichment involving inductive learning was a more appropriate model for teaching the gifted than the deductive learning model of 'schoolhouse giftedness'. The deductive model was one of a prescribed and presented model of instruction – didactics. The inductive model was process-based enrichment. It emphasised:

- the uniqueness of the learner
- the role of enjoyment
- personalisation of learning
- methodological resources
- a focus on products and services.

Based on 20 years of research, it maintained that all students' learning should be enriched by the inclusion of opportunities to develop higher-order thinking skills, creative productivity and opportunities to pursue more rigorous content in mixed ability 'enrichment clusters' (Renzulli and Reis, 2008: 165). They proposed the study of real world problems in which creative and productive skills might be developed and used.

The Total Talent Portfolio (TTP)

TTP is a component of the Schoolwide Enrichment Model and the purpose is:

- To collect several types of information
- Classify it in terms of abilities, interests and styles
- Review and analyse the data to make decisions about future opportunities
- Negotiate various options and opportunities
- Use the information and materials for personal, educational and career counselling

Thinking Actively in a Social Context (TASC)

Wallace (2009) described the development of the TASC problem-solving approach with disadvantaged learners and how they named the project after she had moved from Essex to South Africa in the 1980s. An outline of the TASC wheel appears earlier and is another contribution to the process approach to teaching and learning. It offers a wide range of materials and resources (http://tascwheel.com/).

DISCOVER and REAPS

Maker (2013) has updated Discovering Intellectual Strengths and Capabilities while Observing Varied Ethnic Requirements (DISCOVER) to incorporate real problem-solving methods and materials as Real Engagement in Active Problem Solving (REAPS). She developed DISCOVER as a creative curriculum model with colleagues in a range of countries but found that teachers needed more guidance on how to implement it and so she combined it with other models such as real problem solving and the TASC approach to form REAPS.

Evaluating the provision

Effect size

It would seem that the calculation of effect size (ES) (Rogers, 1998) is the ultimate in evidence-based research in education: that an effect of 0.50 really is twice as big as one of 0.25 and therefore that the curriculum method is best. However, not all that is measurable is most valuable. Content knowledge is easily quantified, but not cognition or process.

The statistical measure known as ES is popular. It is determined by dividing the standard deviation of the control group into the difference between the mean scores of the treatment and control groups.

$$\text{Effect Size} = \frac{(\text{Mean of Treatment Group}) - (\text{Mean of Control Group})}{\text{Standard Deviation of Control Group}}$$

In classroom terms an effect size of 1.00 is approximately equal to one school year. An effect size of 0.33 would mean that the treatment group outperformed the control group by one-third of a school year, or about three grade-equivalent school months.

However, what is not usually known, even from the full research details, is whether what was called 'enrichment' really was. If there is grouping by ability compared with mixed ability teaching, have the methods of teaching been controlled and factored into the design? If not acceleration will 'win' in didactic systems.

Some 'effect' sizes for acceleration

Acceleration	– content based	0.57
	– telescoping	0.40
	– grade skipping	0.49 (academic effect)
		0.31 (socialisation effect)
	– early entrance and exit	0.49
	– advanced study courses	0.27
	– dual enrolment	0.22

(Rogers, 1998)

Curriculum compacting effect sizes

	– within class grouping	0.34
	– pull-out grouping	0.65 (extending regular programme)
		0.44 (focus on thinking skills)
		0.32 (focus on creative skills)
	– full-time ability grouping	0.49 (yearly effect primary – all subjects)
		0.33 (yearly effect secondary all subjects)
	– mentor programmes	0.47 (socialisation effect)
		0.42 (self-esteem effect)
		0.57 (academic effect)

(Rogers, 1998)

Hattie (2011) has been engaged in a meta-analysis of research on teaching and effect size over three decades. It encompasses 60,000 research projects and 250 million subjects. His conclusions were that the only variable producing an *effect size* of any value and significance was the quality of teaching. However, when

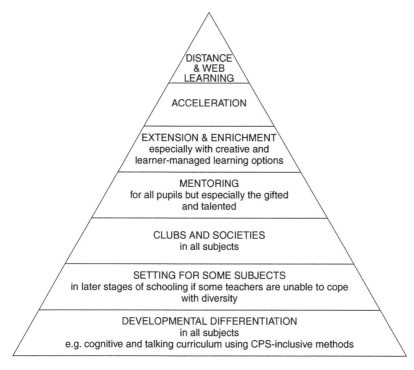

Figure 7.5 Seven levels of provision in effective schools

variables were held constant no differences were found between private and state education; length of years of schooling improved health not achievement; homework in primary school had zero effect and 5–10 minutes in secondary school was as good as 1–2 hours.

Auditing the provision

It is essential that an audit is made of the general provision in a school when there is an intention to improve the quality of education going on within it. Good primary schools (they had won the NACE Challenge Award) offered all the seven levels of provision shown in Figure 7.5.

At the lowest level the aim should be that every class and subject teacher should be trained in and offered developmental differentiation so as to be inclusive for as long as possible until study options may be needed as skill levels and interests become too disparate. Setting and acceleration are only necessary when teachers lack the resources and skills to differentiate properly. Acceleration may be an option for a few individuals in a single subject, usually maths.

Analysing teaching

FIAC teacher talk

In the 1960s Flanders had supervised a number of research projects using Flanders Interaction Analysis Categories (FIAC) and found:

> ... it appears when classroom interaction patterns indicate that pupils have opportunities to express their ideas, and when these ideas are incorporated into the learning activities, then the pupils seem to learn more and to develop more positive attitudes towards the teacher and the learning activities. (1970: 401)

In 1970 he quantified the types of interaction between teachers and their pupils and every three seconds the observer noted the type of interaction occurring in the classroom in relation to a sampling frame. He found that teachers occupied 70 per cent of the talking time in class, leaving 30 per cent to be shared by the pupils. (Hattie's 2011 data indicated that teacher talk occupied 80 per cent of lesson time!)

Flanders' result was replicated in my MA distance learning programmes; only about 1 in 50 teachers ever produced a reverse result, even in individual dyslexia tutorials. It is therefore crucial that in the management of change a teacher makes a 20-minute audio recording of the first section of a typical lesson to analyse in relation to the FIAC categories with tally marks in a table every 3–5 seconds to find the amount of their teacher talk.

FIAC categories

- *Teacher responses:* accepts feelings; praises or encourages; accepts or uses students' ideas. Teacher questions: asks questions. Teacher initiation: gives facts or opinions; gives directions.
- *Pupil responses:* responds to teacher; questions teacher; initiation (students talk expressing own ideas).
- *Other:* including silences. FIAC of course only counts the verbal not the non-verbal interactions.

Teaching quality

The classroom observations described in Chapter 6 (Montgomery, 2002) were used as a sampling frame to evaluate teacher performance. A running record with asides related to the five principles (CBG, 3Ms, PCI, TLP, AfL) was made during the observation of a lesson. It was followed by a feedback interview when the record was read to the teacher and points discussed as they shared in the process. Points of development were identified in relation to the frame and a short agenda set for their achievement.

The appraiser returned after an interval of at least three weeks to evaluate another lesson, with the same class and another running record was made. In the debriefing interview the record was again read and discussed and points for development identified and progress and good work affirmed.

The result was that successful teachers found what it was they were doing that constructed their success. All the participant teachers improved their teaching skills and those who had been failing and due to be dismissed were able to retrieve their positions and became satisfactory. Others moved on to become good teachers. Rarely some were difficult to help and they were usually nervously ill.

The method was taught in the five distance MA programmes and was successfully learned by the students. It worked effectively in their own situations demonstrated in their peer case analyses. It also helped cement supportive relationships between staff in the schools and transferred to positive attitudes to the pupils and non-teaching staff.

Analysing learning

The principles of learning have a long and complex research history and it is now possible to answer the question: What kind of learning processes should we want students to develop and use in order to attain competent performance? Research on learning in classrooms has given a series of seven empirically supported characteristics of effective learning processes (De Corte, 2013). These can be used as assessment criteria when evaluating provision.

Effective learning processes

- *Learning is constructive* – Learners are not passive recipients of information; they actively construct their own knowledge and skills. It requires cognitive processing on the part of the learner. Methods of transmission and passive absorption of knowledge in common use are the antithesis of this. This locates learning in education in the constructivist theory framework.
- *Learning is cumulative* – There is an important role in learning of formal as well as informal prior knowledge. On the basis of what they know learners construct their new learning and derive new meanings and skills.
- *Learning is self-regulated* – This refers to the metacognitive nature of effective learning especially in the managing and monitoring activities during the learning process.
- *Learning is goal-orientated* – Although some learning is incidental, an explicit awareness of and orientation towards a goal facilitates effective and meaningful learning.
- *Learning is situated* – Learning and thinking are more than just information-processing techniques; they have a context and social conception. Thus learning best occurs when it is anchored to real life contents.
- *Learning is individually different* – The processes and outcomes of learning vary due to individual differences in aptitude, prior knowledge

and experience, interest and motivation, self-esteem and self-efficacy and so on.

- *Collaborative learning* – Effective learning is facilitated by the exchange of ideas, comparing solution strategies and discussing arguments. Interaction and cooperation also mobilise reflection and thus foster the development of metacognitive knowledge and skills.

These requirements for effective learning are a significant advance upon the early studies that concentrated upon repetition, contiguity and reinforcement, the principles underlying behaviourist approaches. Cognition, knowing and understanding underpin the cognitivist approach that De Corte's list of effective learning strategies fits into. It can be used as a checklist to evaluate learning provision within lessons.

Authentic assessment of learning

1. Authentic assessment of real world tasks and processes. Gardner (1993) emphasised the role of authentic assessment in MI schools and classrooms, that is pupils should be set real world problems and activities and then assessment should be based on their performance on these, not IQ tests.

2. The Nebraska Starry Night (NSN) Project (Griffin *et al.*, 1995) is an example of authentic assessment in practice and the early identification of more able/creative children.

The title and metaphor is derived from the State of Nebraska Project that found the need for alternative assessments in the early identification of children from non-traditional populations that were under-represented in the overall 'gifted' education population. These were children from families where English was not the home language, those from small rural schools and/or ethnically or racially different families. The purpose was to develop unbiased and age-appropriate means by which teachers could assist in the early identification of able/creative children.

NSN is a general screening device expected to identify 12–15 per cent of children functioning at above grade level. There is no precise score or label.

Initial research identified a number of descriptors in common use in research and practice that identified the target behaviours, and there were multiple citations. Instead of putting them in categories with labels such as 'cognitive', 'affective', 'social', 'creative' that teachers might use as memory hooks, they used non-traditional informal ones such as:

- *'Act hunger'* – *strong need* – Wishes to express him/herself, eager to be involved, attempts to be centre stage.
- *Curious* – *questions* – Wants to know about things. Asks difficult questions. Questions often challenge inconsistencies and/or class rules.
- *Engages* – Given the choice, will draw others into his/her enquiry. Shares information with other children informally. Reaches out to others and includes them.

Overall there were 17 of these non-traditional categories in the NSN. The teachers were given a prompt sheet showing them as a constellation cue card and were trained in its use. They were asked to use it to write a script about each of the children in their class. The categories were: act hunger, fantasy, imagery, explorer, curious questions, independent, focus, knows, vocabulary, moving and doing, observant, sensitive, sees big picture, shares/volunteers, recognised by others, engages, humour.

The teachers were enabled to identify children who were more able or creative. It was also found that after further factor analyses there were four profiles or types that emerged:

- Type 1: the knowing, verbal, independent child;
- Type 2: the curious, moving, and doing explorer child;
- Type 3: the quiet, focused, unexpectedly humorous child;
- Type 4: the socially interactive, engaging, 'on stage' child.

A second result from the three-year research was:

- *Teachers with a directive, behaviour-based approach* (traditional non-constructivist) could identify children showing early signs of able/creative behaviour.
- *Teachers in child-centred, constructivist classrooms* had more opportunities to identify able/creative behaviours and therefore found more children with these abilities.

Evaluating curriculum materials

Curriculum evaluation using Bloom's taxonomy

Bloom's (1956) taxonomy is often used in curriculum design and evaluation for gifted groups. However, the taxonomy is also helpful in any curriculum evaluation and assessment for learners.

1. *Knowledge* – The remembering/recall of previously learned material from specific facts to complete theories. Knowledge represents the lowest level of learning outcomes in the cognitive domain.
2. *Comprehension* – The ability to grasp the meaning of material and represents the lowest level of understanding.
3. *Application* – The ability to use learned material in new and concrete situations. It includes the application of rules, methods, concepts, principles, laws and theories.
4. *Analysis* –The ability to break down material into its component parts so that its organisational structure can be understood. This may include the identification of the parts, analysis of the relations between parts and recognition of the organisational principles involved.

5. *Synthesis* – The ability to put parts together to form a new whole. This may involve the production of a unique communication (theme or speech), a plan of operations (research proposal) or set of abstract relations (scheme for classifying information). Learning outcomes in this area stress creative behaviours, with major emphasis on the formulation of new patterns or structures.

6. *Evaluation* – The ability to judge the value of material (statement, novel, poem, research report) for a given purpose. The judgments are based on definite criteria. These may be internal criteria (organisation) or external criteria (relevance for the purpose) and the student may determine the criteria or be given them. Learning outcomes in this area are highest in the cognitive hierarchy because they contain elements of all of the other categories, plus conscious value judgments based on clearly defined criteria.

It is expected that the materials and methods for engaging gifted and talented learners will involve the three higher levels of Bloom's taxonomy. It is also to be expected that with suitable preparation and development all learners will be enabled to work at these higher levels and not just operate at low-level memorisation.

Difficulty versus complexity
There is a tendency for teachers when making provision for the more able to go for 'difficulty' rather than complexity. For example:

- name one EU country
- name all the countries in the EU
- give the order of their admission to the EU.

These questions are at the knowledge (recall) level of Bloom's taxonomy. Difficulty describes the amount of effort we have to put into a mental operation (Sousa, 1993).

Complexity refers to the level of operation in which we are working in Bloom's taxonomy.

- explain why the capital of one EU country is situated where it is (analysis) + (difficulty)
- name one identifying feature of Paris (knowledge) + (complexity).

Long and short-term evaluations

The evaluation of schools and curricula take place regularly most often by assessing pupils' learning outcomes such as in examination results and international League Table tests, e.g. PISA and TIMSS. These test the traditional diet and are not particularly effective at that when they compare things that are not comparable, e.g. maths teaching in different countries is given different curriculum time, weights different aspects, uses different methods.

In the USA 'Operation Headstart' failed to show the intended outcomes using these standard measures until after 15 years. They were measuring the wrong things! In Headstart the Perry preschool provision for the disadvantaged protected the pupils from delinquency in later years and converted many of them into lifelong learners. They were the pupils who had enjoyed Weikart's 'cognitive curriculum' rather than traditional school curriculum provision of the 'mat and chat' type or the highly structured controlled format of Direct Instruction System for Teaching Arithmetic and Reading (DISTAR) provision (Weikart, 1967).

6. Case studies in effective school provision

> Case study methodologies are an important tool that provide a comprehensive picture of any issue which could be a complex one. Case study also helps to extend experience or add strength to what is already known through previous research. Case studies emphasise detailed contextual analysis of a limited number of events or conditions.
>
> (Flyvbjerg, 2006: 219)

As part of a NACE research project six primary and six secondary schools that had won the NACE Challenge Award had case studies made of them (Wallace *et al.*, 2009). All the schools used a range of identification procedures and the identification of the more able pupils took place by both qualitative and quantitative procedures and a comprehensive picture was built up of each child's progress and performance. There was also school-based monitoring and lesson observation. The learning outcomes were monitored by gender, ethnicity, special educational needs and stages of language acquisition. The strong commitment to extending the opportunities for all pupils enabled those with special ability and talent, who may not have been observed in the normal curriculum, to be identified.

The general ethos of the primary schools and classrooms observed (Montgomery, 2009) was positive, quiet, orderly and self-controlled. In each one the children were moving around the school in a purposeful manner talking quietly. The teachers' voices were quietly spoken as they led or followed their classes. There was no rushing, pushing or shouting.

Pupils of all ages dealt with visitors in an easy and polite manner. They talked openly and pleasantly and had a good measure of interested curiosity. They enthused about their school and their teachers and current work they were engaged upon. 'Philosophy for Children' was going down very well as were master classes in Art and Dance and Drama, choir and orchestra, French lessons, 'Brain club', country dancing, opera and many more.

The pupils, parents and staff viewed the school as 'the family'. There was an easy, welcoming and good relationship between them all. Each was accorded proper respect.

All the schools were committed to making inclusive provision while at the same time providing the widest range of opportunities so that no pupil and no talent would be left out. In evidence all the seven levels of curriculum provision described above were available.

The mainstream curriculum provision was backed by an extensive range of lunchtime, after hours and out of school clubs, and specialist local learning opportunities. Specialist sports coaches, ICT experts, specialists in science and the performing arts, and in art and culture were all in evidence at some point in the school calendar. The schools went to great lengths to foster all talents, recruiting expertise from every source they could find and it had paid great dividends for the pupils.

There were creative partnerships and resident artists came in to work with pupils. This was evidenced in the huge numbers of two and three-dimensional displays of all kinds to be seen. One primary school had made African masks and both girls and boys talked excitedly about the experience and the drums. In another of the schools the art coordinators ran master classes based on the style of the apprenticeship system to the great painters and the walls were covered with 'Lowrys', 'Matisses', 'Cezannes' as they worked on composition and style. The standard was very high.

In Dance one school had recruited a professional male dancer as instructor and had set up boys' dance as a regular part of the curriculum as well as mixed dance classes with some fine performances as a result. Another put on an opera based on fairy stories coached by members of the English National Opera.

Drama was a strong component in the curriculum of all the schools as well as related classes from writers in residence and college experts linking drama and writing in master classes for the pupils on the G and T register. Those still working on their Literacy Hour levels had their own specialist enrichment lessons.

Music was another area of talent in which no child was left out. There were opportunities to join the choir, sing for the elderly and join local choirs. In one school LSO musicians came to teach gamelan and identify pupils with musical ability. Another of the schools involved Local Authority experts and the local community and introduced 70 per cent of its pupils to playing a musical instrument. A range of violin, cello, clarinet and brass lessons took place as well as orchestra practice.

One of the schools was twinned with a school in Shanghai and the pupils were looking forward with great excitement to a 'China week'. With all of these initiatives the pupils were assured that if they had a desire to learn something a way would be found for them to do it; no stone would be left unturned.

Through the differentiation, extension and enrichment strategies in lessons teachers were able to use curriculum-based identification findings to extend the pupils' range of skills and develop the cognitive stretch.

Through effective planning, assessment and record keeping and liaison with the children's previous teachers they established what the pupils had previously done to prevent repetition. They then provided challenges through high quality tasks and planned work so that there was always differentiated work and extension material available. By assessing performance on these tasks it was then possible to set individual, more challenging targets and individual homework.

The pupils were allowed to make choices about and to organise their own work. They were expected to carry out, unaided, tasks that stretched their capabilities and helped develop their abilities to evaluate and check their work. Pupils set their own targets in Upper Junior classes and monitored their own progress through self-assessment and marking each other's work.

The Pupil Review process enabled all aspects of each child's progress and attainment to be considered and ideas shared and action taken to intervene as necessary. This process also engaged staff in a continuous cycle of self-reflection and development. In one school it was supported by team teaching and teaching partners.

The inner city school was particularly strong in its pupil review process. It took place termly between head teacher, class teacher and SENCo. For example, they discussed 'V' and all agreed she was a 'star', forthright and stubborn and they laughed fondly. She already went to the Arsenal Study Centre on Thursday mornings and was on the G and T register. Her literacy work was regarded as outstanding and it was at first decided to start a writers' club for her and pupils like her in Year 5. Then it was considered whether she might move into the Year 6 writers' group. When another pupil D., a friend, was also considered capable of joining her, this was the action decided so they would have each other for support amongst the Year 6.

The schools were all performing very well in the national league tables and in Ofsted inspectorial reports, despite some having lower than the national average entry scores.

Personalising learning

In earlier decades this was expressed as making provision for individual differences. In SEN Individual Educational Plans (IEPs) are drawn up to meet special needs. In some instances gifted and talented children also have them and all with DME need them.

Personalised learning (PL) means a tailor-made education for each child (DCFS, 2008b). It can be compared with the trend towards customisation in business where goods and services are tailor-made but at the cost of mass production. In education it means meeting the needs of learners more fully than before but at the same cost!

International comparisons had shown that the system in England and Wales did well on excellence but did not achieve equity in achievement. For example 58 per cent of 11-year-olds who had free school meals reached the expected level in English whereas 81 per cent of the rest did. It was hoped that PL would break the link between disadvantage and attainment. At the same time PL was designed to stretch and challenge the more able, thus bringing together the best features from several different initiatives.

The Personalised Learning programme (DCFS, 2004–2009) was linked with IQS, the Institutional Quality Standards:

- Assessment for Learning (AfL)
- effective teaching and learning
- a flexible curriculum – extension and enrichment
- organising the school for a pupil focus
- beyond the classroom – community involvement, partnerships.

The aim was to create an education system that focused on the needs of the individual child. This meant extra stretch for the gifted and talented and every pupil being able to extend their learning and develop their interests and aptitudes through extra support and tuition beyond the school day. Most important of all, it meant excellent, tailored whole-class teaching with all the resources available, from extra support staff to improved ICT being used to ensure that every pupil received the education they needed.

One of the drivers behind personalised learning was the need to develop *life-long learning* to create a more flexible, knowledgeable and continually upskilled workforce. This was especially important as the developing societies take over large areas of production and do it more cheaply. In order to prepare learners in schools now for this future scenario they needed to learn how to learn and to become accustomed to managing their own learning – *self-regulated learners*, a major work in progress. Would this be enough to fix a broken system?

Constructivist teachers

Constructivism originated in the early twentieth century in the work of Bartlett (1932) in the UK and Piaget, Rey and Inhelder in Paris at about the same time. Essentially it emphasised that in order to learn individuals have to participate in and construct their own knowledge. They are meaning-makers – the process that Piaget termed 'accommodation'. Critical thinking theory as proposed by Resnick (1989) and Paul (1990) belongs to this realm.

Learners in the new millennium need to be self-starters, self-regulating and self-motivated. Gifted pupils in particular are stimulated and extended in situations that offer such opportunities and it is constructivist methods that can facilitate this.

According to Brookes and Brookes (1993) there are 12 guiding principles in the approaches of constructivist teachers. They:

- encourage and accept student autonomy and initiative;
- use raw data and primary sources, along with manipulative, interactive and physical materials;
- use cognitive terminology when framing tasks;
- allow pupil responses to drive lessons, shift instructional strategies and alter content;

- inquire about pupils' understanding of concepts before sharing understanding of them;
- encourage pupils to engage in dialogue both with the teacher and each other;
- encourage pupil enquiry by asking thoughtful, open-ended questions and encourage pupils to ask questions of each other;
- seek elaboration of pupils' initial responses;
- engage pupils in experiences that might engender contradictions to their initial hypotheses and then encourage discussion;
- allow wait time after posing questions;
- provide time for pupils to construct relationships and create metaphors;
- nurture pupils' natural curiosity through frequent use of the learning cycle (spiral model).

As can be imagined teachers once versed in these skills find it hard to work in didactic environments.

Conclusions

Pupils with DME need a constructivist approach to learning and teaching and especially benefit from alternative modes for recording information. They also need a challenging and interesting curriculum suitable for the gifted and to be active participants in the learning process. They need opportunities for more legitimate pupil talk and peer collaboration. These are the needs of all children and if we meet the needs of pupils with DME then the school experience and achievement of all children will be raised.

There need to be more opportunities for creativity in all subjects, and for autonomous learning. Guidance on becoming a self-organised learner will be needed and can be accomplished by teaching research and study skills within all subjects and how to learn from failures.

Teachers educated in a didactic system will need help to develop the necessary knowledge and skills to design problem-based learning and CPS. This is best effected by changing the nature of teacher education to give them direct experience and then using CPD to develop and maintain the skills.

Policies on developmental handwriting and spelling will be needed at both primary and secondary levels to overcome the hidden difficulties that lead to underachievement. All teachers should be expected to address these issues and follow the policies.

There should be structure and order in classrooms and agreed routines with quiet areas and times. The school behaviour and discipline policy should be constructive and supportive, implemented by all staff in a consistent and fair manner. The pupil voice should form part of the structured formal and informal feedback to help maintain and improve the system. A positive classroom ethos and school climate is generated by a respectful and supportive environment and feedback.

What makes a DME-friendly school?

In the school:

- a belief by the head and the senior management team that DME exists and the school can and will do something to identify and support its pupils with DME;
- a lead teacher who may not be the SENCo or Head of Learning Support who will raise the agenda and keep up to date on current thinking and methods of intervention, and run CPD on DME;
- a special budget ring-fenced for DME resources and teacher updating and publications;
- an educated teacher workforce committed to being DME friendly;
- a special resource quiet area for DME pupils to meet and to help each other and do research;
- agreed whole-school policies for cursive handwriting and spelling teaching and for real problem-based and CPS approaches to teaching and learning.

In the classrooms:

- no dictations; no copying notes from the whiteboard; no reading aloud round the class, volunteers only;
- no extended writing periods without support or assistive technology;
- different modes of response encouraged;
- extended and legitimate pupil talk to be encouraged and built into lesson plans;
- discreet attention training and social skills development;
- quiet structure and routine.

A positive, supportive classroom climate:

- teachers model respect for pupils and each other;
- give praise and support for effort;
- a sympathetic attitude to writing and reading problems;
- enable pupils to talk about their ideas before they write;
- encourage TPS, the Think – Pair – Share strategy;
- give handouts to support learning and cut down note taking;
- provide alternative methods of presentation than writing;
- give unobtrusive help with written work;
- encourage peer tutoring and buddy support;
- arrange mentoring from older pupils who have had problems;
- systematically use CPS across all subjects;
- explain new concepts carefully and clearly with examples;
- keep instructions brief; have protocols written down and agreed;
- give homework briefing time;

- give written notes for essentials;
- cut tasks into smaller sections so they can be followed more easily;
- ensure all pupils sit still and make eye contact with the teacher whilst listening to instructions;
- ensure that tasks have built-in success points;
- organise lessons to have a Tactical Plan.

Specialist provision. Ensure that:

- diagnosis occurs early, soon after entry into Reception, junior or secondary school;
- a lead teacher is identified and trained to work with dyslexics, Asperger, etc. cases;
- a specialist programme is used with dyslexics, not a 'pick and mix' one;
- progress is carefully monitored to achieve the 'catch up' rate;
- pupils can re-enter specialist programmes for top-ups, especially for spelling;
- bullying should be discussed with the pupil and dealt with quickly;
- tutorial provision should be discreet;
- specialist programmes should not be attempted during other lessons;
- all pupils have a mentor.

Postscript

Schools have historically been most conservative, uncritically passing down from generation to generation outmoded didactic, lecture and drill-based models of instruction (Resnick, 1989). There has been a failure to develop higher order cognitive skills in schools and colleges.

The result was that students, on the whole did not:

- learn how to work by, or think for themselves;
- learn how to gather, analyse, synthesise and assess information;
- learn to enter sympathetically into the thinking of others nor how to deal rationally with conflicting points of view;
- learn to become critical readers, writers, speakers or listeners and so did not become literate in the proper sense of the word;
- critically analyse their own experience and would find it difficult to explain the basis of their own beliefs; and so
- gain much genuine knowledge.

They therefore lacked the traits of mind of a genuinely educated person, such as intellectual humility, courage, integrity, perseverance and faith in reason.

In schools and colleges around the world instructional practice presupposes a didactic theory of knowledge, learning and literacy despite the fact that we know that these methods are particularly unsuitable. This is also despite the fact that employers in the developed nations now realise that they must increasingly generate workers who can think critically, who can reason and work in a flexible and creative manner.

As societies become less isolated and more complex, lack of rationality at both global and local level becomes increasingly dangerous for the maintenance of human existence. To combat these dangers of didactic education that brings with it its own kind of ignorance and prejudice, education worldwide needs to change (Paul, 1990).

In the twenty-first century we have seen the effects of this education based upon traditional memorisation methods on our vulnerable youths. Education worldwide needs reframing to become constructivist in approach. Schools that meet the needs of pupils with Dual and Multiple Exceptionalities will be in the lead.

References

Adams, J., Eyre, D., Howell, J. and Raffan, J. 1993 *The Motorway Project; Village of Edenfield; and Townscapes* Wisbech: Learning Development Aids

Addy, L. 2004 *Speed Up* Wisbech: Learning Development Aids

Allcock, P. 2001 'The importance of handwriting skills in Keystage 3 and GCSE Examinations of more able pupils' *Educating Able Children* 5 (1) 23–5

Alloway, T. P. 2009 'Cognitive training: Improvements in attainment' *PATOSS Bulletin* 22 (1) 57–61

Alston, J. 1993 *Assessing and Promoting Writing Skills* Stafford: NASEN

Amundson, S. J. 1995 *Evaluation Tool for Children's Handwriting (ETCH)* Horner AK: OTKids

APA 1994 *Diagnostic and Statistical Manual of Mental Disorders DSM-IV (4th Edition revised)* Washington DC: American Psychiatric Association

APA 2000 *Diagnostic and Statistical Manual of Mental Disorders DSM-IV-TR* Washington DC: American Psychiatric Association

APA 2006 *Diagnostic and Statistical Manual of Mental Disorders DSM-V* Washington DC: American Psychiatric Association

APA 2011 *Diagnostic and Statistical Manual of Mental Disorders DSM-V* Washington DC: American Psychiatric Association

Appleby, M. and Condonis, M. 1998 *Hearing the Cry* Sydney: Rose Training

Ashlock, R. B. 1982 *Error Patterns in Computation 3rd Edition* Columbus OH: Merrill

Asperger, H. 1979 'Problems with infantile autism' *Communication* 13 45–52

Attwood, T. 2008 *The Complete Guide to Asperger's Syndrome* London: Jessica Kingsley

Ausubel, D. P. 1968 *Educational Psychology. A Cognitive View* New York: Holt Rinehart and Winston

Ayres, A. J. 1976 *Sensory Integration and Learning Disorders* Los Angeles: Western Psychological Services

Baddeley, A. 1985 *Human Memory: Theory and Practice* Boston MA: Allyn and Bacon

Baddeley, A. 2007 *Working Memory: Thought and Action* Oxford: Oxford University Press

Bandura, A. 1977 *Social Learning Theory* Engelwood Cliffs NJ: Prentice Hall

Barber, C. 1996 'The integration of a very able pupil with Asperger Syndrome into mainstream school' *British Journal of Special Education* 23 (1) 19–24

Barkley, R. A. 1997 *Defiant Children: A Clinician's Manual for Assessment and Parent Training* (2nd edition) New York: Guildford

Barkley, R. A. (ed) 1998 *Attention Deficit Hyperactivity Disorder: A Handbook for Diagnosis and Treatment* (2nd edition) Hurstpierpoint: IPS Publications

Barnett, A., Henderson, S. E., Scheib, B. and Schutz, J. 2008 *DASH – Detailed Assessment of Speed of Handwriting* London: Pearson

Baron-Cohen, S. 2008 'Theories of the autistic mind' *The Psychologist* 21 (2) 112–16

Baron-Cohen, S., Leslie, A. M. and Frith, U. 1985 'Does the autistic child have a theory of mind?' *Cognition* 21 37–46

Bartlett, Sir F. C. 1932 *Remembering. A Study in Experimental and Social Psychology* New York: Cambridge University Press

Baum, S. and Owen, S. V. 1988 'High ability learning disabled students. How are they different?' *Gifted Child Quarterly* 32 (3) 321–6

Bennathan, M. and Boxall, M. 2000 *Effective Interventions in Primary Schools* (2nd edition) London: David Fulton

Benner, G. J. 2002 'Language skills of children with EBD: A literature review – Emotional and Behavioural disorders' *Journal of Emotional and Behavioural Disorders* 10 43–56

Berninger, V. W. 2004 'The role of mechanics in composing of Elementary students: A review of research and interventions' Keynote, Annual DCD Conference, Oxford, April

Berninger, V. W. 2008 'Writing problems in developmental dyslexia. Underdiagnosed and undertreated?' *Journal of School Psychology* 46 1–21

Berninger, V. W. and Graham, S. 1998 'Language by hand: a synthesis of a decade of research on handwriting' *Handwriting Review* 12 11–25

Berninger, V. W., Abbott, R. D., Nagy, W. and Carlisle, J. 2010 'Growth in phonological, orthographic, and morphological awareness in Grades 1 to 6' *Journal of Psycholinguistic Research* 39 (2) 141–63

Bishop, D. V. M. 1989 'Autism, Asperger Syndrome and Semantic-pragmatic disorder. Where are our boundaries?' *British Journal of Disorders of Communication* 24 107–21

Blagg, N. R., Ballinger, M. P. and Lewis, R. E. 1993 *Development of Transferable Skills in Learners. Research Series* Sheffield: The UK Government Employment Department

Bloom, B. S. 1956 *Taxonomy of Educational Objectives Vol 1* London: Longmans

Blythe, P. and McGlown, D. J. 1979 *An Organic Basis for Neuroses and Educational Difficulties* Chester: Insight Publications

Bond, G. L. and Tinker, M. A. 1967 *Reading Difficulties* New York: Appleton Century Crofts

Bourassa, D. and Treiman, R. 2003 'Spelling in children with dyslexia: Analyses from the Treiman-Bourassa Early Spelling Test' *Scientific Studies of Reading* 7 (4) 309–33

Bowers, S. and Wells, L. 1988 *Ways and Means; A Problem Solving Approach* Kingston upon Thames: The Friends Workshop Publication

Bowlby, J. 1990 *A Secure Base. Parent–Child Attachment and Healthy Human Development* Michigan: University of Michigan Basic Books

Boxall, M. 2002 *Nurture Groups in Schools: Principles and Practice* London: Sage

Boyle, W. and Bragg, J. 2007 '£2 billion schools initiative a "waste of time"' *Guardian* 22 October http://www.theguardian.com/education/2007/oct/22/schools.uk2 (accessed 8 February 2015)

Bradley, C. 1937 'The behaviour of children receiving benzedrine' *American Journal of Psychiatry* 94 577–85

Brand, V. 1998 *Spelling Made Easy* (14th edition) Cheltenham: Lucky Duck Publishing

Bravar, L. 2005 'Studying handwriting: An Italian experience' 6th International Conference on Developmental Co ordination Difficulties, Trieste, 17–20 May

Briggs, D. 1980 'A study of the influence of handwriting upon grades in examination scripts' *Educational Review* 32 185–93

British Dyslexia Association 2015 http://www.bdadyslexia.org.uk/aboutdyslexia.html (accessed 2 February 2015)

Bronfenbrenner, U. 1989 'Ecological systems theory' *Annals of Child Development* 6 187–249

Brookes, J. and Brookes, M. 1993 *In Search of Understanding, The Case for Constructivist Classrooms* Alexandria VA: Association for the Supervision and Curriculum Development

Brown, A. L., Brandsford, J. D., Ferrara, R. A. and Campione, J. C. 1983 'Learning, Remembering and Understanding' in J. H. Flavell and E. Markham (eds) *Carmichael's Manual of Child Psychology Vol 1* New York: Wiley

Bruner, J. 1968 *Toward a Theory of Instruction* New York: Norton and Company

Burnhill, L.P., Hartley, J., Fraser, L. and Young, D. 1975 'Writing Lines: An exploratory study' *Programmed Learning and Educational Technology* 12 (2) 84–7

Butterworth, B. 2010 'Foundational numerical capacities and the origins of dyscalculia' *Trends in Cognitive Sciences* 14 (12): 534–41

Canter, L. and Canter, M. 2002 *Assertive Discipline* London: Assertive Discipline Company

Carper, J. 2000 *Your Miracle Brain* New York: Harper Collins

CBI 2000 *Consortium of British Industry: Director's speech* London: CBI

Cefai, C. 2004 'Pupil resilience in the classroom' *Emotional and Behavioural Difficulties* 9 (3) 149–70

Cefai, C. 2007 'Resilience for all: a study of classrooms as protective contexts' *Emotional and Behavioural Difficulties* 12 (2) 119–34

Chall, J. 1967 *Learning to Read: The Great Debate* New York: McGraw Hill

Chall, J. 1985 *Stages in Reading Development* New York: McGraw-Hill

Chesson, R., McKay, C. and Stephenson, E. 1991 'The consequences of motor/learning difficulties in school age children and their teachers: Some parental views' *Support for Learning* 6 (4) 172–7

Christensen, C. A. and Jones, D. 2000 'Handwriting: An underestimated skill in the development of written language' *Handwriting Today* 2 56–69

Clark, M. M. 1970 *Reading Difficulties in Schools* Harmondsworth: Penguin

Clay, M. M. 1975 *What Did I Write? The Beginnings of Writing Behaviour* London: Heinemann

Clay, M. M. 1979 *The Early Detection of Reading Difficulties* London: Heinemann

Clements, S. D. 1966 *National Project on Minimal Brain Dysfunction in Children: Terminology and Identification Monograph No 3 Public Health Service Publication No 1415* Washington DC: Public Health Services Publication

Coffield, F. C. 2005 'Kinaesthetic nonsense' *Times Educational Supplement* 14 January 17–18

Cohen, N. J., Menna, D. D., Vallance, M. A., Barwick, N. I. and Horodezky, N. B. 1998 'Language, social cognitive processing, and behavioural characteristics of psychiatrically disturbed children with previously identified and unsuspected language impairments' *Journal of Child Psychology and Psychiatry* 39 (6) 853–64

Cole, T., Visser, J. and Upton, G. 1998 *Effective Schooling for Pupils with Emotional and Behaviour Difficulties* London: David Fulton

Connelly, V., Dockrell, J. and Barnett, A. 2005 'The slow handwriting of undergraduate students constrains the overall performance in exam essays' *Educational Psychology* 25 99–109

Conners, K. C. 2007 *Conners Behaviour Rating Scale* London: Pearson/Psychological Corporation

Cooper, P. 2008 'Editorial' *Emotional and Behavioural Difficulties* 13 (4) 333–4

Cooper, P. (ed) 1999 *Understanding and Supporting Children with Emotional and Behavioural Difficulties* London: Jessica Kingsley

Cooper, P. and Ideus, K. 1999 *Attention Deficit Hyperactivity Disorder: A Practical Guide for Teachers* Hurstpierpoint: IPS Publications

Corn, A. 1986 'Gifted students who have a visual difficulty. Can we meet their educational needs?' *Education of the Visually Handicapped* 18 (2) 71–84

Couture, C., Royer, E., Dupuis, F. A. and Potkin, P. 2003 'Comparison of Quebec and British teachers' beliefs about training and experience with ADHD' *Emotional and Behavioural Difficulties* 8 (4) 286–302

Cowdery, L. L., Montgomery, D., Morse, P. and Prince-Bruce, M. 1994 *TRTS – Teaching Reading Through Spelling Volumes 1 to 7* Wexford: TRTS Publishing

Cropley, A. J. 1994 'Creative intelligence: A concept of true giftedness' *European Journal of High Abilities* 15 16–23

CSIE 2015 'What is inclusion?' www.csie.org.uk/inclusion/what.shtml (accessed 8 February 2015)

Curry, M. and Bromfield, C. 1994 *Circle Time* Stafford: NASEN

Dabrowski, K. 1972 *Psychoneurosis is Not an Illness* London: Little, Brown and Co

DCFS 2007 *Teach First Report, 'Lessons from the Front'* London: DCFS

DCFS 2008a *The Education of Children and Young People with Behavioural, Emotional and Social Difficulties as a Special Educational Need* London: DCFS

DCFS 2008b *Personalised Learning. A Practical Guide* London: DCFS Publication

DCFS 2009 *Learning Behaviour: Lessons Learned: the Steer Report* London: DCFS

DCFS 2013 *Statistics in Education 2011–2012* London: DCFS

DCFS 2014 *Statistics in Education 2013–2014* London: DCFS

De Corte, E. 2013 'Giftedness considered from the perspective of research on learning and instruction' *High Ability Studies* 24 (1) 5–20

Dehaney, R. 2000 'Literacy hour and the literal thinker: The inclusion of children with semantic-pragmatic language difficulties in the literacy hour' *Support for Learning* 15 (1) 36–40

Delpire, R. and Monory, J. 1962 *The Written Word* London: Prentice Hall

Dennison, P. E. and Dennison, G. E. 1998 *Brain Gym Handbook* Ventura CA: Edu-Kinaesthetics Inc.

DfE 2014 *National Curriculum, Key Stages 1 and 2: Framework for English and Mathematics* London: DfE

DfE 2014 *Statistical First Release: Schools, Pupils and Their Characteristics* London: DfE SFR/15/2014

DfEE 1997 *Excellence for All Children: Meeting Special Educational Needs* London: DfEE

DfEE 1998 *The National Literacy Strategy Framework for Teaching* London: Department for Education and Employment

DfEE 1999 *Excellence in Cities* London: DfEE

DfEE 2001 *The Code of Practice Revised* London: Department for Education and Employment

DfEE 2001 *The National Literacy Strategy* London: DfEE

DfES 2005 *Excellence and Enjoyment: Social and Emotional Aspects of Learning (SEAL)* Nottingham: DfES Publications

Duke, D. 2002 'The Neurology of NLD' Policy into Practice Conference on Dyslexia Uppsala, Sweden, August

Dweck, C. S. 2006 *Mindset: The New Psychology of Success* New York: Random House

Dyslexia Action 2015 'About dyslexia: A specific learning difficulty' http://dyslexiaaction.org.uk/about-dyslexia (accessed 2 February 2015)

Edwards, J. 1994 *The Scars of Dyslexia* London: Cassell

Ehri, L. C. 1980 'The development of orthographic images' 311–38 In U. Frith *Cognitive Processes in Spelling* London: Academic Press

Elliott, J. G. and Grigorenko, E. L. 2014 *The Dyslexia Debate* New York: Cambridge University Press

Elton, L. 1989 *The Elton Report. Discipline in Schools* London: DES

Feder, K. P. and Majnemer, A. 2007 'Handwriting development, competency and intervention' *Developmental Medicine and Child Neurology* 49 312–17

Fischer, C. 2014 'Mathematically gifted but reading and spelling difficulties. The perspective of learning difficulties' International Biennial ECHA Conference, 17–20 September, Ljubljana, Slovenia

Flanders, N. A. 1970 *Analysing Teaching Behaviour* Reading MA: Addison-Wesley

Flavell, J. H. 1979 'Metacognition and cognitive monitoring' *American Psychologist* 34 906–11

Flyvbjerg, B. 2006 'Five misunderstandings about case study research' *Qualitative Inquiry* 12 (2) 219–45

Forsyth, D. 1988 'An evaluation of an infant school screening instrument' Unpublished dissertation Kingston upon Thames: Kingston Polytechnic

Frederickson, N., Frith, U. and Reason, R. 1997 *Phonological Assessment Battery (PhAB)* London: Pearson

Freeman, J. 1991 *Gifted Children Growing Up* London: Cassell

Frith, U. (ed.) 1991 *Autism and Asperger Syndrome* Cambridge: Cambridge University Press

Frith, U. 2014 'Autism – are we any closer to explaining the enigma?' *The Psychologist* 29 (10) 744–5

Gabis, L., Raz, R. and Kesner-Baruch, Y. 2010 'Paternal age in autism spectrum disorders and ADHD' *Paediatric Neurology* 43 (4) 300–2

Gabor, G. 2007 'An evaluation of the process and progress towards setting up a dyslexia programme in an International School' Unpublished MA SpLD dissertation London: Middlesex University

Gagne, F. 1998 'The prevalence of gifted, talented and multitalented individuals: estimates from peer and teacher nominations' 101–26 In R. C. Friedman and K. B. Rogers (eds) *Talent in Context: Historical and Social Perspectives on Giftedness* Washington DC: American Psychological Association

Gagne, F. 2004 'Transforming gifts into talents: the DMGT as a developmental theory' *High Ability Studies* 15 (2) 119–47

Gagne, R. L. 1973 *The Essentials of Learning* London: Holt Rinehart and Winston

Galaburda, A. 1993 *Dyslexia and Development* Cambridge MA: Harvard University Press

Galloway, D. and Goodwin, C. 1987 *Education of Disturbing Children* London: Longman

Galton, M., Simon, B. and Croll, P. 1980 *Inside the Primary Classroom* London: Routledge and Kegan Paul

Gardner, H. 1993 *Multiple Intelligences. The Theory in Practice* New York: Basic Books

Gardner, T. (ed.) 2000 *Acceleration or Enrichment: UK Mathematics Foundation Report* Birmingham: Birmingham University

Gathercole, S. E. 2008 'Working memory in the classroom' *The Psychologist* 21 (5) 382–5

Gerstmann, J. 1940 'Syndrome of finger agnosia. Disorientation for right and left agraphia and acalculia' *Archives of Neurology and Psychology* 44 589–95

Geschwind, N. 1979 'Specialisations of the human brain' *Scientific American* 241 (3) 158–67

Gibbs, G. 1990 *Learning Through Action* London: Further Education Unit

Gillingham, A. M. and Stillman, B. U. 1956 *Remedial Training for Children with Specific Disability in Reading, Spelling and Penmanship* Bath: Basic Books

Gillingham, A. M., Stillman, B. U. and Orton, S. T. 1940 *Remedial Training for Children with Specific Disability in Reading, Spelling and Penmanship* New York: Sackett and Williams

Glueck, S. and Glueck, E. 1968 *Delinquents and Non-Delinquents in Perspective* Cambridge MA: Harvard University Press

Goddard-Blythe, S. 2009 *Attention, Balance and Coordination: The ABC of Learning Success* Oxford: Wiley Blackwell

Goldberg, M. L. 1956 *Research on the Talented* New York: Teachers College Press

Goleman, D. 1995 *Emotional Intelligence* New York: Bantam Books

Golinkoff, R. M. 1978 'Phonemic awareness skills and reading achievement' 23–41 In F. B. Murray and J. J. Pikulski (eds) *The Acquisition of Reading* Baltimore: University Park Press

Good, T. L. and Brophy, J. E. 1986 *Educational Psychology: A Realistic Approach* London: Holt Rinehart and Winston

Goodenough, F. L. 1926 *Measurement of Intelligence by Drawings* Yonkers, New York: World Book Company

Goswami, U. 2003 'How to beat dyslexia' *The Psychologist* 16 (9) 403–5

Gould, J. and Ashton Smith, J. 2011 'Good Autism Practice' http://www.autism.org.uk/about-autism/autism-and-asperger-syndrome-an-introduction/gender-and-autism.aspx (accessed 3 March 2014)

Graham, L. 2008 'From ABCs to ADHD: The role of schooling in the construction of behaviour disorder and the production of disorderly objects' *International Journal of Inclusive Education* 12 (1) 7–33

Gray, C. 1990 *The Social Stories Book* Arlington TX: Future Horizons

Gray, C. 2003 *My Social Stories Book* London: Jessica Kingsley

Greenfield, S. 2007 'Peer calls for ADHD care review' http://www.news.bbc.co.uk/1/hi/health/7093044.stm (accessed 8 February 2015)

Gregory, K. and Clarke, M. 2003 'High stakes assessment in England and Singapore' *Theory and Practice* 42 66–78

Griffin, N. S., Curtiss, J., McKenzie, L., Maxfield, L. and Crawford, M. 1995 'Authentic assessment of able children using a regular classroom observation protocol' *Flying High* 2 Spring 34–42

Gubbay, S. S. 1975 *The Clumsy Child* London: W.B. Saunders

Hallam, S. 2002 *Ability Grouping in Schools* London: Institute of Education Publications

Hallett, V., Ronald, A., Rijsdijk, F. and Happe, F. 2010 'Association of autistic-like internalising traits during childhood' *American Journal of Psychiatry* 167 (7) 809–17.

Hammill, D. D. and Larsen, S. C. 1988 *TOWL-3: Test of Written Language* Austin: Pro-ed

Happe, V., Ronald, A. and Plomin, R. 2006 'Time to give up on a single explanation for autism' *Nature Neuroscience* 9 (10) 1218–20

Harbinson, H. and Alexander, J. 2009 'Asperger syndrome and the English curriculum: Addressing the challenges' *Support for Learning* 24 (1) 11–18

Harris, A. 1995 'Raising the levels of pupils' achievement through school improvement' *Support for Learning* 11 (2) 62–7

Harris, D. (ed.) 1963 *The Revised Version of the Goodenough Draw a Man Test* New York: Grune and Stratton

Hattersley, C. 2010 'Autism factfile' *Special* 24–6.

Hattie, J. 2011 *Visible Learning for Teachers: Maximizing Impact on Learning* London: Routledge

Helene, M. 2007 'An Investigation of two different remedial approaches to dyslexic difficulties' Unpublished MA SpLD Dissertation, London: Middlesex University

Henderson, S. E. and Green, D. 2001 'Handwriting problems in children with Asperger Syndrome' *Handwriting Today* 2 65–71

Henderson, S. E. and Sugden, D. A. 1992 *Movement Assessment Battery for Children* Sidcup, Kent: The Psychological Corporation

Heng, M. A. and Tam, K. Y. B. 2006 'Reclaiming soul in gifted education: The academic caste system in Asian schools 178–86' In B. Wallace and G. Eriksson *Diversity in Gifted Education: International Perspectives on Global Issues* London: Routledge

Hickey, K. 1977 *Dyslexia: A Language Training Course for Teachers and Learners* Staines: The Dyslexia Institute

Hillman, P. 2014 'Effectiveness of Mindfulness Cognitive Behaviour Therapy with talented youth' European Council for High Ability (ECHA) Conference, 27–20 September, Ljubljana, Slovenia

Hippocrates and Adams, F. 1946 *The Genius Works of Hippocrates* Baltimore: Williams and Witkins Co.

Hjorne, E. and Saljo, R. 2014 'The practices of dealing with children in need of special support: a Nordic perspective' *Emotional and Behavioural Difficulties* 19 (3) 246–50

HMI 2001 *The Teaching of Writing in Primary Schools: Could Do Better* London: DfES

Hodgson, J. 2009 'GCSE mathematics evaluaton study' BBC Radio 4, 5 September

Honey, P. and Mumford, A. 1986 *A Manual of Learning Styles* London: Honey

Hornsby, B. and Farrar, M. 1990 'Some effects of a dyslexia-centred teaching programme' In P. D. Pumfrey and C. D. Elliott (eds) *Children's Difficulties in Reading, Spelling and Handwriting* 173–96 London: Falmer Press

Hornsby, B. and Shear, F. 1978 *Alpha to Omega* London: Heinemann

Howe, M. J. A., Davidson, J. W. and Sloboda, J. A. 1998 'Innate talents, reality or myth?' *Behaviour and Brain Sciences* 21 399–442

Howlin, P. 2006 'Crime vulnerability in ASD' International Conference on ASD, Cardiff, 8–10 May

International Dyslexia Association 2003 *Orton Emeritus Series: Mathematics and Dyslexia* (by H. A. Tomey, J. Steeves and D. L. Gilmour) Baltimore MD: IDA

Iszatt, J. and Waslewska, T. 1997 'Nurture groups. An early intervention model enabling vulnerable children with EBD to integrate successfully into school' *Education and Child Psychology* 14 (3) 121–39

Jaksa, P. 1999 *25 Stupid Mistakes Parents Make* New York: McGraw Hill Professional

James, K. and Engelhardt, L. 2012 'The effects of handwriting experience on functional brain development' *Neuroscience and Education* 1 (1) 32–42

Jenkins, J. 2014 'Out of the ordinary' BBC Radio 4, 3 March

Jerrim, J. 2013 *The Reading Gap* London: The Sutton Trust.

Kagan, J. 1966 'The generality and dynamics of conceptual tempo' *Journal of Abnormal Child Psychology* 71 17–24

Kanner, L. 1943 'Autistic disturbances of affective contact' *The Nervous Child* 2 217–50

Kaplan, M. 2000 'Atypical brain development' 27th International Congress in Psychology, Stockholm, August

Kelly, G. A. 1955 *The Psychology of Personal Constructs, 2 Vols* New York: Norton

Kerry, T. 1983 *Finding and Helping the Able Child* London: Croom Helm

Kibel, M. 2002 'Linking language to action' 42–57 In T. R. Miles and E. Miles (eds) *Dyslexia and Mathematics* London: Routledge

Klingberg, T. 2009 *The Overflowing Brain* New York: Oxford University Press

Kokot, S. 2003 'A neurodevelopmental approach to learning disabilities: Diagnosis and treatment' 7–24 In D. Montgomery (ed.) *Gifted and Talented Children with SEN: Double Exceptionality* London: NACE/Fulton

Kolb, D. A. 1984 *Experiential Learning; Experiences as a Source of Learning and Development* New York: Prentice Hall

Koppitz, E. 1977 *The Oral Visual Digit Span Test (VADs)* New York: Grune and Stratton

Kosc, L. 1974 'Developmental dyscalculia' *Journal of Learning Disabilities* 7 (3) 164–77

Kuczaj, S. A. 1979 'Evidence for a language learning strategy: on the relative ease of acquisition of prefixes and suffixes' *Child Development* 50 1–13

Kussmaul, A. 1877 'Disturbance of speech' *Cyclopaedia of the Practice of Medicine* 14 571–5

Kutscher, M. L. 2005 *Kids in the Syndrome Mix of ADHD, LD, Asperger's and Tourette's and More* London: Jessica Kingsley

Laszlo, M., Barstow, P. and Bartrip, P. 1988 'A new approach to perceptuomotor dysfunction, previously called "clumsiness"' *Support for Learning* 3 35–40

Laufer, M. W., Denhoff, E. and Solomons, G. 1957 'Hyperkinetic impulse disorder in children's behaviour problems' *Psychosomatic Medicine* 19 18–49

Law, J., Lindsay, G., Peacey, N., Gascoigne, M., Soloff, N., Radford, J., Band, S. and Fitzgerald, L. 2000 *Provision for Children with Speech and Language Needs in England and Wales* London: DfES

Law, J. and Stringer, H. 2014 'Introduction: The overlap between behaviour and communication and its complications for mental health in childhood. The elephant in the room' *Emotional and Behavioural Difficulties* 19 (1) 2–6

Lawrence, J., Steed, D. and Young, P. 1989 *Disruptive Children – Disruptive Schools?* London: Routledge

Leites, N. S. 1971 *Intellectual Abilities and Age* Moscow: Pedagogica

Lewis, C., Hitch, G. and Walker, P. 1994 'The prevalence of specific arithmetical difficulties and specific reading difficulties in 9–10-year-old boys and girls' *Journal of Child Psychology and Psychiatry* 36 283–92

Liberman, I. J. 1973 'Segmentation of the spoken word and reading acquisition' *Bulletin of the Orton Society* 23 365–77

Lipman, M. 1991 *Thinking in Education* Cambridge: Cambridge University Press

Lloyd, G. 2005 *Problem Girls: Understanding and Supporting Troubled Girls and Young Women* London: Routledge Falmer

Lockhead, J. 2001 *THINKBACK: A User's Guide to Minding the Mind* London: Lawrence Erlbaum

Loviglio, L. 1981 'Mathematics and the brain: A tale of two hemispheres' *Massachusetts Teacher* Jan/Feb 8–12

Low, G. 1990 'Cursive makes a comeback' *Education* 6 April, 341

Lyth, A. 2004 'Handwriting speed: An aid to communication success?' *Handwriting Today* 3 30–5

McCarty, C. A. and Weisz, J. R. 2007 'Effects of psychotherapy for depression in children and adolescents: What We Can (and Can't) Learn from Meta-Analysis and Component Profiling' *Journal of the American Academy of Child and Adolescent Psychiatry* 46 (7) 879–86

McGhee, E. 2010 'An investigation of working memory training in a sample of dyslexics' Unpublished MA SpLD Dissertation, London: Middlesex University

McGuinness, C. 1999 *From Thinking Schools to Thinking Classrooms* DfEE Research Report No 115 London: DfEE

Mackie, L. and Law, J. 2014 'The functional communication skills of boys with externalising behaviour with and without co-occurring language difficulties' *Emotional and Behavioural Difficulties* 19 (1) 89–105

McManus, M. 1989 *Troublesome Behaviour in the Classroom* London: Routledge

Maker, C. J. 2013 'Real Engagement in Active Problem Solving (REAPS). Practical ideas and research results' Keynote, WCGTC 20th Biennial World Conference, Louisville, Kentucky, 10–14 August

Makins, V. 1991 'Five steps to peace in the classroom' *Times Educational Supplement* 1 Nov p. 23

Marland, S. P. 1972 *Education of the Gifted and Talented. The Marland Report to the Congress of the United States* Washington DC: US Government Printing Office

Marton, F. and Säljo, R. 1984 'Approaches to learning' 36–55 In F. Marton, D. J. Hounsell and N. J. Entwistle (eds) *The Experience of Learning* Edinburgh: Scottish Academic Press

Masten, A. S. and Coatsworth, J. D. 1998 'The development of competence in unfavourable environments. Lessons from research on successful children' *American Psychologist* 53 (2) 205–20

Mathematical Society 2010 *Policy on Enrichment* Leicester: Mathematical Association

Medwell, J. and Wray, D. 2014 'Plotting the significance of handwriting automaticity' *Handwriting Today* 13 3–8

Medwell, J., Strand, S. and Wray, D. 2008 'What should we assess in primary writing?' *Handwriting Today* 7 23–8

Miles, T. R. 1993 *Dyslexia: The Patterns of Difficulty* London: Whurr

Miles, T. R. and Miles, E. 2001 *Dyslexia, 100 Years On* (2nd edition) London: Routledge

Miller, G. A. 1956 'The magical number seven plus or minus two' *British Journal of Psychology* 63 (2) 81–97

Mongon, D. and Hart, S. 1989 *Improving Classroom Behaviour: New Directions for Teachers and Learners* London: Cassell

Monroe, M. 1932 *Children Who Cannot Read* Chicago: Chicago University Press

Montgomery, D. 1977 'Teaching pre-reading through pattern recognition training' *The Reading Teacher* 30 (6) 216–25

Montgomery, D. 1981a 'Do dyslexics have difficulty accessing articulatory information?' *Psychological Research* 43 235–43

Montgomery, D. 1981b 'Education comes of age' *School Psychology International* 1 2–5

Montgomery, D. 1983 'Teaching thinking skills in the school curriculum' *School Psychology International* 3 108–12

Montgomery, D. 1989 *Managing Behaviour Problems* Sevenoaks Kent: Hodder and Stoughton

Montgomery, D. 1990 *Children with Learning Difficulties* London: Cassell

Montgomery, D. 1993 'Fostering learner managed learning in teacher education' 59–70 In N. Graves (ed.) *Learner Managed Learning* Leeds: Higher Education for Capability/ World Education Fellowship

Montgomery, D. 1994 'The role of metacognition and metalearning in teacher education' 227–53 In G. Gibbs (ed.) *Improving Student Learning: Theory and Research* Oxford: Oxford Brookes University

Montgomery, D. 1995 'Subversive activity' *Education* 21 April 16–17

Montgomery, D. 1996 *Educating the Able* London: Cassell

Montgomery, D. 1997 *Spelling: Remedial Strategies* London: Cassell

Montgomery, D. 1998 *Reversing Lower Attainment* London: David Fulton

Montgomery, D. (ed.) 2000 *Able Underachievers* London: Whurr

Montgomery, D. 2002 *Helping Teachers Develop Through Classroom Observation* London: David Fulton

Montgomery, D. 2007 *Spelling, Handwriting and Dyslexia* London: Routledge

Montgomery, D. 2008 'Cohort analysis of writing in Year 7 after 2, 4, and 7 years of the National Literacy Strategy' *Support for Learning* 23 (1) 3–11

Montgomery, D. (ed.) 2009 *Able, Gifted and Talented Underachievers* Oxford: Wiley/ Blackwell

Montgomery, D. 2012 *Spelling Detective* Maldon: Learning Difficulties Research Project www.ldrp.org.uk

Montgomery, D. 2014 'Identifying talented self-regulated learners in preschool and Reception' International Biennial ECHA Conference, 17–20 September, Ljubljana, Slovenia

Morin, M. F., Lavoie, N. and Montesinos-Gelet, I. 2012 'The effects of manuscript, cursive or manuscript/cursive styles on writing development in Grade 2' *Language and Literacy* 14 110–24

Mosley, J. 2008 'Setting up and running Circles of Support' *SEBDA News* Issue 15 Spring 20–3

Mueller, P. A. and Oppenheimer, D. M. 2014 'The pen is mightier than the keyboard. Advantages of longhand over laptop note-taking' *Psychological Sciences* 25 (6) 1159–68

Munro, J. 1996 *Gifted Students' Learning. Basing the Teaching of Gifted Students on a Model of Learning* Melbourne: Educational Assistance

Myklebust, H. 1973 *Development and Disorders of Written Language Vol 2 Studies of Normal and Exceptional Children* London: Grune and Stratton

Naglieri, J. A. 2003 *The Draw a Person Test* London: Pearson

NICE 2008 'Guidance on use of Methylphenidate for ADHD' National Institute for Clinical Excellence http://www.nice.org.uk/guidance/cg72 (accessed 6 February 2015)

Nickerson, R. S., Perkins, D. N. and Smith, E. E. (eds) 1985 *The Teaching of Thinking* Hillsdale NJ: Erlbaum

Niehart, M. 2000 'Gifted children with Asperger's Syndrome' *Gifted Child Quarterly* 44 (4) 222–30

Niehart, M. 2011 'The revised profiles of the gifted: A research-based approach' Keynote, WCGTC 19th Biennial World Conference, Prague, 8–12 August

Norrie, E. 1973 *Edith Norrie Letter Case and Manual* Frensham Surrey: Helen Arkell Centre

NUT 2008 *National Union of Teachers Survey* London: Hamilton House

O'Connor, T. and Colwell, J. 2002 'The effectiveness and rationale of the "nurture group" approach to helping children with EBD remain within mainstream education' *British Journal of Special Education* 29 (2) 96–100

Ofsted 2013 *The Annual Report of Her Majesty's Chief Inspector 2012/13* London: Crown Copyright

Ofsted 2014 *The Annual Report of Her Majesty's Chief Inspector 2013/14* London: Crown Copyright

Oliver, T., Alres, R. A., Castro, S. L. and Branco, M. 2009 'The impact of children's handwriting on text composition' *Handwriting Today* 8 14–17

Oussoren Voors, R. 1999 'Write Dance' *Handwriting Interest Group Newsletter* 70–87

Overvelde, A. and Hulstijn, W. 2011 'Learning new movement patterns: A study on good and poor writers comparing learning conditions emphasizing spatial, timing, or abstract characteristics' *Human Movement Science* 30 731–44

Parrant, H. 1986 'An investigation of remedial approaches to spelling difficulties' Unpublished Dissertation Kingston upon Thames: Kingston Polytechnic

Passow, A. H. 1966 *Youth Talent Project. Ventura Report on the First Phase Operation* Ventura CA: County Superintendent of Schools Office

Passow, A. H. 1990 'Needed research and development in educating high ability children' *European Journal for High Ability* 1 (4) 15–24

Paul, R. W. 1990 'Critical thinking in North America' 18–42 In A. J. Binker *Critical Thinking. What Every Person Needs to Know in a Rapidly Changing World* Sonoma CA: Sonoma State University

Pawley, J. 2007 'Dyslexia – The hidden trigger?' Unpublished MA SpLD Dissertation, London: Middlesex University

Perry, B. D. 2002 'Childhood experience and the expression of genetic potential. What childhood neglect tells us about nature and nurture' *Brain and Mind* 3 79–100

Persson, R. S. 2012 'Cultural variation and dominance in a globalised knowledge economy: Towards a culture-sensitive research paradigm in the science of giftedness' *Gifted and Talented International* 27 (1) 15–48.

Piaget, J. 1952 *Origins of Intelligence in Children* (2nd edition) New York: International Universities Press

Pomerantz, M. and Pomerantz, K. 2004 *Listening to Able Underachievers* London: David Fulton

Poorthuis, E., Kok, L. and Van Dijk, J. 1990 'A curriculum assessment tool' 2nd International Biennial Conference of ECHA, Budapest, October

Powell, L., Gilchrist, M. and Stapley, J. 2008 'Self Discovery Programme: A journey of self discovery involving massage, yoga and relaxation for children with EBD attending primary school' *Emotional and Behavioural Difficulties* 13 (3) 193–9

Radford, J. 1990 *Child Prodigies and Exceptionally Early Achievers* New York: Free Press

Rafalovich, A. 2005 'Relational troubles and semiofficial suspicion: Educators and the medicalisation of "unruly" children' *Symbolic Interaction* 29 (1) 24–46

Raffan, J. 2003 'The learning country' 15th Biennial Conference of The World Council for Gifted and Talented Children, Adelaide, 1–5 August

Raven, J. C. 2008 *Raven's Progressive Matrices* London: Pearson Assessment

Rawlings, A. 1989 Personal communication

Rawlings, A. 1996 *Ways and Means Today. Conflict Resolution Training and Resources* Kingston upon Thames: Kingston Friends Workshop Group, Eden Street

Rayner, S. 1998 'Educating pupils with emotional and behaviour difficulties "Pedagogy is the key"' *Emotional and Behavioural Difficulties* 4 (3) 44–51

Read, C. 1986 *Children's Creative Spellings* London: Routledge and Kegan Paul

Reichelt, C. 2001 'Biochemical basis for autism' The Food Programme, BBC Radio 4, 14 January

Renzulli, J. 1977 *The Enrichment Triad Model: A Guide for Developing Defensible Programs for the Gifted and Talented* Mansfield CT: Creative Learning Press

Renzulli, J. and Reis, S. 1989 *The Schoolwide Enrichment Model* Mansfield Center CT: Creative Learning Press

Renzulli, J. and Reis, S. 2008 'What is this thing called giftedness and how to develop it? A 25-year perspective' 8–36 In J. Fortikova (ed.) *Successful Teaching of the Exceptional Gifted Child* Prague: Triton Press

Renzulli, J., Reis, S. and Smith, L. 1981 'The revolving door model. A new way of identifying the gifted' Phi-Delta-Kappan 62 548–9

Resnick, L. B. 1989 'Introduction' 1–24 In L. B. Resnick (ed.) *Knowing, Learning and Instruction: Essays in Honour of Robert Glaser* Hillsdale NJ: Erlbaum

Reynolds, S., MacKay, T. and Kearney, M. 2009 'Nurture Groups. A large scale and controlled study of effects on development and academic achievement' *British Journal of Special Education* 36 (4) 200–12

Richardson, M. 1935 *Writing and Writing Patterns* New Education Fellowship Conference Papers, St Andrews Silver Jubilee Exhibition

Ridehalgh, N. 1999 A comparison of remediation programmes and an analysis of their effectiveness in a sample of pupils diagnosed as dyslexic' Unpublished MA SpLD Dissertation London: Middlesex University

Riding, K. and Rayner, R. 1998 *Cognitive Styles and Learning Strategies* London: David Fulton

Roaf, C. 1998 'Slow hand. A secondary school survey of handwriting speed and legibility' *Support for Learning* 13 (1) 39–42

Rogers, B. 2007 *Behaviour Management* (2nd edition) London: Sage

Rogers, K. B. 1998 'Using current research to make "good" decisions about grouping' *National Association of Secondary School Principals (NASSP) Bulletin* 82 38–46

Rogers, K. B. 2010 'Thinking smart about twice exceptional learners. Steps to finding them and strategies for catering to them appropriately' Keynote, 11th Asia-Pacific Conference on Giftedness, Sydney, 29 July – 1 August

Rogers, K. B. and Span, P. 1993 'Ability grouping with gifted students. Research and guidelines' 585–92 In K. A. Heller, F. J. Monks and A. H. Passow (eds) *International Handbook of Research and Development on Gifted Education* Oxford: Pergamon

Rommelse, N. N., Franke, B., Geurts, H. M., Hartman, C. A. and Buitelaar, J. K. 2010 'Shared heritability of attention deficit/hyperactivity disorder and autism spectrum disorder' *European Child and Adolescent Psychiatry* 19 (3) 281–95

Ronald, A. 2014 'The times they are a-changin' *The Psychologist* 27 (3) 144–66

Root, R. W. and Resnick, R. J. 2003 'An update on the diagnosis and treatment of ADHD in children' *Professional Psychology Research and Practice* 34 (1) 34–41

Rose, J. 2006 *Rose Review. Independent Review of the Teaching of Early Reading: Final Report* London: DfES

Rosenblum, S. and Livneh-Zirinsky, M. 2007 'Handwriting process and product characteristics of children diagnosed with DCD' *Human Movement Science* 27 200–14

Rosenshine, B. 2010 *Principles of Instruction.* Intenational Academy of Education Geneva: International Bureau of Education, UNESCO

Rumelhart, D. E. and McClelland, R. R. (eds) 1995 *Parallel Distributed Processing Vol 1 Foundations* Cambridge MA: MIT Press

Rutter, M. L. (1985) *Helping Troubled Children* (2nd edition) Harmondsworth: Penguin

Rutter, M. (2005) 'Genetic influences and autism' 425–52 In F. R. Volkmar, R. Paul, A. Kline and D. Cohen (eds) *Handbook of Autism and Pervasive Developmental Disorders* (3rd edition) Hoboken NJ: John Wiley and Sons

Rutter, M. L., Tizard, J. and Whitmore, K. (eds) 1970 *Education, Health and Behaviour* London: Longman

Rutter, M. L., Maughan, M., Mortimore, P. and Ouston, J. 1979 *Fifteen Thousand Hours* London: Open Books

Rutter, M. L., Caspi, A., Fergusson, D., Horwood, L. J., Goodman, R., Maughan, B., Moffatt, T. B., Meltzer, H. C. and Carroll, J. 2004 'Sex differences in developmental reading disability' *Journal of the American Medical Association* 291 (16), 2007–12

Ryan, R. M. and Deci, E. I. 2000 'Self determination theory and the facilitation of intrinsic motivation and social development and well-being' *American Psychologist* 55 68–78

Schneck, C. M. and Henderson, A. 1990 'Discriminant analysis of the developmental progress of grasp position for pencil and crayon control in a longitudinal study' *American Journal of Occupational Therapy* 44 (10) 893–900

Schneider, B. H. 1992 'Didactic methods for enhancing children's peer relations: A quantitative review' *Clinical Psychology Review* 12 363–82

Schoemaker, M. M. and Calveboer, A. S. 1994 'Social and affective problems of children who are clumsy. How do they begin?' In S. E. Henderson (ed.) *Developmental Co-ordination Disorder Special Issue of Adapted Physical Activity Quarterly* 11 130–41

Schonell, F. J. 1943 *Backwardness in Basic Subjects* Edinburgh: Oliver and Boyd

Schwellnus, H., Carnahan, M., Kushki, A., Polatajiko, H., Missiuna, C. and Chau, T. 2012 'Effect of pencil grasp on the speed and legibility of handwriting in children' *American Journal of Occupational Therapy* 66 718–26

Scott MacDonald, W. 1971 *Battle in the Classroom* Brighton: Intext Publications

Selkowitz, M. 2004 *ADHD The Facts* Oxford: Oxford University Press

Sharma, M. C. 2003 'Numbersense. A window into dyslcalculia and other mathematical difficulties' 277–92 In S. Chinn (ed.) *The Routledge International Handbook of Dyscalculia and Mathematical Learning Difficulties* Abingdon Oxon: Routledge

Sharp, R. and Green, A. 1975 *Education and Social Control* London: Routledge and Kegan Paul

Shayer, M. and Adey, P. (eds) 2002 *Learning Intelligence: Cognitive Acceleration Across the Curriculum from 3–25 Years* Buckingham: Open University Press

Shore, B. M. 1991 'How do gifted children think differently' *Gifted and Talented Education Council of the Alberta Teachers' Association* 5 (2) 19–22

Shuard, H. and Rothery, A. 1980 *Children Reading Maths* London: NATFHE

Skilbeck, M. 1989 *School Development and New Approaches to Learning: Trends and Issues in Curriculum Reform* Paris: Organisation for Economic Co operation and Development

Skinner, B. F. 1958 *Science and Human Behaviour* New York: Macmillan

Silva, K., Hurry, J. and Riley, S. 1996 'Evaluation of a focused literacy teaching programme in Reception and Year 1' *British Educational Research Journal* 22 (5) 517–30

Silverman, L. K. 1989 'Invisible gifts, invisible handicaps' *Roeper Review* 12 (1) 37–42

Silverman, L. K. 2002 *Upside-Down Brilliance: The Visual-Spatial Learner* Denver: DeLeon Publishing

Singleton, C. 2006 'Dyslexia and youth offending' 117–21 In S. Thomas and A. Cooke (eds) *The Dyslexia Handbook* Reading: Dyslexia Association

Sisk, D. 2003 'Gifted with behaviour disorders: Marching to a different drummer' 131–54 In D. Montgomery (ed.) *Gifted and Talented Children with SEN* London: David Fulton

Smith, L. 2002 'An investigation of children with EBD with dyslexic type difficulties in two special schools and a PRU unit' Unpublished MA SpLD Dissertation London: Middlesex University

Snowling, M. L. 2000 *Dyslexia* (2nd edition) Oxford: Blackwell

Soloff, S. 1973 'The effect of non content factors on the grading of essays' *Graduate Research in Education and Related Disciplines* 6 (2) 44–54

Solomon, D., Watson, M., Schaps, E. and Lewis, C. 2000 'A six district study of educational change. Direct and mediated effect of the Child Development Project' *Social Psychology of Education* 4 3–51

Sousa, D. A. 1993 *How the Gifted Brain Learns* Thousand Oaks CA: Corwin Press

Spender, D. 1983 *Invisible Women: The Schooling Scandal* London: Writers and Readers

Stainthorp, R. and Rauf, N. 2009 'An investigation of the influence of the transcription skills of handwriting and spelling on the quality of text writing by girls and boys in Key Stage 2' *Handwriting Today* 8 Autumn 8–13

Stainthorp, R., Henderson, S., Barnett, A. and Scheib, B. 2001 'Handwriting policy and practice in primary schools' British Psychological Society Educational and Developmental Section Joint Annual Conference, Worcester University, September

Starr, R. 2003 'Show me the light – I can't see how bright I am. Gifted students with visual impairment' 93–109 In D. Montgomery (ed.) 2003 *Gifted and Talented Children with SEN: Double Exceptionality* London: NACE/David Fulton

Steer, J. 2009 *The Steer Report. Learning Behaviour. Lessons Learned* London: DCFS

Stein, J. 2001 'The magnocellular theory of developmental dyslexia' 27th International Biennial Conference in Psychology, Stockholm

Stevenson, K. R. 2006 'School size and its relationship to student outcome and school climate' *National Clearing House for Educational Facilities* 1–8 April

Stewart, M. A. 1970 'Hyperactive children' *Scientific American*, April 222 (4) 94–9 Offprint 527 932–36

Stott, D. H. 1966 *Studies of Troublesome Children* London: Tavistock

Strauss, A. A. and Lehtingen, C. E. 1947 *Psychopathology and Education of the Brain-Injured Child* New York: Grune and Stratton

Sunderland, M. 2014 'Interrupted learning and enabling children to learn' Keynote, SEND Conference, Dover, Deal and Sandwich, 4th July

Swanson, J. M. 2001 'Clinical relevance of the primary findings of the MTA. Success rates based on severity of ADHD and ODD symptoms at the end of treatment' *Journal of the American Academy of Child and Adolescent Psychiatry* 40 (3) 168–79

Sweedler-Brown, C. U. 1992 'The effects of training on the appearance of bias of holistic essay graders' *Journal of Research and Development in Education* 26 4–88

Taba, H. 1962 *Curriculum Development: Theory and Practice* New York: Harcourt, Brace and World

Tannenbaum, A. J. 1993 'History of giftedness and gifted education in world perspective' 3–28 In K. A. Heller, F. J. Monks and A. H. Passow (eds) *International Handbook of Research and Development of Giftedness and Talent* Oxford: Pergamon

Tatum, D. 1984 'Disruptive pupils. Systems rejects' In J. Shostak and T. Logan (eds) *Pupil Experience* London: Croom Helm.

Taylor, A. F. and Kuo, F. E. 2009 'Children with attention deficits concentrate better after a walk in the park' *Journal of Attention Disorders* 12 (5) 402–9

Taylor, A. F. and Kuo, F. E. and Sullivan, W. C. 2001 'Coping with ADD. The surprising connection to the green play setting' *Environment and Behaviour* 33 (1) 54–77

Teasdale, R. 2000 'A case study in double exceptionality' *Educating Able Children* 6 (2) 41–2

Terman, L. M. 1954 'The discovery and encouragement of exceptional talent' *American Psychologist* 9 221–30

Thomas, F. 1998 'Une question de writing. A comparative study' *Support for Learning* 13 43–5

Tolman, E. C. 1934 *Purposive Behaviour in Animals and Men* New York: Appleton Century Crofts

Torrance, E. P. 1963 *Education and the Creative Potential* Minneapolis: University of Minnesota

Tremblay, R. E., Nagin, D. S., Seguin, J. R., Zoccolilla, M., Zalazo, P. D., Bolvin, M., Perusse, D. and Japel, C. 2005 'Physical aggression during early childhood, trajectories and provisions' *Canadian Child and Adolescence Psychiatric Review* 14 (1) 3–9

Tucha, L., Lange, K. W., Stasik, D., Walitza, S. and Tucha, O. 2008 'Disturbances of handwriting in children with ADHD' *Handwriting Today* 7 29–36

Turner, C. 2000 'A pupil with EBD perspective. Does John feel that his behaviour is affecting his learning?' *Emotional and Behavioural Difficulties* 5 (4) 13–18

Tymms, P. 2004 'Are standards rising in English primary schools?' *British Educational Research Journal* 30 (4) 477–94

Upton, J., Duckett, J. and Boardman, M. 2008 'A Motorway to ABC' *Special* November 17–19

Vellutino, F. R. 1979 *Dyslexia: Research and Theory* London: MIT Press

Vellutino, F. R. 1987 'Dyslexia' *Scientific American* 256 (3) 20–7

Viding, E., Simmonds, E., Petrides, K. V. C. and Frederickson, N. 2009 'The contribution of callow unemotional traits and conduct problems to bullying in early adolescence' *Journal of Child Psychology and Psychiatry* 50 (4) 471–81

Visser, J. and Dubsky, R. 2009 'Peer attitudes to SEBD in secondary mainstream school' *Emotional and Behavioural Difficulties* 14 (4) 315–24

Visser, J. and Jehan, Z. 2009 'ADHD A scientific fact or a factual opinion? A critique of the veracity of Attention Deficit Hyperacticity Disorder' *Emotional and Behavioural Difficulties* 14 (2) 127–40

Vygotsky, L. S. 1978 *Mind in Society* Cambridge MA: MIT Press

Wallace, B. 2000 *Teaching the Very Able Child: Developing a Policy and Adapting Strategies* London: David Fulton

Wallace, B. 2009 'What do we mean by an enabling curriculum that raises achievement for all learners? An examination of the TASC problem solving framework' 59–84 In D. Montgomery (ed.) *Gifted, Talented and Able Underachievers* Chichester: Wiley/ Routledge

Wallace, B. and Erikson, G. (eds) 2006 *Diversity in Gifted Education: International Perspectives on Global Issues* London: Routledge

Wallace, B., Leyden, S., Montgomery, D., Pomerantz, M. and Winstanley, C. 2009 *Raising the Achievement of Able Gifted and Talented Pupils Within an Inclusive School Framework* London: Routledge

Wallen, M., Bonney, M. A. and Lennox, L. 1996 *The Handwriting Speed Test* Adelaide: Helios

Walsh, J. P., Scullion, M., Burns, S., MacEvilly, D. and Brosnan, G. 2014 'Identifying demographic and language profiles of children with a primary diagnosis of ADHD' *Emotional and Behavioural Difficulties* 19 (1) 59–70

Wang, M. C. and Lindvall, C. M. 1984 'Individual differences and school environments' in E. W. Gordon (ed.) *Review of Research in Education II* Washington DC: American Education Research Association

Warnock, M. 1978 *Special Educational Needs: The Warnock Report* London: DES

Warnock, M. 2007 Foreword In R. Cigman (ed.) *Included or Excluded? The Challenge of the Mainstream for SEN Children* London: Routledge

Warwick, I. 2009 'Overcoming class, race and cultural factors in underachievement' 219–63 In D. Montgomery (ed.) *Gifted, Talented and Able Underachievers* Chichester: Wiley/Routledge

Watkins, D. and Wentzel, K. 2002 'Peer relationships and collaborative learning as contexts for academic enabling' *School Psychology Review* 31 (3) 366–77

Webb, J. T., Amend, E. R., Webb, N. E., Goerss, J., Beljan, P. and Olenchak, F. R. 2005 *Misdiagnosis and Dual Diagnosis of Gifted Children and Adults* Scottsdale AZ: Great Potential Press

Webb, M. 2000 'An evaluation of SEN provision to improve literacy teaching at N. school' Unpublished MA Dissertation, London: Middlesex University

Wechsler, D. 2008 WISC – IV *Wechsler Intelligence Scale for Children IV Edition*. London: Pearson/Psychological Corporation

Wedell, K. 1973 *Learning and Perceptuomotor Difficulties in Children* New York: Wiley

Wedge, P. and Prosser, H. 1982 *Born to Fail* London: Arrow Books

Weikart, D. 1967 *Preschool intervention. A Preliminary Report from the Perry Preschool Project* Ann Arbor: Michigan Campus Publishers

Whitmore, J. R. 1982 *Giftedness, Conflict and Underachievement* Boston: Allyn and Bacon

Williams, D. 1996 *An Inside Out Approach* London: Jessica Kingsley

Wills, L. and Munro, J. 2009 'Changing the teaching for the underachieving gifted child: The Ruyton School experience' 89–110 In D. Montgomery (ed.) *Able Underachievers* London: Whurr

Wing, L. 1981 'Asperger Syndrome: A clinical account' *Psychological Medicine* 11 (1) 115–29

Wing, L. 1996 *The Autistic Spectrum: A Guide for Parents and Professionals* London: Constable

Wing, L. 2008 'Asperger Syndrome: A clinical account' http://www.mugsy.org/wing2.htm (accessed 11 March 2015)

Wise, S. and Upton, G. 1998 'The perceptions of pupils with RBD of their mainstream schooling' *Emotional and Behavioural Difficulties* 3 (3) 3–12

Wolff, S. and Barlow, A. 1979 'Schizoid personality in childhood: a comparative study of schizoid, autistic and normal children' *Journal of Child Psychology and Psychiatry* 20 29–46

World Health Organisation (WHO) 1992 *The ICD-10 Classification of Mental and Behavioural Disorders: Clinical Description and Diagnostic Guidelines* Geneva: WHO

Wray, D. 2005 'Raising the achievement of boys in writing' NACE London Conference, April

Zahn, M. (ed.) 2009 *The Delinquent Girl* Philadelphia: Temple University Press

Zhang, K. C. 2008 'Square pegs in round holes? Meeting the educational needs of girls engaged in delinquent behaviour' *Emotional and Behavioural Difficulties* 13 (3) 179–92

Ziegler-Dendy, C. A. 2000 *Teaching Teens with ADD and ADHD: A Quick Reference Guide for Teachers and Parents* New York: Woodbine House

Index